PRAISE FOR JOE GIBBS AND *RACING TO WIN*

Whether in the football arena, the racing arena, or the arena of everyday living, Joe Gibbs clearly has found a successful formula for being a winner. Knowing how to establish a great game plan is second nature to Joe, and I know you will thoroughly enjoy his insights into winning the most important game of all—the game of life.

JAMES R. ANDREWS, MD, Orthopedic Surgeon

Joe Gibbs is a shining example for all of us—a shining example of how to do things the right way.

CHARLES CAWLEY, CEO, MBNA America

Joe Gibbs is a uniquely successful football-coach-turned-NASCAR-owner. He's also a remarkably decent and generous man. Joe's advice is worth hearing.

DONALD E. GRAHAM, Chairman of the Board, *The Washington Post*

Joe Gibbs knows how to inspire men and women to achieve greatness in the face of formidable obstacles. He is the kind of courageous, noble citizen that has made our country great, and we can all learn from his example.

JACK KEMP, Director, Empower America

Joe Gibbs is a fierce competitor who knows how to motivate people and bring out the best in them.

BOBBY LABONTE, 2000 NASCAR Winston Cup Champion

From the high of winning the Super Bowl to the low of nearly losing his cherished wife, Pat, to a brain tumor, Joe Gibbs has seen more dramatic ups and downs in the twenty years I've known him than most people experience in a lifetime. Yet even in his darkest hours, I've never seen him lose his grace, integrity, or humility. In Racing to Win, Joe teaches us his high-octane formula for handling life's triumphs and trials—a rock-steady reliance on faith and family.

J. W. MARRIOTT, JR., Chairman and CEO, Marriott International

When Joe Gibbs announced he was getting involved with NASCAR, he told me he was going to win *and* enjoy his family more than ever. Little did I know Joe would win another Super Bowl—the Daytona 500—and a Winston Cup championship with a formula that can bring victory to anyone. It's all here in *Racing to Win*.

GEORGE MICHAEL, **The Sports Machine**

Russ Grimm and I made plans to go to the Kentucky Derby, but Coach Gibbs wouldn't let us out of the Redskins mini-camp; so instead he set up televisions outside so we could watch the Derby. Joe did so many things to encourage and humor us.

JOE JACOBY, **Four-time Pro Bowl lineman, Washington Redskins**

When I'm right in the middle of the action, as I have been from the beginning of Joe Gibbs Racing, I don't have to judge by a man's promises; I can judge by what I have actually experienced: Joe Gibbs practices what he preaches.

NORM MILLER, **Chairman, Interstate Batteries**

I have long been an admirer of Joe Gibbs. He embodies the qualities that make great leaders and inspire others to excel. He will stretch your horizons and challenge your imagination.

BOB NARDELLI, **Chairman, president, and CEO of The Home Depot**

My mind's eye will always see Joe Gibbs in our locker room at halftime, in complete control commanding his coaches and players. Regardless of the circumstances, his approach was always the same—calm and deductive with a genuine vision for victory. And his vision continues to inspire in his teams confidence, the cornerstone of all success. To paraphrase that old saw regarding parents, it amazes me how smart Joe's gotten since I've been out of football.

JOHN RIGGINS, **Hall of Fame running back, Washington Redskins**

Joe Gibbs has proven again and again that the principles he lives by actually work!

TONY STEWART, **2002 NASCAR Winston Cup Champion**

RACING TO
WIN

JOE GIBBS
WITH
KEN ABRAHAM

Multnomah Publishers, Inc., *Sisters, Oregon*

RACING TO WIN
Published in association with the literary agency of
Alive Communications, Inc., 7680 Goddard Street, Suite 200,
Colorado Springs, CO 80920

© 2002, 2003 by Joe Gibbs

International Standard Book Number: 1-59052-155-2

Cover image of Joe Gibbs by David Bailey Photography

Background cover image by CIA Stock Photography

Unless otherwise indicated, Scripture quotations are from:

The Holy Bible, New International Version © 1973, 1984
by International Bible Society, used by permission of
Zondervan Publishing House.

Multnomah is a trademark of Multnomah Publishers, Inc.,
and is registered in the U.S. Patent and Trademark Office.
The colophon is a trademark of Multnomah Publishers, Inc.

Printed in the United States of America

For information:
MULTNOMAH PUBLISHERS, INC.
POST OFFICE BOX 1720
SISTERS, OREGON 97759

Library of Congress Cataloging-in-Publication Data

Gibbs, Joe J.
    Racing to win / by Joe Gibbs with Ken Abraham.
        p. cm.
    ISBN 1-57673-947-3 (hardcover)
    ISBN 1-59052-155-2 (pbk.)
    1. Success--Religious aspects--Christianity. 2. Gibbs, Joe J. I. Abraham, Ken.
II. Title.
    BV45983.G53 2002
    248.4--dc21   2002000873

03 04 05 06 07 08—10 9 8 7 6 5 4 3 2

CONTENTS

THE GAME PLAN

SUCCESS IN YOUR CAREER

YOUR FINANCIAL SUCCESS

SUCCESS IN BUILDING YOUR TEAM

SUCCESS IN YOUR PERSONAL RELATIONSHIPS

SUCCESS AND YOUR MORAL CHOICES

SUCCESS AND YOUR HEALTH

THE FINAL LAP

FOREWORD

BY J D GIBBS AND COY GIBBS

You can imagine the anxiety experienced by a brand-new head coach of the Washington Redskins whose team starts the season with five losses in a row. What people tend to overlook is the stress felt by that coach's family. Picture yourself as the new kid in school whose dad promptly leads the local NFL team to a rousing 0-5 start. Believe me, kids in school can be a lot more cruel than your average sports reporter. Thankfully our dad was able to turn things around, and we learned a few life lessons by observing Mom and Dad's trust in the Lord.

Whether it was watching our dad handle a crisis on the field or seeing him deal with a situation at home, we learned what it meant to be a man after God's own heart. Now, we're not saying he's perfect—just ask Mom if you want some proof—but we grew up with a dad who knew right from wrong and was willing to stand up and take the blows life dealt him. In the process he showed us how to be men who trust in the Lord and keep our priorities in order.

A recurring theme throughout this book, and one of the greatest blessings our dad has passed on to us, is the realization that we are stewards of what God has given us. The moment we believe that we are solely responsible for our own success, get ready—the bottom will soon drop out. Over and over we've heard our dad tell us that all we are going to leave behind are our family and the impact we have on others. One of his favorite sayings is "You never see a hearse towing a U-Haul."

After 'Skins games, when Dad was head coach, we would flip on the radio as we headed out to dinner. The local sports talk host would be taking calls from fans about the day's game. We'll always remember people calling in and bashing Dad for calling a running play on third and long or for starting the wrong player. Dad would then explain the playbook to us boys and tell us why he made certain calls. Many times the fans had no idea what they were talking about.

Our dad taught us that often in life we are like those fans without playbooks. But instead of yelling at a coach about the play he called, we lash out at God about our lives without ever turning to *His* playbook, the Bible. Whether our concern is with finances, careers, relationships, health, or just making a tough choice, God has already given us the answers to life's questions.

Thanks, Dad and Mom, for pointing us in the direction of the ultimate Coach and His Playbook. And thanks for allowing us the freedom to choose our own paths. No matter how far we strayed, we could always cast our eyes back on you and truly see God's image.

ONE

RACING
TO WIN

W atch out! Trouble on the backstretch!"
The excited voice of Eddie Masencup, the spotter for our Interstate Batteries #18 car, crackled in my headset, piercing the din at the Homestead-Miami Speedway. Eddie's job was to warn our driver Bobby Labonte of impending traffic around him, and with race cars streaking by at nearly 150 miles per hour, Bobby needed the extra "eyes" Eddie provided. One small bump by another hurtling NASCAR missile could send Bobby's car careening out of control, crashing into another car, or worse yet, smashing into the thick concrete wall surrounding the race track.

Anyone associated with NASCAR knows the risks involved with racing high-speed stock cars on tracks not much wider than the roads in front of most American shopping malls. Four cars running behind Bobby smashed into one another like bumper cars at an amusement park—only these bumps were costly, dangerous, and anything but amusing to our race team.

As rescue crews hurried to the scene of the accident, I strained to see what was going on down in turn four, the last turn before the homestretch leading to the start-finish line. For a long moment, I couldn't tell whether Bobby had made it through the rising smoke and metal strewn across the track. Nor could I locate Tony Stewart, the driver of our #20 car, who had

been leading the race. From where I was standing in the pits, it was difficult to see the entire race track. More than 75,000 race fans had jammed
into the enormous grandstand to see the 2000 Pennzoil 400, and I craned
my neck along with them, trying to catch a glimpse of our guys.

Unable to see the crash site, I paced back and forth in the pit area,
waiting anxiously for information to come over the headset. As a former
head coach of a National Football League team, I was accustomed to the
tension. I was used to having to recover and regroup when plays didn't
pan out the way I had meticulously drawn them up in our game plan. I
knew the joys and the frustrations of building a strong team, fighting and
clawing to get to the top, and overcoming adversity.
I knew what it felt like to win, to succeed in front
of a worldwide audience. I also knew how it felt to
fail in front of friends, family, and people I had
never met but who knew all about me—or at least
thought they did.

*I knew what
it felt like to win.
I also knew how it
felt to fail.*

But all that heightened exponentially when I
got involved with NASCAR—the National Association for Stock Car Auto
Racing, as the organization has been known since 1949. The competition
in NASCAR was just as intense as in the NFL.

I had coached the Washington Redskins for only two years before we
won a Super Bowl. Now, in my ninth year as owner of one of the premier
NASCAR racing teams, I could almost taste our first Winston Cup championship. Joe Gibbs Racing had grown to nearly 150 employees, including my
two sons, J D and Coy. We all wanted this one badly.

Bobby Labonte had grown up a Dallas Cowboys fan. "I hated the
Washington Redskins!" Bobby once admitted to me. No matter. Today,
Bobby and I were on the same team. He was my "quarterback" on the
Interstate Batteries #18 team. Jimmy Makar, our crew chief, was the coach
who called the shots. Tony Stewart drove the Home Depot #20 car, while
Greg Zipadelli was that team's crew chief. When I coached the Redskins, I
designed the offense and helped call the plays, so I could control the foot-
ball team's destiny to some extent and help make it happen. Not so in racing.
On our race team, Jimmy and Greg are the technical guys; they are the

ones making the tough decisions. Bobby and Tony drive the cars. And my job as the owner...well, truthfully, my job is to let the guys do their jobs while I stay out of the way. As the owner, my main function is to pace and worry. What a job description!

OUR RACE DAY ROUTINE

During the prerace interviews that morning, Bobby and Tony joked and laughed casually with the press. One reporter asked Bobby, "How'd you sleep last night?"

"Best night of sleep I've had the whole time down here," Bobby replied.

Another reporter piped up, "What was your first thought when you woke up this morning?"

"I've got to go to the bathroom," Bobby deadpanned. He was obviously going to enjoy this day. Bobby had been here before. His older brother, Terry Labonte, had won the Winston Cup title in 1984 and 1996, and Bobby himself had finished second in the championship points race in 1999. He wasn't about to let the pressure get to him.

Although the Sunday race was not scheduled to begin until one o'clock, the flurry of activity had begun early for all of us. Dressed in my usual race day garb—a white shirt sporting the Interstate Batteries and Home Depot logos, black slacks, and black running shoes—I had flown in to join Bobby and Tony in visiting the hospitality tents, the areas in which our corporate sponsors entertain their clients before, during, and after the race. The drivers and I went from group to group—Bobby to visit with the #18-car sponsors, Tony to greet the #20-car sponsors, and I to do both—meeting and greeting myriad people, many of whom were avid race fans and many others who knew me from my twenty-eight years as a football coach. Bobby, Tony, and I shook hands with fans, posed for pictures, and signed autographs for several hours, right up until it was time for the drivers to get ready for the race. Although Bobby and Tony have risen to what could be equated with superstar status in other sports, they remain extremely accessible to the NASCAR fans.

Finally, just before race time I returned to our transporters, the eighteen-wheelers in which our race cars are hauled to the track. Parked in the NASCAR garage area, the transporters carry everything from spare lug nuts and an extra engine to a complete backup car. The transporters also serve as our portable offices at the track.

I picked up my headset and headed for the pits, pressed by a throng of reporters and fans each step of the way. It was a chaotic scene. Pit crew members from various teams, dressed in brightly colored uniforms decked out with a wide variety of corporate logos—McDonald's, Tide, Coca-Cola, etc.—scurried in every direction. Curious fans, sporting the credentials which gave them "backstage access" to the pit and garage areas, watched for any glimpse of their heroes. The crowd—a strange mix of corporate executives, ruddy mechanics, immaculately dressed women, and the jeans-and-T-shirt crowd—all surged harmoniously along. A young woman bearing a sign, *NASCAR Garage Tour,* led a group of Japanese fans through the garage area, while a translator conveyed her words to the tour members listening on headsets. A sea of faces blurred in front of me as I passed by, many people calling out words of encouragement and reporters pelting me with last-minute queries.

I tried my best to answer the reporters' questions as we moved through the crowd. When asked how I was doing, I told them the truth: "I'm nervous." Just as I had experienced so many times on a football field, I had an anxious excitement in anticipation of the race. I felt sure that this was going to be a big day for both our racing teams.

With all but two of thirty-four races already run, Bobby had won four times during the 2000 season. He had accumulated 4,505 points, leading the hard-charging, always competitive Dale Earnhardt by a mere 218 points. "The Intimidator," as Dale was known by legions of his fans, was pursuing his eighth NASCAR championship with a passion. Jeff Burton trailed right behind him, and Dale Jarrett stood just 356 points shy of first place.

The Winston Cup points system looks complicated, but it's really quite simple: The winner of a race receives 175 points, second place gets 170, and the points awarded drop 5 per position until seventh place, where the points drop 4 per spot down through twelfth place. The points drop is then 3 per position down to last place. Five bonus points are awarded for leading a lap, and the driver who leads the most laps in each race receives a 5-point bonus. Points earned each week are added to the cumulative season totals, and the team with the most points at the end of the season wins the championship.

Since every car that starts a race receives some points, drivers and teams will race like mad even when they know they have little possibility of winning a particular race. If a car crashes or has a mechanical problem that forces it out of the race, the driver drops to the bottom of the points for that race. That's why race teams work feverishly to get banged-up cars back into the race after a wreck or other problem, because the points earned even in a losing effort will be important in the year-end championship tally.

Bobby had owned first place in the point standings for most of the 2000 season, even as Dale Earnhardt pressed ever closer. Before the Miami-Homestead race, Dale admitted that Bobby had the inside track: "Bobby has a pretty solid lock on things...but we're going to keep fighting till it's over."

The Pennzoil 400 would be a key race. If Bobby could finish in fifth place or better, he would clinch his first NASCAR championship—and accomplish the dream of a lifetime. We would take home the Winston Cup trophy and a check for more than $3 million at the awards ceremony to be held at the Waldorf-Astoria in New York the first week in December.

Should Bobby fail to place fifth or better, he'd still have a good chance to win it all in Atlanta the following week, but that would only increase the pressure. Besides, close is never good enough in NASCAR. Anyone associated with motor racing well understands that anything can happen at any moment on the track. Although Bobby had finished every race he had started during the year, all it would take is one spinout in the third turn, one blown tire, one broken valve, or one serious miscue by a competing driver—and dreams of winning our first championship after nine years of racing could be shattered.

We had almost gotten to the place of not wanting to talk too much about the championship to the press, or even around the race shop, for fear that we might jinx our chances or become overconfident.

Now at Homestead, I was really sweatin' it out, thinking, *We've come all this way, after thirty-two weeks of racing, and we still haven't won this thing!* We didn't want to go into the last race of the season having to place in the top ten or else. We wanted to win this thing today!

Four F-16 jets from Homestead Air Force Base streaked across the sky following the singing of "The Star-Spangled Banner." Then former United States Senator Howard H. Baker stepped to a microphone and gave the traditional call: "Gentlemen, start your engines!"

A roar of gas-powered thunder pealed across the track as forty-three drivers simultaneously cranked their motors. Few feelings in all of sports can compare to the enormous adrenaline rush people experience when they hear that sound—the sound of sheer power.

I prayed briefly with our team members prior to the race: "Lord, let us have a great race today, and please keep the guys safe. Let everything we do today bring honor to You."

We wanted to win this thing today!

Steve Park, driving the #1 Pennzoil car, sat on the pole—the number one starting position— which he had earned by posting the fastest speed in the field during qualifying. Ricky Rudd had qualified on the front row with Steve. Bobby started the race in row number two. Tony Stewart, who had won the Pennzoil 400 in his first full year of NASCAR racing in 1999, was in row seven, driving our #20 Home Depot car. Today there was a printed reminder on his dashboard: PATIENCE. With his outgoing personality and sometimes risky racing style, Tony needed all the patience he could muster, especially as he was the reigning champion of this race. Telling Tony to take it easy was like telling Tiger Woods to lay up.

The greatest stock car racers in the world compete every week of the NASCAR season. The list of drivers gathered at Homestead-Miami Speedway that day read like a *Who's Who* of racing—Dale Earnhardt, Jeff Gordon, Mark Martin, Dale Jarrett, Rusty Wallace, Bill Elliott, and the legendary Darrell Waltrip, who was winding down his on-track career. Jeff Burton was there, too, as was Terry Labonte, Bobby's older brother. Dale Earnhardt Jr., known as "Little E" to many of his colleagues, sat behind the wheel of the #8 car.

The 400-mile race meant 267 grueling laps around the one-and-a-half-mile, sun-baked track. Even in November, the heat on the track would be horrific. Most of the cars' crew chiefs would call for a change of tires every fifty to sixty laps to prevent their cars from slipping on the hot asphalt track. Fresh tires are crucial to winning races, because the track gets slicker with every lap, and as the rubber on the tires wears, traction diminishes, heightening the possibility of accidents and hampering the ability of drivers to handle their cars at blazing speeds. A wall of tires stood ready, stacked four-high with lug nuts in place, at the rear of our pit area. Even at $1500 per set, I knew that we'd probably use five to eight sets of tires before the race was over.

The racers slowly followed the pace car around the track, weaving slightly to "scrub in" their tires, creating a sticky quality to the rubber to help with traction. I watched nervously from pit road, the stretch of track where the cars come in during the race for adjustments, fresh tires, and fuel. Pit locations are picked according to the order in which teams qualify, with faster drivers receiving first choice. The choices are not made lightly. Strategy is involved in the pit selection, with the crew chiefs and drivers usually preferring locations closer to the pit road exit leading back onto the track, though not always. Sometimes the crew chief will select a stall farther down pit road, especially if the stall has an opening behind or in front of it, allowing his driver's car to get in and out of the pit area more easily—and hopefully faster. A fraction of a second saved during a pit stop can easily be the difference between winning and losing.

I donned my headset so I could hear the radio communications between Bobby and our Interstate Batteries crew. Crew chief Jimmy Makar sat perched in a chair atop the pit cart, a mobile "tool chest" housing a television monitor connected to a satellite dish, several computers, and a raft of tools and equipment. In front of Jimmy was another television screen and a computer monitor on which he received constant updates on the speed and status of every car on the track. Stock car racing has come a long way from its humble beginnings during Prohibition, when bootleggers took a break from running moonshine to test their automobiles and driving skills against one another on the back roads of the South. Today NASCAR racing is a national obsession—a multimillion-dollar venture utilizing advanced space-age technology.

THE RACE IS ON!

The pace car dropped off the track, and the green flag was waved. The drivers accelerated, and with a deafening roar the cars surged across the start-finish line. Steve Park, Joe Nemechek, Casey Atwood, and Bobby Labonte quickly took advantage of their starting positions to open a gap between themselves and the rest of the pack. Tony Stewart dropped back to ninth position, but I wasn't too worried. The #20 car was running very fast, and in prerace interviews nearly everyone in the garage area had tapped Tony as a potential winner of today's race.

Ten laps into the race, Dale Earnhardt "got into" another driver, bumping the car ahead of him and bending his own fender in the process. Earnhardt radioed his crew chief, Kevin Hamlin, concerning the damage, and they started anticipating a caution period when he could bring the car into the pit to be repaired without losing too much valuable track position. The yellow flag wasn't long in coming out.

Bobby and Tony were running in third and fourth positions on lap 25 when Scott Pruett and Andy Houston got into trouble. Scott's #32 car nicked the rear bumper of Andy's #96, sending both Fords into a spin. The cars veered across the track, and the #96 McDonald's car violently impacted the track wall, crunching the rear of his vehicle like an accordion. The caution flag came out as rescue crews quickly made their way to the scene of the accident. Amazingly, both drivers walked away from the mishap without a scratch. Scott and Andy were teammates driving for the same owner, so I could easily imagine that postrace conversation!

During the caution the pace car returned to the track, and the field maintained their positions, making their way slowly around the track as clean-up crews cleared debris from the racing surface. Tow trucks hauled the damaged vehicles behind the wall to the garage area, but the damage was too severe for the cars to be repaired.

Bobby Labonte and several other leaders took advantage of the caution laps to make an early pit stop. Our crew hurriedly filled Bobby's gas tank, changed two of his tires, took a pound of air pressure out of both left-side tires, and made a handling adjustment to "loosen" the #18 car. Early in the race, Bobby's car had been too tight, "pushing" the front end up the track in the corners. These adjustments were made quickly but with precision, because if the car were to get too loose, its rear end would have a tendency to slide in the turns.

"How's the track?" Jimmy asked Bobby over the headsets.

"I think it's gonna get slick real quick," Bobby replied. Hot tires speeding across the asphalt surface leave a thin layer of rubber on the ground, quickly turning areas of the race track into a virtual skating rink. Heat on the track also causes the tires to pick up oil from the track, making driving even more treacherous. If you've ever been driving along dry pavement and then suddenly hit a patch of ice or oil, you know how difficult it is to control your vehicle. Imagine hitting the same slick spot at 150 miles per hour!

Tony Stewart piloted the #20 car back onto the track after his pit stop, losing two positions, dropping from third to fifth place during the stop. Bobby emerged from the pits in seventh place. The excellent pit stops would prove to be lifesavers.

In contrast, Ward Burton entered the pits in eleventh position, but as his crew was changing tires, the car rolled off the jack momentarily, costing Ward several precious seconds. He returned to the track in twenty-fifth place, but—far worse—the delayed pit stop would put Ward Burton in the wrong place at the wrong time.

The green flag waved again at lap 32, and the cars roared back to racing speed. But as the field rounded turn three, contact with Dale Earnhardt caused Ward Burton to lose control of his #22 car. Ward crashed hard into the wall, the car spinning about and coming to a stop on the track facing oncoming traffic. The cars behind him had nowhere to go and, in a fraction of a second, that section of the race track erupted in fire, smoke, and flying sheet metal. It looked more like a war zone than a sporting event.

Earnhardt slipped on by; so did Darrell Waltrip. But Geoffrey Bodine wasn't so lucky. He got hit hard from behind, took a nasty shot to the driver's-side door, hit the wall, and then slammed into Burton. As Stacy Compton tried to avoid the mess, he and Mike Bliss rammed each other and bounced into the wall, sending more smoke and debris into the air.

It was about that time that I was straining to see where our drivers were in the mayhem. "God, help them!" I prayed instinctively. It was all happening so fast, I had no time to think that our nine-year quest for a NASCAR championship might be obliterated instantaneously in the crash. You don't think of championships, money, or machinery at a moment like that—you just pray that everyone is okay.

Thanks to their great pit stops just prior to the wreck, Bobby and Tony had been running ahead of where the crash took place. Nevertheless, as they rounded the track, they had to negotiate the crash area. They darted through the tangled mass of machinery, expertly steering away from trouble, as our spotters shouted instructions in their headsets. A race car driver has to trust his spotter completely—there's no time to argue, negotiate other options, or attempt to outguess the spotter. With cars caroming off one another like bumper cars and a wall of smoke blocking the view ahead, the driver must react instinctively to the voice of the spotter, relying on the spotter's direction to get him through the melee—using his own driving ability, for sure, but knowing that the spotter has a better overall view of the track. The spotter can see what is up ahead of the driver and what is behind the driver, and he must often make split-second decisions to help the driver avoid disaster.

I swallowed hard and breathed a sigh of relief as I saw both the #18 and the #20 emerge from the smoke. "Whew! That was close," I said aloud to no one in particular. I squeezed my eyes shut as I tried to hear clearly the voices in the headsets that were describing the accident.

Clean-up crews went to work clearing the damage from the five-car crash. After only thirty-eight laps, seven cars—each one costing more than $150,000—had been towed to the garage area. For the drivers of those cars, the race was over.

Following the caution period, the race restarted with Jeremy Mayfield leading Ricky Rudd and Dale Jarrett into the first turn. Ricky had been on a roll, finishing in the top ten in nine of his last twelve races, and he had a great car again today.

Hot on the leaders' tails was Tony Stewart. Bobby hung back a bit in seventh position as he waited patiently for an opportunity to advance. In a long race with more than 200 laps yet to go, Bobby knew that he'd get his chance.

Mayfield and Jarrett soon fell back, and Tony swept into second position behind Ricky Rudd. Tony then boldly slid under Ricky, passing him on the left and moving into the lead. The two traded the lead back and forth as they ripped around the race track, with Tony finally pulling ahead of Ricky Rudd by less than a second.

By lap 67, Tony had caught and nearly lapped the cars at the tail end of the field. Bobby had moved into fifth position—right where he needed to be if we were to win the championship. Tony was gunning for victory in the race; Bobby was chasing a championship dream!

PRECISION TEAMWORK

Tony kept in close radio contact with his crew chief, Greg Zipadelli—Zippy, as he is known around our race shop. Tony updated him on the car's engine temperature, gauges, and overall feel. The #20 car was running great. "I'm just babying the car," Tony quipped as he roared by the grandstands.

With 180 laps to go, Tony now led Ricky Rudd by more than one full second. Bobby was about twelve seconds behind the leaders, and Jeff Gordon hovered in ninth position, 17.8 seconds behind Tony. Jeff had won the Winston Cup championship in 1995, 1997, and 1998, so nobody ever counted him out of a race; but a 17-second lead is tough to overcome, even for a great driver.

Tony completed lap 92, and Zippy instructed him to pit for fresh tires and fuel. Watching the pit crew work is like watching artistry in motion—a symphony played on finely tuned instruments by experts performing at a level few novices can ever hope to achieve. It is a true team effort, each member of the pit crew contributing his talent to the overall accomplishment of the team.

Like a precision military unit, our pit guys stood poised on the wall, ready to respond. They leaped over the wall just as Tony whipped the car into the Home Depot pit. Wearing a protective helmet, our gas man, Gooch, carried an eleven-gallon tank to the car and filled Tony's tank. Meanwhile, Marcus, the jack man, hoisted the car as the tire changers went to work with their powerful pressurized air wrenches, whizzing the lug nuts off the wheels, the whirring, high-pitched sound piercing the air like two loud and very large dentist's drills. Two tire carriers hauled the large, fresh tires and threw them onto the wheels, and the air wrenches whirred again, replacing the lug nuts. The hot tires just removed from the car were bounced out of the way. The tire guys made it look easy, like a perfect pass around a befuddled defender on a basketball court. The process was repeated on the car's left side, while two team members used long-handled brushes to scrub the car's windshield and grill area. In 15.4 seconds, Tony was heading back into the race with four new tires, a full tank of gas, and a clean windshield. Try *that* at your local service station!

A lap later, Bobby Labonte pulled onto pit road. Bobby had smartly stayed out on the track while the other race leaders came in for their pit stops, thereby pulling into the lead of the race and picking up five more points toward the 2000 NASCAR championship. As soon as Bobby picked up the bonus points, he headed for pit road, where the Interstate Batteries team whipped into action. With a blur of motion, the crew refueled the car, changed tires, and took one pound of air pressure out of both rear tires—all in an astonishing 14.9 seconds!

I have a standing bonus program for our pit crews. For every pit stop completed in less than sixteen seconds, I pay our crew a bonus. For every pit stop that takes more than sixteen seconds, the crew pays me! Watching Bobby as he roared off pit road and back into the race, I knew that stop was going to cost me—a bonus I was glad to pay!

As soon as the pit crew hauled the used tires back into the pit, one of our tire guys took a torch and smoothed off a plane of rubber across each tire to rid the tire of any road debris or crud collected from the track. Tread-depth gauges were inserted into each tire, and the wear was measured and recorded. A pyrometer measured the tires' temperatures. We want to know exactly how far our drivers can go on each new tire, and the only way to do that is to closely monitor the wear and tear on our used tires. Information is then recorded and entered into our computers aboard the pit cart for future reference.

I paced back and forth, slowly but incessantly, in the #18-car pit area. There's not much room in the pit, and with the pit cart in front of me and stacks of tires behind me, I was forced to confine my pacing to a relatively tight area, but I kept moving nonetheless. I focused intensely, oblivious to everything and everybody except the action on the track. To a casual observer, I must have looked much as I did along the sidelines during my coaching career in the NFL, radioing plays to the quarterback over my headset microphone. Now, however, I wasn't saying anything at all, but the microphone and my sunglasses helped to conceal my anxiety. I struggled to maintain a cool, calm demeanor, while inside my heart was pounding. *We really might win this thing!* I thought.

One hundred fifty-five laps to go! Tony continued leading the race, lapping cars all around the track. Most of the lapped cars simply got out of the way, but not Dale Earnhardt. As Tony came up behind Dale, "The Intimidator" was not about to go easily. Dale was in hot pursuit of Bobby for the 2000 championship, and whether it was losing points or pride, Dale didn't take kindly to going a lap down to the leader.

Tony moved up behind Dale and attempted to slide by him on the inside. But then Dale roared back and cut Tony off, costing him valuable time as Ricky Rudd picked up nearly half a second on the leader. Tony backed off momentarily, allowing Dale to move slightly ahead, as both cars bore down on a pack of others in front of them. One by one, Tony slipped past the other race cars, but he couldn't get around Earnhardt. Consequently, Ricky Rudd loomed ever closer in Tony's rearview mirror. This was NASCAR racing at its best! Even when Dale Earnhardt was not in contention to win the race, he was a fierce competitor and a force on the track.

Finally, Tony found an opening. He powered past Dale, but even then Dale wasn't done. As Tony rounded the turn in front of Dale, the black #3 car nearly nudged the back of Tony's car. Had Dale gotten into Tony's bumper, the #20 car could easily have careened out of control. Fortunately, Earnhardt slid off higher on the track, and Tony picked up some breathing space between them. In doing so, Tony helped his teammate's quest for the championship by putting Bobby's closest challenger a lap down.

Now all we had to do was hope and pray that Bobby could finish near the front at Homestead.

Two

VICTORY LANE

Unlike the thirty-one-degree banking found at super speedways like Daytona International, which allows drivers to achieve speeds of more than 200 miles per hour, the Homestead-Miami track has a banking of only six degrees. Top drivers at Homestead dare not push their machines much faster than 150 miles per hour for fear that the centrifugal force they create will whisk their car right out of the race track.

Tony Stewart, however, loves that kind of track. For the next hour, Tony streaked around the nearly flat track, at times running two full seconds ahead of second-place Ricky Rudd. Meanwhile, Bobby raced for the championship, patiently biding his time in seventh place. Throughout the day, Tony called over the radio, "Where's Bobby?" or "How's Bobby doing?" This was a team effort, and although Tony wanted to conquer the field at Homestead for the second year in a row, he was nonetheless concerned for Bobby and his bid for the Winston Cup.

Tony came in for a pit stop at lap 150, but just as he did, Rick Mast pulled his car out of a pit stall right in front of Tony! Tony slammed on the brakes to keep from hitting the #14 car, and the delay cost him precious time getting to our pit.

But the #20 crew was up to the challenge! Over the wall they flew to refuel the car and change all four tires in an astounding 14.5 seconds.

Tony's tires were already spinning as the jack came down. A slight but disconcerting puff of smoke came from the car as it left pit road.

Tony had been distracted during the pit stop. While the crew worked on the car, one of our guys passed Tony some ice to help him stay cool in the sweltering Florida heat. Tony unzipped his fire suit and dumped the ice inside his suit. As he roared out of the pit stall, he was rezipping his fire suit when he suddenly realized that he was accelerating too rapidly. He was about to break the forty-five-mile-per-hour pit road speed limit! Tony slammed on the brakes, causing the puff of smoke from his right front tire. Breaking the speed limit on pit road results in a fifteen-second penalty—an eternity in races often won or lost by hundredths of a second. Worse yet, had Tony not slowed down abruptly, the infraction would have occurred as he was exiting pit road. He would have had to run a lap, return to pit road, and stop for fifteen seconds—which would have cost him even more time and, undoubtedly, the race.

Despite the valiant efforts of our pit crew, Ricky Rudd jumped out ahead of Tony during the delayed stop. Ricky now led by 2.7 seconds, and Tony would have a tough time catching him. Ricky's #28 car had been running well all day, and he really wanted to win this race. A late-race wreck had cost Ricky a win the week before in Phoenix, which made the Rudd team all the more determined to win at Homestead. Nevertheless, Tony's Pontiac Grand Prix was running great—a full one mile per hour faster than Rudd's car—so I felt confident that Tony could eventually regain the lead, barring any unforeseen incidents.

Bobby Labonte now pulled into the pits, and the #18 team burst into action. This was a make-or-break pit stop for Bobby. He couldn't afford to fall behind, not even by a few seconds, if he hoped to finish the day with a championship. The pit crew made a few minor adjustments to the car, put on four fresh tires, and got Bobby on his way in 14.9 seconds.

Back on the track, Bobby worked the Interstate Batteries Pontiac up through the pack. A shout went up in our pit when Bobby lapped Dale Earnhardt, his closest pursuer for the points championship; the move virtually ensured our team a Winston Cup title. All Bobby needed to do now was to finish in front of Dale and Jeff Burton...and make it through this race without incident.

At lap 172, Tony closed the gap to one second behind Ricky Rudd. Jeff Gordon and Mark Martin followed closely behind. This was still anybody's race. A few laps later, Tony roared up right behind Ricky, putting the pressure on. At lap 184, Tony passed Ricky and regained the lead. What a race!

With 66 laps to go, Tony pulled up alongside Dale Earnhardt and was about to slide by him when his car got a little loose and swerved within a few inches of Dale, both cars flying along at nearly 150 miles per hour. Dale slid off toward the wall, and Tony blew by him, putting another lap on the legendary driver. Another close call, but Tony was still in good shape.

LUG NUTS AND LOST CYLINDERS

Late in the race, the leaders came chugging down pit road for their final stop. The #20 team worked feverishly on the left rear tire of Tony's car, but a lug nut flew off as they were replacing the tire. Slowing things even further, Tony had trouble getting more ice under his suit, and the pit stop took seventeen seconds, while Ricky Rudd got back out in just over fourteen seconds. My stomach churned as I watched our guys give up valuable time to the #28 team. Tony managed to retain the lead, but the gap had closed considerably.

Bobby radioed Jimmy Makar and said, "I want to come in and take new tires. I don't like the set I've got on." I knew that even if we had a bad pit stop, with only eight cars remaining on the lead lap, Bobby was almost guaranteed to come in at least eighth in the race.

But for the first time in my career, I thought that finishing in the middle of the pack might not be so bad. It had been nine frustrating, expensive, and extremely difficult years getting to this point. Now Bobby was in position to win the championship. All we had to do was to maintain the status quo. We didn't have to press so hard. We didn't have to compete so furiously, vying for first place. Bobby could cruise comfortably around the Homestead track for the remainder of the day, without taking on new tires, and we'd all go home champions.

I rarely offer any advice to my crew chiefs during a race, but I couldn't help myself this time. I climbed up the side of the pit cart, looked up at

Jimmy Makar, and said, "Jimmy, we can just run the rest of the race in the back of the pack and still win this thing!"

Jimmy looked down at me incredulously, as though he couldn't believe what he'd just heard. "We can't do that," he said with a wry smile.

I knew Jimmy was right, and I "repented" for my momentary lapse into complacency. To this day, every time I think about this incident, it makes me laugh.

Meanwhile, Bobby had a great pit stop, and Jimmy told him that he remained in position to win the championship. I sensed that Bobby was smiling behind the tinted mask of his helmet. The Interstate Batteries pit crew sensed that victory was near. A few seconds later, the bright green #18 car began to gain on the leaders.

Jeff Gordon encountered a problem with his throttle, forcing him to stop twice so his crew could work under the hood, causing him to lose precious time in the pits. Although he would reenter the race, the extended stop eliminated Jeff as a contender for the remainder of the day.

Tension mounted as the race came down to a battle between Tony and Ricky Rudd. Jimmy Spencer in the #26 car, Jeremy Mayfield in the #12, and Mark Martin in the #6 ran together a few car lengths back, with Bobby closing in on them—as safely as possible—in his quest for the championship.

With thirty-five laps to go, Tony stretched his lead over Martin and Rudd to 3.2 seconds. Tony seemed confident. "Guys, I haven't even begun to push this car yet!" he radioed.

In the #18-car pit, Norm Miller, chairman of Interstate Batteries, paced almost as nervously as I. Norm wore a four-inch button with the slogan GO, BOBBY on it. Norm had ordered the buttons made for all 800 of his employees at Interstate Batteries, and during the entire month prior to the Homestead race, Norm's Dallas-based employees wore the GO, BOBBY button every day! If Norm came across one of his employees without a button, he'd ask, "Where's your button? Go put it on." I had never seen my friend Norm—our first and only major sponsor of the #18 car—so excited!

Ricky Rudd's engine suddenly lost a cylinder with only five laps to go, dropping him to sixth place behind the leaders: Tony, Jeremy Mayfield, Mark Martin, and now Bobby. Five more laps. After more than 390 miles of racing, you'd think that five laps would pass in a flash—but they didn't.

My nerves jangled. Perspiration dampened my entire body, while my mouth felt like I had opened wide in the face of a desert sandstorm. Four laps. *Easy, Tony. Hang in there, Bobby!* These guys were racing at twice the speed of cars on most interstate highways; yet to me the cars seemed to be moving in slow motion, barely inching their way around the track. I thought I could hear my heart pounding above the thunderous roar of the cars as they streaked by.

Three laps. *Don't do anything foolish, guys. We're almost there.* It seemed to take forever for the cars to get around the track.

Two laps to go. After nine years, all our efforts were coming down to a little more than a minute. I wanted to shout. I wanted to jump for joy! But we weren't home yet. Last-minute accidents had destroyed the hopes and dreams of many a NASCAR team and driver. I dared not relax until the race was over.

The white flag! *This is it, guys—the last lap!* In a fraction of a second, my brain yelled to our drivers a thousand instructions, none of which made it to my dry tongue.

Here they come! Tony's car rounded the last turn ahead of the pack, followed closely by Mayfield and Martin.

The checkered flag! *Way to go, Tony!*

Already on their feet, the fans leaped up and down, cheering wildly as Tony Stewart crossed the finish line first, winning the race! He had led 167 laps of the 267-lap event.

Jeremy Mayfield roared by, and then Mark Martin. Right behind them came Bobby Labonte! I thought my heart was going to explode as Bobby thundered across the finish line, and the #18-car team erupted, jumping into each other's arms, slapping each other on the back, and sharing high fives all around.

Bobby Labonte was the 2000 NASCAR Winston Cup champion! In the stock car racing organization's fifty-one-year history, only twenty-three other drivers had won the NASCAR championship. Now Bobby Labonte joined his brother, Terry, as a member of that elite group.

In an inspiring display of team spirit, Tony and Bobby drove a victory lap together around the Homestead track—Tony as the Pennzoil 400 winner, Bobby as the Winston Cup champion. Then Tony pulled into Victory Lane, allowing Bobby to run a championship lap by himself. It was a moving moment.

THE SWEET TASTE OF VICTORY

There I was with a bunch of grown men hugging one another in joy. Marty Snider, an interviewer from NBC Sports, grabbed me and asked, "Joe, is this as or more gratifying than the three Super Bowls?"

I could barely talk, but I said, "I don't know how to describe it.... It's been nine long, hard years.... I wouldn't trade those Super Bowls for anything; but I'll tell you, this is fantastic!" I caught my breath and tried to explain.

"It's been a total team effort. A lot of these people have devoted nine years of their careers working for us, being part of our team. The Lord blessed us with a great day. I'm just thrilled!"

You win with people.

Marty pressed the comparison between football and racing: "It took you only two years to win a Super Bowl, nine years to win the Winston Cup—which was harder?"

"They're both team sports, and you've gotta have great people," I exclaimed. "You win with people. With this one, I had a lot less to do with it, but it's just as much fun." I wasn't telling Marty anything new. I had been winning with people for nearly forty years. I had learned long ago that you don't win with machines or methods, helpful as they may be. You win with people, by helping to bring out the best in others.

"I get a kick out of seeing all our people enjoy it, too," I told Marty. "We have only a handful of people on our team that have ever been part of a championship, so it's a thrill for them. The Lord gave us a great year."

I climbed over the wall separating the pit area from pit road and headed for crew chief Jimmy Makar. People were clasping my hand and clapping me on the back as I moved through the crowd. When I got to Jimmy, we embraced tightly and slapped each other on the back. "You did it, Jimmy. You deserve this! Nine years later, man. You deserve it. You made it happen."

Bob Dyar, our team chaplain, led us in a prayer of thanks. Then both of our teams, along with Bobby's wife Donna, their little boy Tyler, and their daughter Madison, moved toward Victory Lane. Tony's car was already in place as the winner of the race, but, in a self-effacing and gracious gesture, Tony stayed in his car longer than usual so the attention could be directed toward Bobby, the new Winston Cup champion. The NBC interview team clamored around Tony's car to get his comments. Only then did Tony reveal that he had suffered from the heat throughout the race, that the pit crew had been pouring ice into his fire suit to cool him down and keep him from becoming nauseated. In fact, Tony talked more about Bobby's achievement than his own performance.

Meanwhile, Bobby was directed to an area in front of the huge Winston Cup championship sign. Bobby climbed out of his driver-side car window, where family, friends, and an army of cameras and microphones awaited him. He stepped up on his door and bounded onto the roof of the car, where he leaped into the air in jubilation. He was wearing a green-and-black Interstate Batteries cap when he got out of the car, but someone handed him a red NASCAR championship hat, which Bobby promptly plopped onto his head.

Two NASCAR officials hoisted the large, heavy Winston Cup championship trophy to Bobby atop the car roof, and the weight of the trophy nearly knocked him off balance. For a moment it looked as though the new champion might drop the enormous trophy, but Bobby regained his footing and raised the trophy high above his head, as the Homestead crowd erupted in cheers. Bobby allowed the NASCAR officials to safely retrieve the trophy. Then he held up an Interstate Batteries case, honoring our main sponsor of the #18 car. Norm and Interstate truly deserved a lot of the credit for getting us here!

The TV microphones were waiting for him as Bobby scampered down. "Bobby, you are the 2000 NASCAR Winston Cup champion. How does that sound?"

"Well, I guess we can talk about it now, right?" Bobby quipped, referring to his reluctance to talk too much about the heightened pressure as the season wore on. Sitting atop the roof of the #18 car with his son, Tyler, at his side, Bobby took a moment to praise our corporate sponsors, whose names were displayed on the car.

And then confetti and champagne were flying in every direction, as Bobby sprayed our team members with a giant bottle of bubbly. About that time, Tony Stewart came running in, champagne bottle in hand, and soaked our new Winston Cup champion. It was a wonderful display of team spirit as our #18-car team and #20-car team celebrated together.

It was fitting that both teams should share in the victory. At our race shop, most of the guys work on both cars—a rather unusual relationship. Many multi-car teams tend to become extremely competitive with each other. But our guys really do work together as one unit on both cars. When one car wins, both teams share in the success—and in the rewards that accompany success.

THE FUN THING IS GETTING HERE

I was exhausted and exhilarated at the same time. What a day! Two teams, two champions. What a year! Much as I had done when the Washington Redskins won three Super Bowls, in the midst of the euphoria I took some time to reflect. I looked around at all the people who had worked so hard for so long to get us to this place. Their nine-year struggle had finally paid off.

There was Bobby Labonte, a young guy who had come to us in 1995 as a relatively inexperienced driver on the NASCAR circuit. He hadn't won a Winston Cup race yet, but he had a ton of talent. He had said, "This is the place where I want to stake my career. I want to race with Joe Gibbs Racing." As I watched him celebrating with his family, I couldn't help thinking back to the first race we ever won with Bobby behind the wheel, the 1995 Coca-Cola 600 in Charlotte. I had stood there that day with Bobby's wife, Donna, and our family members, and there wasn't a dry eye among us as we cheered his first victory. Bobby won two more races that year. Over the years since then, I had watched him progress as a driver—he'd now won sixteen Winston Cup races—and I had admired his growth as a loving husband and father. Bobby was every inch a champion.

I looked over and saw my son J D celebrating with our crew. J D had initiated our involvement in racing soon after graduating from college. Although he was a fine athlete and a bright leader, J D had said, "Dad, I don't want to coach football. I'd rather go into something like racing." Together, J D and I began to dream about one day developing a race team. This victory belonged to my son as much as to me.

I glanced around and saw Norm Miller standing next to me, and I nearly broke into tears. Norm had believed in our team from the very beginning— I mean the *real* beginning.

When I first went to Dallas, Texas, to pitch Norm on the idea of sponsoring our race team, I had absolutely nothing to show him. I didn't have a nut or a bolt. I didn't have a car, a driver, a garage, a motor—nothing! And I was asking Norm to invest millions of dollars in our dream of putting together everything we needed to create a winning race team. It's a wonder he didn't throw me out of his office!

I had never before met Norm Miller, but I knew a bit about him. He had a reputation as a highly successful Christian businessman and a great sports fan—in Dallas, of all places. In case you've forgotten, the rivalry between the Dallas Cowboys and Washington Redskins has long been one of the fiercest in the NFL. Nevertheless, one day I telephoned Norm on a cold call, and we hit it off immediately. We talked for nearly forty-five minutes, and I shared with him a few of my ideas about putting together a race team.

"Come on down to Dallas and tell me more about your idea," Norm said, and so I did.

Rick Hendrick, who owns several highly successful NASCAR teams, including those of Jeff Gordon and Terry Labonte, had graciously agreed to lease engines to us to get us started. Rick also offered the assistance of his general manager, Jimmy Johnson, and Jimmy accompanied me to Dallas to help pitch our idea.

There we met with Norm, his brother Tommy Miller, the president of Interstate Batteries, and Norm's management team, Charlie Suscavage and

Len Ruby. They listened attentively and promised to get back to me. A few days later, when I hadn't heard from Norm, I called him back. In the interim I had come to realize the enormous risk involved for Norm, and the ludicrousness of my proposal hit me. Norm's company was already involved in racing on a small scale. Why would he want to get involved with me, someone with absolutely no professional racing experience?

"Norm, I've had a chance to think about it," I began hesitantly, "and I've realized that maybe this is too big for you. How about becoming an associate sponsor and I'll try to find someone else to be the major sponsor of our team?"

"Well, we're talking about doing the whole thing," Norm replied.

"The whole thing?" I about fell out of my chair!

Now, doused in champagne mixed with sweat and tears, I hugged Norm and remembered how we struggled through our first year without winning a race, finishing nineteenth in points for the season. But Norm had never wavered from his commitment, even when it was costing him millions of dollars with little to show for it. Now Norm was the major sponsor of the Winston Cup champion!

I looked over at Jimmy Makar, another astonishing story. Jimmy, too, had been with me from the beginning, but his coming to our team was a total surprise and a blessing from God. Jimmy had been the crew chief for the Roger Penske racing team, one of the best jobs in racing with one of the top teams on the track. When I began building a race team, my advisors instructed me, "The two key guys you need to hire are a top-notch driver and a great crew chief."

First we hired a young up-and-coming driver, Dale Jarrett. Then I went after a crew chief. I had a list of five top NASCAR crew chiefs, one of whom was Jimmy Makar, but everyone said, "Don't even bother to talk to Jimmy, because he's got a great job and he just won a championship a few years ago."

But when I hired Dale, he said to me, "I'd like to talk to Jimmy Makar about being our crew chief."

"So would I," I said, "but everyone says there's no way we could get him."

"I'd like to try," Dale replied.

"What makes you think you can get him?"

"Because he's my brother-in-law," said Dale, smiling.

"Well, hey, knock yourself out," I told Dale.

A short time later, we hired Jimmy Makar as our first crew chief. Jimmy was excited by the challenge of starting a race team from scratch. Nine years later, he had once again achieved the pinnacle of success in his field.

Basking in the warm glow of the NASCAR championship, I recalled an incident that took place on the football field, after the Redskins defeated the Buffalo Bills in Super Bowl XXVI at the Metrodome in Minneapolis. As I walked out onto the field after the hoopla had died down a bit, I saw Redskins defensive end Charles Mann staring dreamily around the stadium. Charles looked at me and with awe in his eyes said, "You know, Coach, the fun thing is getting here."

Charles was right. The taste of victory is sweet, the trophy is awe-inspiring, and the financial reward is real. But the thrill of the journey—the anticipation, pain, work, fun, frustration, practice, struggles, shoestring wins, gut-wrenching losses, leaving the stadium with your head down, the grit and grind—that's the truly rewarding aspect of winning a championship. The same thing hit me about our NASCAR championship. Getting here had been half the fun!

MY GAME PLAN FOR SUCCESS

So how does a kid from a small town in North Carolina get to the top of the sports world?

I've been asked thousands of times, "Joe, how do you do it? How have you achieved such success?" "How do you motivate people?" "Why do you keep coming up with winners in some of the most competitive sports in the world?" "How can *I* be successful?"

My answer is "I follow a good game plan." As a football coach, I found it was crucial to have a good, solid, well-conceived game plan if I ever hoped to win. The same is true in NASCAR racing. Much the same is true for your career, your acquisition and use of money, and other key areas of your life, as well.

I have experienced both exhilarating success and crushing failure, both on a personal and professional level, and I have identified six areas of my life where success must be achieved if I am to be truly content: my career, my finances, my ability to build a team and manage people, my personal relationships, my values and moral choices, and my physical and spiritual health. In each of these areas, through success and failure I have discovered several key principles that have helped guide my decisions and, if followed, point the way along the path to true success.

In this book, I want to share my game plan with you.

I've always been competitive, and I've always wanted to win. But over the years, I've discovered that success on the playing field or in business doesn't necessarily make me a success in life. How can I know whether or not I have achieved real success in life? Can my bank statement tell me? Should I measure success according to what my friends and family think? The media have called me both a genius and an idiot. Can either of these really be true?

Success on the playing field or in business doesn't necessarily make you a success in life.

The lessons I've learned weren't taught in a classroom. They've been learned the hard way: on football fields and race tracks, in NFL locker rooms and NASCAR pits, in boardrooms and around the dinner table. What you will find within these pages will not be high-fallutin', hypothetical gobbledygook or theoretical mush. I've tested these down-to-earth principles for achieving success in my own life, and I'm here to tell you, they work! I'm convinced that if you will adopt these principles, you can shorten your learning curve by ten years or more. I wish that when I was in my twenties or thirties, someone would have told me what I am about to tell you. Besides being saved a lot of hard knocks, heartache, and financial loss, I could have been much richer today in every way—if someone had just shared with me this blueprint for success.

So jump in the driver's seat, buckle up, and hold on—this could be the ride of your life!

THE GAME PLAN

Success in Your Career

Joe Gibbs and I have shared many exciting moments, especially during the 2000 run for the Winston Cup championship. Joe is a fierce competitor who plans to win, and he's a great friend. He knows how to motivate people and bring out the best in them. Joe Gibbs has been a true inspiration to me and my family.

Bobby Labonte is the driver of the #18 Interstate Batteries Chevrolet Monte Carlo and the 2000 NASCAR Winston Cup Champion.

Patience, patience, patience...is not one of my strongest traits. But the longer I work with Joe Gibbs, the more I discover how patience is a key element to success in any career—yours or mine. Joe never gives up. He has incredible faith in God, in himself, and in the people he surrounds himself with.

Tony Stewart is the driver of the #20 Home Depot Chevrolet Monte Carlo and the 2002 NASCAR Winston Cup Champion.

Now that you know a bit about where I spend my time and energy today, let me fill you in on how I've gotten to this point—and share with you the most important lessons I've learned along the way. I want you to discover what real success is and how you, too, can achieve it.

The remainder of this book will be divided into bite-size chunks, focusing on how to be successful in six key areas:

1. Career
2. Finances
3. Building a team
4. Personal relationships
5. Making moral choices
6. Health and physical fitness

Each section will be a few chapters in length, with lots of stories from my personal and professional experience. I'll then provide you with several cornerstone principles on which I have built my life. Following the six key areas, there's a comparison between sports and life that you won't want to miss!

I'm not a professor, so you won't find a lecture here. What you will find are the key elements that have helped me achieve success and enjoy it. We'll also explore a few areas where I made costly mistakes. I hope you can learn from both my victories and my defeats.

I'm an extremely competitive guy, so let's start where the competition is most intense for many of us—our careers.

In this section, you'll find:

- The foundations on which I've built my life.
- How to make good career decisions.
- My own spiritual struggles and growth.
- Why I retired from football.
- How we started a winning racing team.
- How we won a *second* Winston Cup championship.

DO WHAT YOU LOVE

R acing and football. Football and racing. My dual loves have colored my life as far back as I can remember. Of course, in my youth I could never have imagined a career in which I led superstar football players to three NFL championships in front of millions of people on television. Nor could I possibly imagine that my occupation would one day involve racing $150,000 cars at speeds of 200 miles per hour in front of more than 100,000 fans. As I was growing up, I was excited just to play sandlot football and race in our local soap box derby.

But I could dream!

HUMBLE BEGINNINGS

I grew up in the small town of Enka, North Carolina, near Asheville. My brother Jim and I loved to play all sorts of sports, and our mom was glad to get us out of the house. Our dad, Jackson Cephus Gibbs, was a big man—a highway patrolman and a rough, tough, rumbling type of guy with a generous heart and friendly personality. But Dad drank too much, too often. He had grown up in a home with an absentee father and had never finished high school. He met Winnie Blalock, and they married young. Dad was a hard worker, and he provided well for our family—and he always took care of my mother. I learned from him early on that a man could do pretty much whatever he put his mind to, as long as he didn't give up.

Because both Mom and Dad worked outside the home, I spent a lot of time at the home of my Aunt Louise and Uncle Walter, my mother's brother. It was Uncle Walter who first helped make soap box derby racing carts for

> *If you're going to build a great career, you better have a strong foundation.*

Jim and me. I loved cars and grew up fascinated with hot rods and racing. I couldn't wait to get behind the wheel! The town had a few streets built on steep hills, and my first sensation of speed came from racing down the streets, thinking, *This is as fast as anyone has ever gone!* My soap box cart was probably pegging all of twenty miles per hour.

In the wintertime the town shut off the streets, and we replaced the carts with sleds, streaking down the hill on the snow and ice. I mean, we hauled it down those hills!

Whether on wheels or on runners, I was fascinated with speed. We can build it better, Uncle Walter. We can make it go faster!

SPIRITUAL FOUNDATIONS

If you're going to build a great career, you had better have a strong foundation. My career has been built on rock-solid values that I first learned as a child at home and in church. As a nine-year-old boy, I committed my life to Jesus Christ. Looking back now, I can see how that one decision has impacted every aspect of my life. Of course, when I walked to the front of that little church to acknowledge my faith in God and my need of a Savior, I had no idea just how far-reaching that choice would prove to be. All I knew was that I was being taught in school that my life was an accident, that a couple of amoeba had met in a puddle a few million years ago and eventually evolved into a man and woman. My science teachers were teaching me that I was nothing more than a bunch of grown-up goo.

But my mother, my grandmother, and my Aunt Louise made sure that I attended church. In church, my pastor and Sunday school teachers confronted the evolutionary theory head-on. They taught that God loved me and had made me special, and He put me on this earth with special abilities. They said He had an important plan for my life and that if I'd trust Him, He would lead me in the right direction and show me what He wanted me to do.

As I weighed these two contrasting concepts, I concluded that evolution didn't make a lot of sense. Surrounded by the world, its beauty, and the order I saw in nature, I felt sure there must be a Creator. When I look at my wristwatch I think, *This is a complicated piece of machinery, and I know that where there is a watch, there is a watchmaker.* I extended that logic to the world around me and realized there must be a God. Looking at this world and the way it's put together, I said, "Hey, listen, I am not real sharp, but I know this: Where there is a world, there is a World Maker!"

That's what prompted me to go forward at that church service and commit myself to the One who had created me. I prayed, *God, I know You're there. I know You made me and that I am not an accident. I want to live for You.* More than a half-century later, I've never regretted praying that prayer.

CALIFORNIA DREAMIN'

When Aunt Louise and Uncle Walter moved to California, my mom and dad decided to follow. We settled near Whittier, and in no time I was a starter on my high school baseball, basketball, and football teams. As the starting quarterback at a small school, I led an active social life.

I was a "rounder," out cruising in my car with the guys, carousing, and generally goofing off. I wasn't the romantic type, and I rarely dated the same girl for more than a few weeks—until I met Pat, a beautiful, dark-haired cheerleader. We continued dating after high school, but it took me eight years to convince her to marry me! We finally married on January 29, 1966, and our first anniversary fell in the same month as the first AFL-NFL Championship game, which is today known as the Super Bowl. To this day, when anyone asks Pat how long we've been married, she quips, "What number of Super Bowl is it?"

I wasn't a great athlete in high school—I really wasn't—but through a lot of hard work I was named the school's Athlete of the Year when I graduated in 1959. Football was my favorite sport, and I hoped to receive a scholarship to a major university, with dreams of one day playing for a pro football team. When no scholarship offers came from the schools I wanted to attend, I elected to go to nearby Cerritos Junior College. But my quarterbacking days were over. The coach decided I was better suited as an end, so I worked hard and won a starting job on the team.

I wasn't a particularly great student, either. Throughout college, I'd sit in the front row of the class, point to my letterman's jacket, and beg my teachers, "Please, Prof! I need a C to be eligible to play." I was focused on my goal of playing pro sports. I played hard and eventually got noticed by Don Coryell, head coach at San Diego State University, the "Harvard of the West." He offered me a half scholarship to play football, and he didn't have to offer it twice. I went for it!

I played guard, tight end, and linebacker for Coryell, and I quickly discovered that the man was "football brilliant." He was an incredible strategist, constantly devising new plays, trying new alignments—anything that might help us win a game. In the back of my mind, I thought, *If I can't play pro football, I want to be a coach like Don Coryell.* Coryell would one day become the successful head coach of the San Diego Chargers, and *Sports Illustrated* would name him one of the top three professional football coaches of all time.

When it came time for me to pick a major in college, I glanced down the list of possible careers. I skipped over neurosurgeon, nuclear physicist, and astronaut. *What am I qualified to do?* Finally, I thought, *I've got it! Physical education! I can do that. Handball, recreational dancing—this is perfect!* So I embarked on a physical education major, which I regarded at the time simply as a stepping stone to a career in professional sports.

I was a junior in college when, one day, I looked at my body in the mirror and realized that I wasn't big enough, fast enough, or talented enough to make it in football at the pro level. This was a shock to my system, and at first I panicked!

What am I going to do to make a living? I had a degree in physical education, but I didn't really want to teach. Suddenly, it dawned on me. I know! I'll coach! What does a coach do? He stands on the sidelines and tells people, "Run faster! Jump higher! Hit 'em! Kill 'em!" I can do that!

I went to see Coach Coryell and volunteered to work for no pay as part of his coaching staff. By now, Pat and I were planning to be married and I was in graduate school, so working for no money was not exactly a glamorous prospect. But I believed in what I wanted to do, and Pat believed in me. Together we were willing to sacrifice and work hard to see our dreams come true. As it turned out, the experience and football knowledge I soaked up under Coryell's leadership was worth it.

I believed in what I wanted to do, and Pat believed in me.

On Coach Coryell's staff was a big, gregarious guy named John Madden. My main job as junior member of the coaching staff was to go to the local fast-food joint at night and pick up hamburgers and tacos for the other coaches. The only time I got into trouble was when I inadvertently left something off John's taco order. Madden, of course, went on to an outstanding career as head coach of the Oakland Raiders and is now one of the most highly respected football analysts in broadcasting.

He's also well-known for his television commercials. The man has no shame! He's done all those Ace Hardware commercials, but he can't fool me. I've been to Madden's home, and he doesn't know a bolt from a belt sander!

I was visiting the Maddens' home one Christmas when John gave his wife, Virginia, a set of crescent wrenches as a gift! She does all the mechanical work around their house. And it's a good thing, because John doesn't have a clue! One day, John was leaving for work when he got a flat tire. He went to his neighbor's house and called *his wife* to come fix the flat!

But John *does* know football, and together with Coryell, they provided me with an education in coaching. I was privileged to learn from the best.

My job at San Diego State soon turned into a paid position. I was coaching the offensive linemen, earning a grand total of $6200 that first year. It wasn't much of an income, but Pat and I were ecstatic, and we decided to go ahead and get married. In 1966, my first year as a paid coach, San Diego State went 11-0 and won the small college national championship. We were off to a great start!

CROSS-COUNTRY COACHING

Following that season, I got a phone call in the middle of the night from a guy who spoke in such a thick Louisiana accent that I could barely understand him. Don Breaux was an assistant coach at Florida State University. They had somehow heard about me and wondered if I'd be interested in joining their staff. Besides making more money for coaching at a bigger school, the move would give Pat and me the opportunity to buy our first real home. We decided it was an offer I couldn't refuse.

Pat stayed behind in San Diego while I traveled to Florida to begin a new chapter in my career. I saw the move to Florida as a step up the ladder of success in my field.

It was certainly a step up in salary—I was making twice as much money at FSU as I had been in San Diego. Better yet, a booster of the athletic program gave me an incredible deal on a brand-new, 1,800-square-foot home on a corner lot in a new subdivision. "Give me four hundred dollars down and we'll do the deal," he said.

Few feelings in life can compare to the joy of stepping across the threshold of your own home.

"Four hundred dollars!" I exclaimed. "Sold!" I bought the house without ever stepping inside it! Pat excitedly sent me a checklist, wanting to know what sort of features were in our new home. Wondering whether the kitchen had a double stainless-steel sink or some other style, Pat had written, "Sink?" Beside her query I wrote, "Yes," and sent it back to her.

Nevertheless, when Pat finally saw our first home, she was so elated she wept. The little house was so pretty, far beyond our wildest expectations—and it was *ours*. Few feelings in life can compare to the joy of stepping across the threshold of your own home.

At Florida State, I coached under Bill Peterson, one of the hardest-working coaches I have ever met. Coach Pete was football's version of Yogi Berra, butchering the English language with humorous malapropisms—describing a close game as "a real *cliff dweller*" or boasting to the other coaches that he had such great *repertoire* with his players. Coach Pete once described two people missing each other as "two ships *crashing* in the night." When he got steamed, he sometimes warned, "Don't forget who's the *head football* around here!"

Bill Peterson may not have made it on the professional speaker's circuit, but the man developed a tremendous program at Florida State. And he knew how to win football games.

We went 15-4-1 during my two-year stint with the Seminoles. I was becoming addicted to winning. I thrived on it! So far in my fledgling coaching career, I had been a part of forty-two victories, with only eight losses and a tie. Coaching with Bill Peterson whetted my appetite for being a head coach, and that became my goal.

The standard career track was to move up from assistant coach to coordinator to head coach, the guy in charge of it all. That's who I wanted to be. Looking back, I can see clearly that God placed that desire in my heart and then maneuvered me into the positions where He could bring it to pass. Unfortunately, it would take a number of years and a lot of frustration before I realized that He could promote me much more effectively than I could promote myself. I became obsessed with wanting to be a head coach. I was willing to pay any price to get there...and I almost did.

FOUR

CHASING DREAMS

Transitions are tough for most of us, especially when you have settled into something you enjoy doing. I wanted to be a head football coach, and although I learned a lot during my two years at Florida State, when I got the opportunity to work at the University of Southern California with legendary coach John McKay, I couldn't resist.

USC was a national powerhouse, catapulting players and coaches to fame, glory, and success—or at least what looked like success. Even though it meant hauling everything we owned back across the country, Pat and I were excited about going home.

Pat was pregnant with our first baby, so I put her on a plane from Florida to California, and I drove our dream car—a tan 1968 Oldsmobile Toronado that we had hocked just about everything to purchase. I loved that car, but by the time I arrived at USC, I felt as though I had become permanently glued to the Toronado's front seat! No matter. I couldn't wait to get started with Coach McKay.

I was a good assistant football coach. I'm convinced that to reach your own goals and dreams, you must learn how to assist others in reaching theirs—and I can tell you that you'll never be a great head coach until you've learned how to be a good assistant.

When it came to being a supportive, encouraging, expectant father, however, I was a mess. Pat's labor seemed to go on forever, and I felt every contraction. Well, it seemed that way to me. Three times I was called into

To reach your own goals and dreams, you must learn how to assist others in reaching theirs.

the delivery room for the big event, only to discover that Pat was still struggling. I have a high tolerance for pain, but I couldn't stand to see Pat hurting, so I told the nurses, "Don't call for me again until the baby's ready to be born!"

So much for being a supportive spouse!

About four in the morning, after eighteen hours of labor, Pat gave birth to Jason Dean Gibbs. We started calling him J D as a baby, and he goes by the nickname to this day. J D's birth changed the focus of our life.

At USC, I immersed myself in John McKay's winning tradition. Coach McKay was a brilliant tactician who was involved in every facet of the game—offense, defense, and special teams. Although he tended to be caustic, controlling, and domineering, I learned a lot from his management style. We won fifteen of nineteen games during my first two years there, and I probably would have stayed at USC a long time had I not received another phone call from my buddy, Don Breaux. Don had left Florida State and moved on to Arkansas, another college football dynasty headed by Frank Broyles, one of the most respected coaches in the nation. Don was calling to let me know that the Arkansas offensive-line coaching job was open.

EVALUATING CAREER CHOICES

How do you make decisions regarding your career and its direction? If you're like me, you lay out all the positives and negatives and evaluate them in relation to how they will affect you and your family. I considered the pluses and minuses of the Arkansas job opportunity and came up with several strong negative factors: I'd have to leave USC, one of the most sought-after coaching positions in college football; I'd be taking another assistant coaching job, a lateral move instead of a step up; and I would have to move our family back east again.

"A lot of head coaches have come out of Arkansas." Don Breaux dangled the statement like a ping-pong ball hovering lazily above the net, just begging to be spiked.

Head coach? That was all I needed to hear. Suddenly the negatives disappeared, and all I could see was what *I* wanted to do. So Pat and I started packing once again.

Your strongest ally in making career choices is your spouse, the person who knows you at your best and at your worst. If you are single, seek out a mentor, a good friend, or a pastor who can serve in that advisory role. But if you are married, you and your spouse should be in agreement on any major career changes either of you makes. And you shouldn't have to trick, manipulate, or coerce your spouse into seeing things your way. If you and your spouse can't agree on the change, then it's probably not in your family's best interests to pursue it, regardless of how good the opportunity looks on the surface.

The Bible talks about surrounding yourself with wise counselors, of having people in your life to whom you are accountable—someone who can look you in the eyes and say, "That's a good idea," or "I don't think that's a good move for you." And if you listen carefully and are willing to hear, you might just hear the voice of God speaking through your spouse and other close advisors.

Unfortunately, I wasn't ready to bring God in on my career choices yet. I prayed occasionally for God to have His way in my life, but in the back of my mind there was a disclaimer: *God, have Your way in my life...as long as I get to call the shots.*

Despite my headstrong approach to climbing the ladder of success, God had a plan for my life, although I was not aware of it. He was giving me opportunities to learn from the best.

As it turned out, coaching with Frank Broyles in Fayetteville, Arkansas, was a significant juncture in my career and personal life.

Broyles was radically different from my previous head coaches.

Don Coryell was passionately intense. He was totally consumed with coaching, living and breathing football from the time he woke until the time he went to bed. On Saturdays when the whistle blew, I sometimes thought he might race onto the field to help cover the opening kickoff.

It's a wonder we didn't get penalized every game for having twelve men on the field!

Bill Peterson wrenched results out of his players and staff through sheer determination and hard work.

John McKay had a razor-sharp tongue and used fear as a motivator.

Frank Broyles took a different approach to coaching. Frank was a smooth, polished salesman—a real Southern gentleman who could sell *anything*. From Frank I learned that it wasn't enough to have the right product, with all the *X*'s and *O*'s in place; I had to be able to sell our program to potential players and their parents, as well as to alumni and supporters of the university.

True success is impossible without a strong spiritual commitment.

I traveled all over Texas recruiting high school players to attend Arkansas. Believe me, it was no small feat convincing players in Texas—home of the Texas Longhorns, the Baylor Bears, the Aggies of Texas A&M, and about a dozen other football dynasties—to play football twelve hours away from home in Arkansas.

On one such trip, I was in Houston when a ringing telephone woke me at six o'clock in the morning. A voice on the line said that Pat had gone into labor with our second child. I was frantic. I was responsible for fifteen high school boys who were scheduled to fly back with me that morning to Arkansas, but I had a hard time concentrating on them as we hurried to the airport. To make matters worse, we got snowed in at Fort Smith and couldn't get to Fayetteville.

Flustered and frazzled, I called the hospital from a pay phone. "Give me the waiting room for having babies!" I practically shouted into the phone.

Apparently the operator was accustomed to nervous fathers, because she interpreted my statement well enough to connect me. An elderly gentleman with a deep Arkansas drawl answered the phone and informed me that they "already done had that baby." I felt awful that I hadn't been able to get back in time for the birth. But Pat and I welcomed to our family another boy, and a big one, too—ten pounds. We named him Coy Randall Gibbs.

SPIRITUAL STIRRINGS

Today I'm convinced that true success is impossible without a strong spiritual commitment. Yet for more than twenty years, I virtually ignored my relationship with God. Oh, sure, I prayed occasionally and attended church services regularly. But from the time I committed my life to Christ as a child, I had plotted my own course with little concern for what God wanted me to do or to be. Mostly when I prayed, I made lists for God, describing what I wanted and asking Him to help me fulfill my dreams. It never occurred to me to ask what *His* plan for my life might be.

Now in my early thirties, I was frustrated, discouraged, and confused concerning my future. I was obsessed with becoming a head coach in college football, and I often asked God to help me make it happen. *God, why am I not getting ahead? Where are the best opportunities?* I felt stuck coaching the linemen at Arkansas. Indeed, God had a much bigger plan in mind; I just wasn't ready for it yet.

While we were living in Florida, Pat had found a fresh relationship with the Lord. Raised in a Catholic church, she, too, had left her faith on a shelf somewhere. We attended a small Baptist church in Tallahassee simply because our friends did and because it was the socially acceptable thing to do.

But in Tallahassee, Pat began to develop a genuine hunger to know God. She was no longer satisfied with going through the motions, performing certain rituals and ceremonies yet not having an exciting relationship with the living God. She knew there *had* to be more. The church that we attended frequently extended an invitation for people to step forward to the front of the sanctuary at the close of the service—similar to invitations extended at Billy Graham crusades—to ask God for forgiveness of their sins and to trust Jesus Christ as their Savior. One evening when the invitation was given, much to my surprise, Pat answered the call! She committed her life to Christ and found the deeper relationship with God that she had been seeking.

Almost immediately, I saw changes in her. She became fascinated with the Bible. She read it voraciously and was excited about what she learned. She spent much of her free time with friends from the church, talking about the Lord and learning how she could better live the faith she had found.

Of course, I was thrilled for her! Even though my anemic faith had stagnated a long time ago, I still believed in Jesus as "the way, the truth, and the life." I just wanted to live my way, according to my truth, and run my own life. But the Lord kept surrounding me with witnesses of a life that was unknown to me—people with a faith and an ability to cope with life's ups and downs that went far beyond church attendance or casual assent to some basic spiritual truths. They had something real, and I began to take notice.

One of the guys I noticed was Raymond Berry, the legendary receiver for the Baltimore Colts and a frequent target of Hall of Fame quarterback Johnny Unitas. Raymond now worked on the coaching staff at Arkansas, and he was one of the first Christians I knew who really lived out his faith in the workplace without compromise. A quiet, straightforward, honest man, Raymond's presence seemed almost saintly. I admired his poise, his confidence, and most of all, his integrity. Raymond's life was a light to me, although I didn't like what I saw when my life was exposed by the light. Unlike Raymond, I was proud, rigid, demanded my own way, and tended to blow people off when they didn't see things the way I did. But Raymond Berry's life showed me that there was a better way.

Don Breaux was another person who greatly influenced me. When I had worked with Don previously, he was like me—a hard-driving, razor-tongued, win-whatever-the-cost coach. Now, two years later, Don was a different person. His language had changed. His relationships with his wife, Harleen, and his daughters had changed. His outlook on work had changed, as well. Although he was still intensely competitive and wanted to field the best team possible, Don seemed to possess a deep inner peace—a peace that I didn't have.

One day, I couldn't take it anymore. "Don, what's happened to you?"

"I gave my life to Christ," Don answered, as though it were the most logical thing a person could do. Don's words brought me up short. I thought back to the commitment I had made to God as a child. I still believed in God, but my relationship with Him had grown cold, like a campfire that had once burned brightly but, through lack of attention, had been reduced to flickering embers. I wondered what it might take to rekindle the flame.

About that time, I was attempting to recruit a high school player, Mike Kirkland, from Pasadena, Texas. Besides being a tremendous young athlete, Mike possessed an unusual level of maturity and spiritual commitment. A devout Christian, Mike attended church not only on Sunday mornings and evenings, but on Wednesday nights, too! And in a day when many teenagers were rebelling against their parents, Mike and his parents seemed to enjoy an incredible love for each other. They spoke well of one another, ate dinner as a family, communicated well, and listened to one another.

One day Mike's dad was showing me some of the trophies Mike had won, when he casually mentioned that Mike was not his natural son but that he and his wife had adopted Mike. I stood in awe of the love this family shared. It was obvious that they loved God and each other, and their example of what a family could be blew across the embers of my heart, and I felt a flicker. I wanted what I saw in the Kirklands: a family centered around the Lord. I wanted to be that kind of father who loved his child so unselfishly. I wanted that amazing love to permeate our home, and I knew that Pat did, too.

As I looked at the lives of these people that God had placed in my path, it became increasingly obvious that although I believed in God and had committed my life to Christ as a child, I was not living for Him. I wanted to be in charge, so I was chasing what I felt would make me happy, fulfilled, and successful. I tipped my hat to God every so often, thinking that I was doing Him a favor by going to church, when in fact I barely knew Him.

AN UNLIKELY MENTOR

Some people just know how to make a way for themselves, and those were the types of achievers I had long admired. I looked up to race car drivers and football players, anyone who could go faster, maneuver better, or knock someone out of their way. Raymond Berry, Don Breaux, and Mike Kirkland all had a football connection, so I suppose it was natural that I should be affected by what I saw in them. Ironically, the man God used to impact me the most spiritually was a fellow who ran a different sort of race—someone who may never have thrown a football in his life.

George Tharel taught the adult Sunday school class at the church Pat and I attended in Fayetteville. A musician and a reader, George managed a JC Penney's store and was known as a pillar of his community. Quick to smile, always loving and kind, he exuded a peace in his life as he walked with God. George and his wife, Nathalie, had a great relationship and an immense love for their kids. Often after class I talked with the two of them, and I found myself more intrigued each week.

George had something that I wanted. He didn't just have head knowledge about God; he had a vibrant, heart-to-heart relationship with Him. George became a "spiritual father" to me. Through George's example and our conversations, I became convinced that I had been moving in the wrong direction and that I needed to get my life straightened out. I not only wanted to know God, I wanted to live in a way that pleased Him.

I wanted to be a better man.

One night as Pat and I sat in church, the Spirit of God was tugging at my heart. I wanted to be a better man. I wanted to be the kind of husband Pat deserved. And I wanted to be the kind of father my boys could look to one day and say, "That's what it means to be a man." I knew that the only way I could be that sort of person was with God's help.

Sitting there in the church, I prayed the only way I knew how: Hey, God. I know You're there. I gave my life to You before, but I haven't been living for You. I want to rededicate my life to You. I got up from my seat and walked to the front of the church, symbolically making a statement that from now on, I wanted to be a man who God could use. I wanted to be an active player on His team.

No fireworks exploded; no lightning bolts struck. I didn't feel any different at the front of the church than I had in my seat. But an important transaction took place that night. It was an act of my will, acknowledging my need for God and asking Him to take over in my life.

WHAT DOES GOD HAVE TO DO WITH IT?

What does all this "God talk" have to do with being a success? Simply this: My faith in God became the foundation for every major decision I made from that point in my life. Faith became the formation out of which I ran every play, the engine that gave me inner power for every race I won or lost. If you miss this point, you may understand the principles of success that have guided my life, but you won't understand the true source of my power—or yours.

The commitment I made to God was genuine, and His commitment to me was equally real. But that didn't mean life was going to be easy. Could I allow God to call the plays in my career, an area where I had always insisted on being in charge? And if I did let Him run things, what would that mean?

God promises in His Word that if we will trust Him, He will direct our steps. I believed that, but I still wasn't prepared for what He had planned for me.

DREAM CHASING

As I approached my mid-thirties, discontent about my career began to really eat at me. My dream to be a college football head coach continued to elude me, and I seemed bogged down doing something I wasn't really excited about—coaching the offensive linemen. While I enjoyed my interaction with Frank Broyles and the Arkansas players, I knew that most head coaches were drawn from the ranks of offensive and defensive coordinators, not from among the line coaches.

After my second season with the Razorbacks, I talked to Frank about my role with the team, and he agreed to let me coach the linebackers. It wasn't much of a promotion, but at least it was a new challenge.

About that time, I received a telephone call from Don Coryell. "Joe, I've just been named head coach of the St. Louis Cardinals," he said excitedly. "How 'bout coming to St. Louis with me and coaching the offensive line?"

Talk about mixed emotions! I was elated that Coryell was jumping from the college ranks to the NFL, and I was honored that he would consider me for one of his assistant coaching positions. On the other hand, I disliked the idea of continuing to coach the offensive line.

Almost without thinking, I answered, "Congratulations, Don. I know you'll do a great job with the Cardinals, and I appreciate your offer. I really do. And I'd love to coach in the pros. But I'm tired of coaching the line, so I think I better stay right here in Arkansas and coach on defense."

I could hardly believe my own ears! I was still fretting about getting a head coaching job on the college level. I had contacted several colleges about head coaching jobs, and they wouldn't even talk with me. Now Don Coryell was handing me a chance to compete with the pros—and I turned him down! I must have been temporarily insane!

For a few days, I kicked myself all over Fayetteville for my foolish decision. Then, amazingly, Coryell called back. "Hey, Joe! Jim Hanifan has agreed to coach the offensive line. How about coming to St. Louis and coaching the offensive backs?"

Don Coryell's flexibility once again astonished me. Not to mention his humility. Most coaches who had been blown off by a subordinate (the way I had rejected Don) would never condescend to call again with another opportunity. But not Coryell. He was more interested in building his team than protecting his feelings. Moreover, by rights he shouldn't have put Jim Hanifan on the line; Jim was a backfield coach. But the wisdom of this move was proven again and again over the years as Hanifan went on to become one of the premier line coaches in the NFL. In fact, when the Washington Redskins won the 1992 Super Bowl, Jim Hanifan was coaching our offensive line.

I coached at St. Louis from 1973 through 1977, longer than anywhere I had been previously. Coaching the offensive backs cranked my motor, and working with Don Coryell was one of the highlights of my career. We turned a losing team into a bona fide contender, and we even won a few division titles. Our success with the Cardinals also positioned me perfectly to make the jump to head coach, and I was ready—or at least I thought I was.

But God knew I needed to learn how to handle adversity, so He arranged to have me take a job with the lowly Tampa Bay Buccaneers.

The move came about unexpectedly. In our fifth year at St. Louis, we lost a key game against Washington, nixing our chances to make the play-offs that year. Coryell blew up at a press conference following the game, and things went downhill from there. The next weekend, I went to work and the locks were changed.

I called Pat and said, "What other part of the country would you like to live in? I think we're done here."

Soon after that, my former boss John McKay invited me to be the offensive coordinator with the Tampa Bay Buccaneers. This was an offer I had been looking for all my adult life! I could hardly have guessed that I was signing up for one of the most difficult seasons of my coaching career.

TROUBLES IN TAMPA

The Tampa Bay area is gorgeous and picturesque. With its white sand beaches and long bridges spanning the sparkling bay, it is easily one of the most beautiful places in America. But in 1978 its professional football team left much to be desired.

The Bucs were a fledgling franchise, a relatively new expansion team struggling to post their first respectable season. We had our work cut out for us, so I didn't have much time to enjoy the swaying palm trees or the pristine beaches. One of my first days on the job, Coach McKay said, "Joe, go work out the quarterbacks and see what you think we've got."

So I ran our QBs through a series of drills. When we came in later that day, Coach McKay asked, "What do you think about our quarterbacks?"

"I don't think we have one," I said bluntly.

"Me neither," McKay replied. "Let's go find one."

He assigned me the job of checking out Doug Williams, a talented black athlete with an incredible arm and plenty of "football smarts." I spent a lot of time with Doug and decided he was a great pro prospect. Never before had a black quarterback been selected in the first round of the annual NFL draft, but Coach McKay didn't let that keep him from drafting Doug with the very first pick in the 1978 draft. John McKay didn't care whether the man was black, white, or purple. If he could do the job with excellence, he was our kind of guy.

We signed Doug and he earned the starting job in his rookie season. Doug Williams's eventual emergence as an NFL star did much to open the quarterback position to talented young men, regardless of their skin color.

We started the season by winning four of our first eight games. Unfortunately, midway through the year, Doug went down with a broken jaw, an injury that sidelined him for the rest of the year. The entire team felt the crunching blow to Doug's jaw as our season suddenly fell apart. Nothing we tried seemed to help. We devised whole new ways of losing games! The fans and the Bucs' management were getting restless.

Have you ever prayed about your job? I mean really *prayed?* I don't mean those saccharine-sounding prayers like, *Lord, please bless my work today* or *Help me be kind to everyone at work.* I mean the kind of wrenching prayer where you spill your guts to God and cry out, "God, HELP!"

We didn't care whether a man was black, white, or purple, so long as he could do the job with excellence.

That's the way I prayed that year—a bunch. The pressure was on, and I knew that this was a pivotal point in my career. I'd hoped to eventually use the Tampa Bay job as a springboard to a head coaching job. Now, in my first year as an offensive coordinator, everything was going down the toilet. I called out to God again and again, "Why? What's going on here? Why is this happening? I believe you brought me here to Tampa Bay—but for *this?* To be humiliated? To fail at my first chance to do what I really want to do? Did you put me in this position just to make a fool of me?"

God didn't speak a word.

It's bad enough to be floundering in your career. But when you believe that God is directing your path, it's even more frustrating when you can't understand what He's doing with you. I knew intellectually that God was there, but I felt abandoned—like a boat, adrift and bobbing helplessly on the bay during a bad storm, just waiting for the next big wave to come crashing in and sink the whole deal.

I was a nervous wreck. I couldn't eat right, I couldn't sleep at night— I'd wake up in the middle of the night sweating through the latest calamity at work. During the day, my hands were literally shaking like a leaf. Our season went from bad to worse. I dreaded going to the stadium. I had never been part of a losing team. I was a winner on the field and off; everywhere I had gone in my career thus far, we had turned out winners. Now we were losing big-time, and I felt responsible. This wasn't fun anymore.

Not surprisingly, at the close of that disastrous season, Coach McKay decided he needed to make some changes. He wanted to get back to calling the offensive plays himself, which under the circumstances made a lot of sense. But what would that mean for me, the offensive coordinator?

Change was also in the wind for the San Diego Chargers. They had hired none other than Don Coryell to be their new head coach. It occurred to me that there might be a job there as one of his assistants, since we had worked well together at St. Louis before the infamous press conference explosion. But I didn't want to leave Coach McKay and move my family across the country again unless I was sure that God was leading me in that direction.

I prayed fervently, *Don't let Don call me, Lord, unless You want me to go with him.*

The next day, Don Coryell called. "Joe, I need you to coach the offensive backfield," he offered enthusiastically.

"You mean you don't need an offensive coordinator?" I ventured.

"Nope. I already have one. Ray Perkins will be handling that for us."

My heart sank, and I felt my ego deflating like a balloon with a slow leak. Ray was a bright offensive strategist and clearly NFL head coaching material. As frustrating as the past year had been, I wasn't sure I wanted to sign on for a job that would have me backpedaling in my career, even if it meant being reunited with my mentor and friend Don Coryell.

Making career decisions is always tough, especially as we get older and begin to see our opportunities through more myopic lenses. I knew that time was running out for me to "make it" in my career, that if I were ever to achieve my goals and be a success, it was now or never. And the job with Coryell looked like a step down in the wrong direction.

"Give me some time to think it over, Don, and I'll get back to you," I told my former boss.

"Okay, fine. But don't wait too long. We've got a lot of excitement around here, and I want to get this team together and moving soon."

I hung up the phone and started pacing. *Should I go or should I stay?* My mind was in a quandary, and my ego was in a quagmire. I talked about the possibilities with Pat. I talked with our pastor. I still wasn't sure. How was I to interpret these things? I had prayed about Coryell's call, and Don had indeed called me. Was that a sign from God or simply a call from an old friend?

I met with Coach McKay. I told him about Don's offer and that I was considering a change. Coach McKay was extremely complimentary and positive about my role at Tampa. "I think you ought to stay here," he said. I thanked him for the vote of confidence, but I didn't commit myself. We agreed to talk again the following day.

That night was one of the longest of my life. I couldn't sleep, so I just tossed and turned and prayed. The next morning, as I was about to leave to meet Coach McKay, Pat offered some advice. "Why don't you just let Coach McKay do the talking," she suggested.

I agreed and even prayed in the car as I drove to work, "Lord, what-ever Coach McKay says, I'm going to make my decision accordingly." I resolved not to say a word until the coach spoke. I mean, I was prepared to sit there in silence all morning if I had to, but I was not going to try to steer this conversation! I had committed it to God, and I was going to trust Him to guide me through it—whatever the coach said.

As soon as I sat down in Coach McKay's office, he pulled out a yellow legal pad containing numerous scrawled notes. McKay began, "After our conversation last night, Joe, I made some notes about a few things we should talk about." From there, he talked about our disastrous season and some of the decisions he'd made concerning next year. He made it clear that he intended to be more involved in calling the plays when next season rolled around.

This was the sign I had been looking for. I hadn't said a word, and Coach McKay had indicated that even if I were still the offensive coordina-tor in Tampa, I would not be fully in charge of the offense.

"Coach, I think I need to go to San Diego," I said calmly.

McKay nodded knowingly and didn't try to dissuade me. He said, "You know that I don't want you to go, and you'd always have a job here as long as I'm here. But I understand." John McKay and I shook hands and parted amicably as friends.

As soon as I left McKay's office, I called Don Coryell and accepted his job offer.

Done. Decision made. My mind should have been at peace, right? That's what I thought, too. Instead, from the moment I hung up the phone with Don, I slipped back into a dungeon of doubt. For the next few days, I was miserable, pondering, *Am I doing the right thing? Did I act presumptuously? Is this really God leading me, or did I operate out of my own foolishness?* I didn't know, and I had to find out.

There was only one man I knew who could help me sort through this. I needed to talk with my spiritual father, George Tharel. The diminutive Sunday school teacher and I had remained close friends after I left Arkansas. Over the years, I'd learned to trust his advice and spiritual wisdom. I decided it would be worth the time to sit down and talk with him, so I arranged to check out a few football prospects in the area and planned a hasty trip to Fayetteville.

I thought I was going to meet with George and wrestle through my career issues, but the man I met instead and the wrestling match in which I engaged was reminiscent of the story of Jacob, the Old Testament patriarch who wrestled with God and was never the same.

FIVE

BRUSH WITH AN ANGEL

Hey, are you guys going to Fayetteville?" I asked the two men standing near the exit at the Fort Smith airport. My flight from Tampa to Fayetteville had been diverted to Fort Smith, Arkansas, because of a nasty snowstorm. I was reminded all too much of the time when inclement weather had kept me from being there for the birth of our second son, Coy. Most people don't think of Arkansas and snow in the same sentence, and granted, it usually doesn't snow a lot in that part of the country. But when it does, watch out!

With our flight grounded due to the weather, I'd overheard the two fellows talking about renting a car and driving the fifty-some miles to Fayetteville. I'd never seen them before, hadn't spoken to them on the plane, and didn't know anything about them. All I knew was that I was determined to see George Tharel, and these guys were going my way!

One of the fellows answered in a deep Georgian drawl, "Yeah, we're drivin' to Fayetteville. Why?"

"Well, I'm going with you." I didn't ask the guys for a ride; I just told them! Apparently the look on my face must have convinced them that this was no time to argue. My jaw was set. I was going to Fayetteville! They shrugged their shoulders and started walking toward their rental car. I trudged out into the snow, threw my suit bag and briefcase into the backseat, and climbed in after them.

As soon as we got on the main highway, I knew this was a mistake. *Oh, great!* I thought. *If these guys are from Georgia, they probably have no idea how to drive in the snow.* My worst fears were soon confirmed. The snow swirled around us, making it almost impossible to see the road ahead. The pavement was covered with a thin layer of ice, with light snow atop the glassy road—and the driver was yanking on the steering wheel as though he were spinning on *Wheel of Fortune!* The car was swerving all over the road, and I knew that at any moment we were going to slide off the highway and into a ditch or, worse, another car. After a few miles, I couldn't take it anymore.

"Pull over!" I shouted from the backseat. "I want to get out."

"Gladly, pal," one of the guys grunted.

The weather had been warm when I left Florida, and I figured that even on a winter day in Arkansas I would need only a topcoat over my suit. I wasn't exactly dressed for a walk in a winter wonderland. But I wrapped my coat tightly around me and climbed out of the car. I was abruptly met by a fierce gust of snow stinging my face. I scrambled across the highway and plowed through the snow piled in the median, dragging my bags behind me.

I started walking back toward Fort Smith, watching over my shoulder for approaching headlights and hoping that drivers could see me hitchhiking. My glasses fogged and my body covered with snow, I became more enraged with every step. The cold and darkness of the night mirrored my soul. *Why, God?* I kept asking. *What do You want from me? Here I am, trying to get to my spiritual counselor, wanting to do Your will, and what do I get? A snowstorm! In Arkansas! God, what in the world are You doing to me?*

Fortunately, the headlights of an approaching vehicle jarred me out of my self-pity. I stuck out a thumb and nearly shouted for joy when I saw the vehicle slow to a stop in front of me.

I made it back to the Fort Smith airport and lugged my bags to the ticket counter. "Got any flights back to Tampa tonight?" I asked hopefully.

"We sure do," the far too chipper ticket agent replied. "There's one boarding in twenty minutes."

I paid for a ticket, dragged my bags to the gate, and slumped into a chair, angry, tired, and dejected. I resumed my questioning. *Why, God? Why are You putting me through this? You know that I want to be a head coach. I know that sometimes I haven't had my priorities straight, but I'm trying to do what I think is right...*

Then I happened to glance down the row of seats, and there on the corner stand was a Bible! That's strange, I thought. How often do you see a Bible just setting out in an airport? Maybe the Gideons are expanding their Bible program to airport concourses. Probably someone took it out of a hotel room and left it here.

For some reason, I reached over and picked up the Bible. I thumbed idly through the pages before I let it fall open to the book of James. I began reading chapter one, a passage related in part to making decisions and discerning the will of God in one's vocation. I had studied the chapter previously and knew that it was about staying committed and not allowing yourself to be tossed and turned by circumstances.

I had read a paragraph or two when I sensed someone sitting near me. I hadn't noticed anyone there earlier, but I've always been good at getting into "a zone," focusing on a subject almost to the point that I am oblivious to everything and everyone around me. Just then I felt someone tap me on my shoulder. A man about my own age was peering over my shoulder at the Bible. "I claimed that chapter in my life about six months ago," he said, pointing to the passage in James.

> *"My career meant more to me than anything in my life," he said. "I was obsessed with it."*

I squinted my eyes at this stranger and managed to say, "What?"

"Yes," he said, "I claimed that chapter. Let me tell you what happened." And the man launched into his story. I had never met him before. I hadn't seen or heard him sit down. I didn't really want to talk to him now. Yet there he was, telling me his tale in such a rapid-fire fashion that I couldn't get a word in edgewise. So I just sat and stared at him, listening.

"I was a pharmacist in Texas," he told me, "and my career meant more to me than anything in my life. I was obsessed with it. I had studied and worked hard all my life to reach my goals. One day I got a job offer in Oklahoma with a much bigger pharmacy. I believed God wanted me to take the job, so I quit my job in Texas and moved to Oklahoma.

"Upon my arrival, my new employers informed me that I would have to take a certification test to be qualified to dispense drugs in that state. The test was technical and demanding in nature, and I was extremely concerned. There was no way I could pass such a test without adequate time to study. I'd been out of school for more than five years, so I felt sure that I didn't have a chance at passing. I was scared that I'd fail the test, that I'd lose my job in Oklahoma and have to return to Texas to start over at a smaller store or take a job as a backup pharmacist someplace.

"I worried myself sick. I couldn't sleep, couldn't eat. I felt sure that I had made a big mistake in leaving my previous job and that I was going to lose everything my family had.

"About that time, I read that same passage in James, and I said, 'Okay, Lord, You know what I want and what I need. I'm turning this whole thing over to You, and I'm going to leave it in Your hands.'

"I studied the best I could in the short amount of time and then went in and took the test. Want to know what happened?" The stranger finally took a breath.

No words formed in my mind. I was still too amazed that this total stranger was telling me his life story. What amazed me even more was how similar the man's experience had been to my own. Finally, I nodded my head.

"I passed the test with flying colors!" He beamed. "It was a miracle! By rights, it shouldn't have happened that way, but it did. I came to the conclusion that I had been giving my job top priority in my life. It had become the most important thing to me. When I finally let go of it, turned it over to Him, and allowed God to have control, I could relax. Funny thing. He didn't take my job away; He simply put it in its proper place in my life and gave it back to me to use for Him. From that point on, my career really took off!"

The announcement that my flight was boarding brought the man's story to a close. I realized that throughout the "conversation," I hadn't uttered a word—as though I had been mesmerized by what he was telling me. I stood and thanked him and said good-bye. I never saw the man walk away, nor did I see him get on my flight. I had never seen the man before, and I've never seen him since. He was just *there,* at the right time with the right word of encouragement for my life. He may have been an angel, for all I know. He was certainly a messenger from God.

I boarded my plane in a daze. When I settled into my seat, I shut my eyes and prayed, *God, I know You're there. Thank You for sending that guy and getting me to hear what he had to say.*

I thought about how I had been trying to manage my own career, calling my own shots and trying to make things happen. My quest for a head coaching job had consumed me, affecting my relationships and every decision I made. Even though I was a Christian, God was not in charge of my life. I was.

I thought about the pharmacist turning his job over to the Lord and decided I needed to do the same. *Lord, You know I want to be a head coach. Lord, I believe You want me to be great at what I do, but from now on, I'm turning it over to You. You know what I want, and You know what I need. From here on out, I'm going to quit trying to do this myself. I'm going to trust You. I'll work as hard as I can, but You're the boss from now on.*

An overwhelming peace washed over me. I leaned my head back, closed my eyes, and slept like a baby. Sleep, precious sleep! The physical rest that had eluded me for several months now came easily. I could truly relax for the first time, knowing that my life was in God's hands—and that He was able to take care of it.

A week later, I arrived in San Diego to begin working with Don Coryell as his offensive backfield coach. I was still as hard-working and focused as ever, but I had come to the end of doing things my way. I was content to serve wherever God put me—even as a backfield coach—and I was determined to be the best backfield coach the Chargers ever had.

Two weeks after I started the new job, Don called me into his office. He grinned as he said, "Ray Perkins is leaving to be the head coach of the New York Giants, and I'd like you to take over his responsibilities with the Chargers."

I could hardly believe my ears! I had taken my hands off my career, and now God was giving me the desires of my heart! Two years later, I was named head coach of the Washington Redskins.

That was the good news.

The bad news was that the people in Washington take their football *really* seriously. They actually expected us to win!

SIX

FREE TO
SUCCEED

T he fans of the Washington Redskins (not to mention the folks in the front office) consider winning on the field to be the only acceptable outcome. And for most of the franchise's history, they haven't been disappointed. Under their first head coach, Ray Flaherty (1937–42), the Redskins posted a 47-16-1 record. George Allen led the team during most of the 1970s, when he racked up a 67-30-1 record and took the team to its first Super Bowl. Jack Pardee, the coach I was replacing, had started off 1978 by winning his first six games; the following year, Pardee finished 10-6 and was named NFL Coach of the Year.

Imagine, then, the city's chagrin when Joe Gibbs comes to town and promptly loses his first five games as head coach of the Redskins! To say the media was in an uproar would be an enormous understatement. "Joe who?!" sports reporters were screaming. "Where did we get this guy? And why did we bring him *here?*"

I worried that I might be the first NFL coach in history to get fired without ever winning a game! I started looking for different routes to drive home every night, semi-seriously fretting that some irate Redskins fans might be following me! In my lighter moments, I joked with Pat, "You better get rid of the dog, Honey. We don't want to come home some night and find the poor fellow draped over the steps."

Pat didn't think I was a bit funny. And neither did Redskins owner Jack Kent Cooke.

Well-read and always dressed immaculately, Mr. Cooke was one of the brightest, most demanding, most intimidating men I've ever met. He had made hundreds of millions of dollars in real estate, media companies, and sports teams, and he did not take losing lightly. But Mr. Cooke had confidence in me and allowed me the freedom to do what he paid me to do. He supported me both publicly and privately, even when things got tough. I appreciated that, and I really wanted to prove that his confidence had not been misplaced.

Nevertheless, I shook in my chair every time my secretary said, "Mr. Cooke is on the line." But Mr. Cooke was encouraging. "We'll survive this," he'd say, and he was right.

I was convinced that we had a good football team. Our guys had strong skills and good attitudes, and they believed in themselves when nobody else did. We just couldn't bring all the elements of our game together on a given Sunday. We made all sorts of adjustments, tinkering with the offensive formations, going with one running back—anything we thought might help. We made a few personnel changes. We were getting so desperate, we would try almost anything to win a game!

I didn't want to experience that sinking feeling of abject failure ever again.

Interestingly, what I drew from most during those awful times of failure was not my past victories. Instead, I drew strength from the tough times I had endured in Tampa with John McKay— and the spiritual lessons I learned as a result. Looking back, I could better understand how God had been working in my life. *So that's why He allowed me to go through those difficult days. He was teaching me, preparing me so I'd be ready to deal with adversity in the future.* My experiences in Tampa had taught me how to handle losses and setbacks. For most of us, it is not our successes that shape us; it is the pressure of living through adversity that catapults us to future success.

I decided not to panic. The team was beginning to gel, and despite the pressure, I had peace. I worked as hard as I could but never lost the awareness that God was in charge of my life, regardless of whether the Redskins won or lost. For the first time in my life, I was truly free to succeed...or not. That doesn't mean it was easy or that there weren't times when I felt like saying, "I'm outta here!"

Mr. Cooke said one day, "You wouldn't believe what people are calling me as I leave the stadium!" Oh, but I could, because *they were calling me the same names!*

When we finally won a game, defeating the Chicago Bears 24-7, it felt as though we had just won the Super Bowl! It was an ugly, stinkin' game in which we ran the ball nearly fifty times, but it was one of the greatest thrills of my life—my first win as an NFL head coach. And we had snapped the five-game losing streak. We lost the next game to Miami but then rallied to finish the season at 8-8.

In fact, after the loss to Miami, we won thirty-five of our next forty football games and played in two consecutive Super Bowls!

Unquestionably, one of the greatest motivating and character-building factors in our future success was that awful 0-5 beginning. None of us associated with those first five losses wanted to know that sinking feeling of abject failure ever again. And for the next eight years, we never lost more than two games in a row.

I coached the Washington Redskins for twelve years, and together we posted the second-best win-loss record in NFL history, went to four Super Bowl games, and won three championships. I wouldn't mention it (my co-author says I have to!) but I was voted NFL Coach of the Year twice, and in 1996 somebody made a bronze bust of my head and placed it in Canton, Ohio, where I was welcomed into the Pro Football Hall of Fame.

Not bad for a P.E. major!

God has certainly been good to me.

GIVE MY REGARDS TO BROADCASTING

I didn't retire from football because we couldn't win anymore. I retired from football because I couldn't find my family! Our eldest son had already graduated from high school and gone off to college. For years, every summer

Pat and the children and I had gone to football camp together. Pat usually came only on the weekends, but with J D now in college, she had to split her time between going to his football games and spending time with Coy and me. Then Coy took off for Stanford University, all the way out in California, and Pat's time was splintered even more. Our family was spread across the nation for most of the year.

When the boys were young, I used to tuck them into bed each night, read a bit from the Bible, talk with them about what it meant, and pray with them before turning the lights out. Then one night I went up to read and talk, and my baby, Coy, was already asleep. I leaned over to give him a kiss and reared up in shock. *Oh, my gosh! My boy has a beard!* I looked closer and saw to my surprise that my youngest son weighed 220 pounds!

What had happened? I realized that my sons were growing up with an absentee father, even though we were living under the same roof. I was a football recluse, spending far more time with the Redskins than with the people who mattered most in my life, my wife and children. It was time to make a change.

One day I walked into the owner's office and said, "Mr. Cooke, it's time for me to retire." I turned on my heels and walked out.

Suddenly the ramifications of what I'd just done hit me. Now what am I going to do to make a living? I'm a physical education major who spent twenty-eight years coaching, and I just quit my job! What can I possibly do?

I racked my brain, and finally it dawned on me. I know! I'll get me a Coke and a hot dog and an instant replay machine. I'll sit upstairs in a booth and watch football on a screen. And when the coach on the sidelines makes all those split-second decisions, I'll think about it for ten or fifteen minutes and then say, "I'm not so sure that he made the right decision..."

I would become a TV football analyst! Hey, Madden did it. I had read where one network paid John $8 million for one season as a color commentator. I joked with my friends, "I know I am not as good as John Madden, but surely I'm one-eighth as good!"

NBC Sports bought my logic and gave me a job.

I felt sure that sports analyst was the occupation for me—possibly the only one open to me. I thought, This is the one thing I can do to be gainfully employed, so I had better be careful and protect this job with everything I've got. Let's not say or do anything stupid.

Great. So who did NBC give me as a partner? Mike Ditka.

Now, Mike is one of my favorite characters in the world, but the man is definitely not one to mince words, even on TV. And no one ever described Ditka as calm or passive. Have you ever seen him coaching along the sidelines? His face can get so intense that even his hair stands at attention. Every time NBC asked him to do something extra on the show, he started complaining and going nuts. I knew Ditka could blow up at any minute. I tried to calm him down. "Mike, shut up. They're going to fire you, and you're going to take me with you!"

Mike didn't care. He never let a thought interfere with what he wanted to say.

For instance, once we were doing a postgame wrap-up meant to be a lead-in to the following week's playoff showdown between the Kansas City Chiefs and Buffalo Bills. Jim Lampley, our play-by-play announcer in the booth, asked me on the air, "Joe, what do you think about Buffalo?"

I started to answer off the top of my head, and then I stopped short. I thought, Wait a minute. We're going to Buffalo next week! So I said, "I love Buffalo! I'd like to see them win the Super Bowl and get the monkey off their back." It was a truthful, noncommittal answer—and one that wouldn't get me into any trouble.

Lampley turned to Ditka and asked, "Mike, what do you think of Buffalo?"

Mike huffed, "Buffalo? What do I think about Buffalo? Boring, that's what I think." The following day, Ditka's comment was quoted in nearly every paper in New York. What Mike didn't know was that our broadcast booth in Buffalo was out in the open, on a platform in the stadium—within spitting distance of the fans.

Now, I had been on the sidelines my entire life, and I hadn't really paid much attention to the antics of the spectators. But I learned a few things the day we went to Buffalo. Did you know that some football fans drink?! And in Buffalo there is snow to contend with. Piles of cold, wet snow.

When I walked out onto the platform, despite the brisk Buffalo weather, I was greeted warmly by the Bills fans. "Hey, Joe, you're the man! You're okay, Joe. You picked Buffalo to win. Now, where's that Ditka guy?"

I said, "He's right over there."

Sure enough, Buffalo blew out Kansas City, knocking Joe Montana out of the game and winning handily. During the postgame show, Jim Lampley asked Ditka, "Mike, what did you think about the quarterbacks' performances today?"

Ditka started to reply, but before Mike got a chance to open his mouth, some guy in back of the end zone whipped an ice ball at him, smacking him right in the shoulder on live TV. Ditka said, "I'll *tell* you what I think. You come down here, you !@#!$%!!! blankety-blank, and I'll kick your butt!"

Instead of commenting on Ditka's explosion, Jim Lampley, the consummate broadcasting professional, calmly turned to me and said, "Joe, what did *you* think about the quarterbacks?"

When it came time to leave the stadium, I knew we were going to be in trouble. We had to walk to the far side of the parking lot to get to our limousine. Mike had had a hip replacement, so he couldn't run. "You go ahead," he said. "I'll meet you at the car."

As I cut through the parking lot, I heard people cussing and shouting to me, "Ditka! Where is Ditka?"

I said, "I think he's right back there."

When I finally reached the limo, I dived into the backseat like I was diving into a foxhole.

About ten minutes later, there came big Mike Ditka across the parking lot, fighting his way through the abusive crowd. I threw open the door, and Mike plunged in, slamming the door behind him. He straightened his clothing and pulled out a cigar that looked to be about a foot long. As he was lighting up his stogie, he looked over at me and said, "I guess we showed those guys, didn't we?"

It didn't surprise me one bit when, a few years later, despite a history of heart problems, Ditka went back to coaching. The guy is amazing! Although I like to joke about Mike, he has become one of my best friends.

Ditka's antics notwithstanding, our run as network analysts was short-lived. NBC decided to go in a different direction, but I really didn't mind. J D and Coy had graduated, and both had taken a strong interest in auto racing.

I'd always had an avid interest in racing. Back when Pat and I were dating, a friend and I used to build dragsters in a tiny garage. So in the early 1990s when J D suggested we put together a NASCAR race team, I thought, *Now there's something we can do as a family.* And it looked as though we might just be able to make a go of it.

SEVEN

NASCAR NEWCOMERS

T alking Norm Miller into spending millions of Interstate Batteries' dollars on a start-up racing team wasn't nearly as difficult as talking my wife into spending *our* money on the venture. Unlike me, Pat had learned how to hang onto her money, to save for a rainy day. So getting her to see the logic of investing in a bunch of guys driving around in circles at high speeds was going to be quite a challenge!

FROM RETIRING TO RE-TIRING

I went to a friend who was knowledgeable about the racing world and asked, "I want my wife to get a good impression of the racing business, so what's the best race I could take her to?"

"Has she ever been to a NASCAR race?"

"No," I replied, "so I don't want to take her to one of those long races where she has to sit out in the sweltering heat. She won't go for that at all."

"Bring her to the Winston in Charlotte," my friend said. "We have a beautiful race track there. We'll get her a seat up in one of those $250,000 corporate suites, where it's nice and cool, with lots of food to eat and people to talk to. She'll love it! And there are three separate races at the Winston event, so she won't get bored."

The Winston was indeed the perfect race for Pat. The day was just right—the people, the corporate box, everything to help her see how wonderful and exciting the racing business could be. She looked as though she was thoroughly enjoying the prerace hoopla. Finally, we heard, "Gentlemen! Start your engines!" On the track below, the engines roared, and the first race was underway.

Twenty laps into the first race, I looked over at Pat to see how she was enjoying the action—and I was absolutely horrified. She was fast asleep! She didn't know any of the drivers, owners, or other people involved with racing, so she was bored stiff. I knew I had my work cut out for me if I was going to talk her into being a part of this game!

Following the Charlotte event, the boys and I continued to work on her, and eventually we persuaded Pat that NASCAR racing was a growing sport and that we should invest in a Winston Cup team.

THE AGONY OF DEFEAT

Our first race as a team was the 1992 Daytona 500, the first race of the year and NASCAR's premier event—a spectacle on par with football's Super Bowl. Dale Jarrett drove our car, the #18, sponsored primarily by Interstate Batteries. Dale started near the back of the pack, thirty-first out of forty-three cars, because we had gotten caught up in a wreck during the qualifying heat. Jimmy Makar was perched in the crew chief's chair, and Norm Miller and I paced in the pits as the green flag waved for our first real race.

Up in the corporate boxes, Pat was all eyes and ears, sitting on the edge of her seat. She had money invested in a car now, so her interest level soared! Every time the #18 car whizzed past the grandstands, she was on her feet watching her money fly by.

Dale Jarrett did a great job maneuvering his way to the front. After 200 miles, we were running in seventh place! Not bad for a bunch of "green" race guys.

High above us in the suite, Pat was saying, "This is a piece of cake. We're going to win in our very first race! It's not even a big deal."

About 350 miles into the race, more than a dozen cars were racing three abreast down the back straightaway when, suddenly, one car nudged another. "Watch it! Watch out!" I heard our spotter's voice in the headsets. All at once, fourteen cars collided in a tangled mess of metal, smoke, gasoline, and burning rubber! And guess whose car was right in the middle of it?

Suddenly, it was over. We were out of the race.

Dale escaped with only minor bumps and bruises, but our #18 car was torn to pieces. It was one of the worst wrecks we've ever had, and it happened on our first day in competition. What a way to start!

Once we knew that Dale and the other drivers were okay, the impact of the crash hit me. I was discouraged and dejected. We were doing so well, and suddenly it was over. We were out of the race. I apologized over and over to Norm Miller, wishing there was something, anything I could do to make it better! I felt terrible, knowing that Norm had put up so much money, and in the blink of an eye, our hopes had been smashed and shredded.

Norm, on the other hand, had an entirely different outlook. While I lamented our losses, Norm looked up at the television monitors where the crash was being replayed over and over again, each time with our bright green #18 car, emblazoned with the Interstate Batteries logo, right in the center of the camera shot. "Hey, this might not be so bad," Norm quipped. "Look at all the free advertising we're getting!"

From then on, we needled Dale Jarrett, "If you're losing the race, make sure you get in a good wreck so we can get some good TV time!"

While Norm's attitude was incredibly positive, I suspected Pat's view might be somewhat different. I talked briefly to our guys in the garage area and tried to encourage them, and then I went searching for Pat. I went up to the corporate box, but she wasn't there.

"She left and went to the motor home," one of our friends informed me. I beat it down to our motor coach parked in the Daytona infield and hurried inside. There was Pat, lying on the bed. She looked up at me and said flatly but emphatically, "I don't think I like this."

The second thing she said was, "How much did that cost?"

"No problem," I said, trying to ease her mind, "it's in the budget."

Maybe so, but just a few months into racing, we were nearly half a million dollars over budget with little to show for it.

SURVIVOR: DAYTONA

We somehow managed to survive our first year of racing. Dale Jarrett had eight top-ten finishes, including two top-five runs, and we scrambled to finish nineteenth in the point standings that year.

Keeping with tradition, the 1993 racing season opened with the legendary Daytona 500, and the race proved to be one of the most dramatic in Daytona's grand history.

Daytona is the race every driver wants to win, and after 498 miles of pulse-pounding action, it looked as though Dale might just have a chance!

Coming down the final stretch, it was Dale and Dale—Dale Jarrett leading the race in the #18 and Dale Earnhardt in his black #3 car, desperately trying to pass Jarrett and take the checkered flag. For both men, a win at Daytona would be huge! Throughout his storied career, victory at the Daytona 500 had eluded Earnhardt. Several times he had come close to capturing the checkered flag, only to lose the race through some bizarre circumstance. For instance, in 1990 Earnhardt was leading the race on the last lap, but as he whipped around the third turn, one of his tires exploded, dropping him out of contention.

What an incredible feeling it was to approach Victory Lane as a winner!

Dale Jarrett was a respected young driver who had enjoyed great success racing in the NASCAR Busch Series but had won only one Winston Cup race in his first six years on the circuit. To win the Super Bowl of stock car racing would be an incredible achievement.

Ironically, up in the CBS television broadcast booth, one of the announcers calling the race for the TV audience that day was Ned Jarrett, Dale's dad. Ned was a former NASCAR driver himself, a Winston Cup champion, in fact; but he had never won the Daytona 500, either. And as our car sped toward the finish line with his son at the wheel, Ned could hardly contain his excitement.

"Come on, Dale," he called into the live microphone. "Go, baby, go! All right, come on. I know he's gone to the floorboard. He can't do any more. Come on, take her to the inside. Don't let him get the inside of you coming around the turn..."

Ned had long since given up his neutrality and was now openly cheering his boy on, and the television audience was loving it!

Our pit-crew guys were on the wall, fists clenched, tension written all over their faces as the cars roared toward the finish line.

"Here he comes!" Ned Jarrett shouted. Nearly overcome with excitement, Ned called the finish. "Earnhardt's...it's Dale and Dale as they come off turn four.... You know who I'm pulling for as Dale Jarrett's.... Bring her to the inside, Dale! Don't let him get down there. He's going to make it.... Dale Jarrett's going to win the Daytona 500!"

As Dale crossed the finish line in the green Interstate Batteries car, Ned let out an enthusiastic, "All right!" Dale Earnhardt would eventually win the Daytona 500 in 1998, but this day belonged to Dale Jarrett.

The celebration was on! Pat was on pit row with me, half laughing, half crying. Our sons, J D and Coy, were doing forward rolls out on the giant Daytona 500 logo spray-painted onto the infield grass at the Daytona International Speedway. What an incredible feeling it was to approach Victory Lane as a winner rather than as a spectator!

EGO CHECK

For all our newfound success in NASCAR and the respect and accolades that came with it, Pat's down-to-earth approach provided all of us with a reality check.

Dale Jarrett joined the Robert Yates Racing team in 1995. Shortly before we hired Bobby Labonte to replace him in the #18 car, I told Pat, "We don't want to say anything to anyone about who we are talking to about driving this race car." I had been telling Pat how we needed to be cautious about what we said publicly before the deal was in place. We didn't want anything leaking to the press before our agreement was firm.

One day, Pat was in the race shop when Bobby walked out of the office. Spying Pat, Bobby greeted her with a smile and said, "Hey, how're you doing?"

"Do I know you?" Pat asked cautiously.

"Yeah, I'm Bobby," he said, extending his hand.

"Bobby who?" Pat asked innocently.

After that, anytime we needed to deflate Bobby Labonte's ego—which wasn't often—all we had to do was ask, "Bobby who?"

When our new home was still under construction, Bobby stopped by to visit while the house was being framed in. In a downstairs room where we were having a trophy case built into the wall, Bobby scribbled a message on a section of the trophy case two-by-fours: *Save this space for a Winston Cup trophy!*

When we later won the Winston Cup championship in 2000, I hoisted a large cardboard check—in the amount of more than $3 million!—over the head of Bobby Labonte. At the official black-tie awards ceremony in New York, I presented Bobby with the piece of two-by-four frame wood that he had inscribed for Pat and me. I'd had it cut out of our trophy case and fitted with a brass plate bearing an inscription: *Thanks for a great ride!*

EIGHT

AGAINST ALL ODDS

One of the toughest things to do in sports is for a championship team to repeat as champion the following year. A natural letdown takes place after climbing your way to the top, and it usually affects a team in two ways. First, you have the incredible self-imposed pressure of trying to recapture the enthusiasm and emotion that builds throughout a championship season. Second, it's like you're walking around for the next year with a bull's-eye painted on your back—all your competitors are gunning for you. We experienced that letdown with Bobby Labonte and the Interstate Batteries #18-car team after winning the Winston Cup in 2000. Consequently, our performance fell off during the 2001 season, and Bobby finished sixth in the points race.

Meanwhile, Tony Stewart and our Home Depot #20-car team were coming on strong and had the Winston Cup clearly in their sights. Tony had won six races in 2000, finishing sixth in points. The following year, Tony and the team turned in another tremendous season, finishing second to Jeff Gordon in the 2001 points race, with three victories, fifteen top-five finishes, and twenty-two top-tens. Not a bad year! Everyone on the Home Depot team could hardly wait to get back to racing as we prepared for the Daytona 500, the first race of the 2002 season and NASCAR's equivalent of the Super Bowl.

TRAGEDY STRIKES

As usual, we arrived that year in Daytona several days before the big race. While the guys fine-tuned our race cars for what has become known as Speedweeks, I geared up to speak at a Friday morning breakfast for an organization in the Tampa area. A helicopter was to pick me up at 6:00 A.M. for the hop across Florida and back. But when I got up that Friday morning, we were socked in by hazy fog. I looked out the window and thought, *There's no way a helicopter will be flying this morning!* We called to confirm the flight, and the company representative said, "Oh, yes. They left around four-forty-five. They should be there already."

I waited and waited for the helicopter to arrive. When it became obvious that the chopper wasn't coming, I decided to make the quick trip by plane. When I arrived in the Tampa area, I learned the awful news that the missing helicopter had crashed in a swampy area, just a few miles from where they were to pick me up. Both the pilot and copilot perished in the crash.

That morning, I spoke for the breakfast group and tried my best to be upbeat, but news of the tragedy shook me to my core. Not only had I survived a brush with death, but I also deeply grieved for the pilots and their families. Suddenly the Daytona 500, Speedweeks, and other things that had seemed *huge* just a few hours earlier, all now paled in importance.

I still can't fully express the tug-of-war I was feeling in my gut over the next few days. I had to carry on stoically for the remainder of Speedweeks, if only for the sake of the nearly one hundred and fifty employees who worked for our company, for their families, and for our sponsors. But for me the helicopter crash cast a pall over the Daytona 500, a dark backdrop against which everything else would be played out. It was a tough start to what would prove to be a tough season.

STARTING FROM THE BACK OF THE PACK

On the track, Tony Stewart ran great at Daytona. One of the hottest drivers at Speedweeks, Tony won both the Bud Shootout and the International

Race of Champions event, and he looked primed to win the Daytona 500 on Sunday.

Bob Nardelli, CEO of Home Depot, came in from Atlanta to share the moment, and we were all anticipating a great race. The excitement was nearly palpable as four fighter jets streaked above the two-and-a-half-mile track at the conclusion of "The Star-Spangled Banner," and the loudspeakers blared, "Gentlemen! Start your engines!"

Then as quickly as it started, it was over for Tony. In front of two hundred thousand people in the stands and millions more watching on television, the Home Depot car blew an engine on the third lap of the race. Not only did Tony not win, he didn't even finish, placing last. Dead last. What a way to start a new and promising racing season! Bobby Labonte didn't fare much better, finishing thirty-fourth when the Interstate Batteries Pontiac overheated on lap 153.

"We're gonna overcome this. We're gonna win this thing."

I expected Tony would be furious, but he handled the frustration fairly well. Our team pushed the car to the transporter behind the garage area, and Tony just sat in the car for a few minutes, window netting still up, as though he wanted to be alone for a while. When he finally emerged, the NBC-TV cameras and Motor Racing Network radio microphones were waiting for him, and he did several "live" interviews. He was clearly dejected and disappointed, but he tried to be optimistic. Although the DNF (Did Not Finish) at Daytona got us off to a lousy start for the season, there were still thirty-five races to go, and he was extremely upbeat with the press. "There's still a lot of racing left," he said. "No one better count us out. Let's see what they say when we win the championship."

Tony was equally positive with his team members. "It's okay," he declared confidently. "We're gonna overcome this. We're gonna win this thing anyhow."

And we all believed him!

Tony watched most of the 2002 Daytona 500 from a motor home parked in the infield. When there were forty laps to go, he decided to drive home to North Carolina instead of flying. For Tony, driving is his job, but it's also his favorite pastime; and in this case, it may have even been a bit of therapy for him. On the way home, he stopped at a Waffle House in South Carolina, and when several people recognized him, he picked up all the customers' tabs.

Interestingly, Greg Zipadelli, crew chief for the #20 car, and one of Tony's best friends, drove himself home from the race as well. For both Tony and Zippy, driving is a way to relax, chill out, and get their mental game together. Zippy is as intense as Tony during a race, even though he doesn't usually show it. The guys are similar in that when setbacks happen, they choose to learn from them. Driving home, both of them were already focusing on the upcoming race at Rockingham.

Apparently, it was time well spent.

The following week at "the Rock," Tony finished fourth. The week after that, in Las Vegas, Tony led most of the way, finishing fifth in the race and moving up to eleventh in the points standings. Then at Atlanta, Tony again led the most laps and this time came home with his first win of the season, which vaulted him to fifth place in the points race.

We had one of the best cars at Darlington in March, and Tony was poised for another win. He was leading the race when his car got tangled up with the #44 of Buckshot Jones, who had fallen a lap behind. Buckshot got loose coming off turn one and swerved unexpectedly into the path of Tony's Pontiac. The impact sent the #44 into the wall and the #20 careening across the track where it came to a near stop—just in time for Jimmy Spencer's #41 car to slam into Tony's passenger-side door. It was a bad wreck, even by NASCAR standards. Tony had sustained a severe blow to his shoulder and was experiencing pain in his lower back, as well as numbness and tingling in his left foot. He was airlifted to a local hospital, where an MRI and other tests checked out okay. Tony was discharged from the hospital early Monday afternoon, but he was still mighty sore all week long.

The following Sunday we were in Bristol for five hundred of the most grueling and demanding laps in racing. Still smarting from the accident at Darlington, Tony led the Bristol race at several points, but on lap 366, he told Greg Zipadelli over the headset, "I've got to get out of the car." Fortunately for us, Todd Bodine, an experienced driver, was available, and we pressed him into service to finish the race for Tony. Todd is built similarly to Tony, and he fit in the car comfortably. Todd drove well and filled in admirably, keeping the #20 car on the lead lap. Had he not done so, Tony would likely have scored 44 fewer points that race—points which could have made a crucial difference by the end of the season.

Sitting atop the points standings was Sterling Marlin, who was having a stellar year. Sterling had overcome the emotional trauma of being involved in the crash that had taken the life of Dale Earnhardt at Daytona in 2001. Since then, Sterling had raced harder and better than ever. In 2002, he was driving as though he were on a mission—Sterling was the guy to beat. He shot to the top of the points race and stayed there for much of the season.

Mark Martin was also having an outstanding year. Always a contender, Mark kept inching his way up through the standings and, by midseason, was rapidly closing the gap on Sterling.

Meanwhile, Tony's season pitched between the jagged mountaintops of three victories and the low valleys of six races he didn't finish, as well as a couple offtrack incidents that threatened to end his season early.

GETTING SIDETRACKED

Although Bobby Labonte and the #18 team were mired deep in the standings, the #20 team was especially cranked up for the Brickyard 400 in Indianapolis. Our pulses were running almost as fast as our cars. Tony was sitting on the pole at the start of the race, having clocked the quickest lap in time trials—and to start in the number one spot on the track of his childhood dreams was no small deal to Tony. We knew we had one of the fastest cars at Indy, and we were all psyched for a win. Tony's car ran great for much of the race, leading forty-three laps. But near the end, the car suddenly seemed to just die. Tony's speed dropped off, and he slid back to the twelfth spot.

Tony was bitterly disappointed. Having grown up in nearby Rushville, Indiana, Tony really wanted to win at the Indianapolis Motor Speedway, and for most of the race, it had looked as though he had the car to do it.

When the race ended, he despondently pulled the car off the track into the garage area. Gasoline Alley, as it is called, was already teeming with fans, photographers, and reporters.

Now, when a quarterback in the National Football League throws an interception, then comes off the field to the sidelines, he isn't subjected to a battery of reporters' questions. He may be grilled in front of the media later, but he's buffered a bit by time, other players, coaches, and the events of the game. He usually has at least a few minutes to get his emotions under control. But in NASCAR, because the garage area is generally open to fans and the media, a driver is immediately confronted the moment he climbs out of his car.

When Tony crawled out of his car at the Brickyard, it was obvious he didn't want to talk to anyone. He started trotting toward our transporter. A photographer freelancing for *The Indianapolis Star* jumped in front of him in an attempt to snap a photo of the dejected driver. Tony kept jogging toward the gate that separates the garages from the transporter parking lot, while the photographer ran along in front of him, apparently trying to get a shot of Tony's face. Tony, however, was in no mood for such posturing. As he neared the gate, he angrily grabbed the photographer, aggressively shoved him out of the way, and stormed off toward the #20-car hauler.

I arrived at the hauler within minutes after the incident, and the photographer involved in the altercation was waiting for me. "Hey, Joe. I need to talk to you," he said. "Tony Stewart physically shoved me and went after me right after the race. I was just doing my job, trying to get a picture."

I talked with the photographer for a while and was convinced he was telling the truth. I apologized to him and assured him that we'd look into the matter. "Look," he said to me, "I don't want to blow this out of proportion or make a bigger issue out of this than what it should be, but it did happen. And I think Tony owes me an apology."

I apologized further and said, "All right. We'll deal with this." We exchanged business cards and promised to keep in touch. Later there were some wild rumors that I had paid the photographer to go away, which was patently untrue.

The photographer and I talked several times by phone during the following week. We were both content to deal with the incident as a private matter, but with Tony's high profile in NASCAR, and the warnings he'd received for unsportsmanlike conduct the year before, that wasn't going to happen. We weren't surprised when the media caught wind of the story almost before I did. Mike Arning, Tony's publicist from Home Depot, and Eddie Jarvis, the PR guy for our race team, hustled Tony out of the area and back to his motor home. Meanwhile, I met with members of the media and explained what had happened. "We're working toward getting this resolved," I told them. Nevertheless, the following day the story made headlines across the country.

NASCAR slapped Tony with a ten-thousand-dollar fine and placed him on probation for the remainder of the 2002 season. In most professional sports, that would be the end of the issue, but not in the world of NASCAR.

When I was in the NFL, if one of our players got in trouble on or off the field, if he paid the fines and met the NFL's requirements, he could still play. The same goes for the National Basketball Association and most other professional sports organizations. But a major factor in the workings of our sport that's unique to Winston Cup racing is the enormous investment of our sponsors. The standards for an athlete's behavior on and off the track are higher, because when there is a problem, the repercussions with our sponsors can be costly.

To the public, Tony represented Home Depot, the primary corporate sponsor of the #20 car. Not surprisingly, following his run-in with the photographer, one of our first meetings the next week was with representatives from Home Depot. We met in a conference room at our race shop—Tony, his manager Cary Agajanian, representatives from Home Depot, J D, and me. Nobody in that room contested the inappropriateness of Tony's actions or the fairness of NASCAR's punishment. The only question was, "What are we going to do about this incident?" I knew that no matter what we did, it wasn't going to be pretty.

Tony never tried to make excuses for his conduct. Immediately after the incident, he admitted, "It was wrong; I shouldn't have done it." He apologized to Home Depot and issued a public apology to the photographer he'd accosted. In our meetings with Home Depot, he readily admitted his responsibility and acknowledged that he needed some help in controlling his anger.

Fortunately, Tony's relationship with Home Depot was strong. He and Bob Nardelli had become good friends over the past few years, and beyond that, the company knew of Tony's little-publicized behind-the-scenes work for charity. Tony had often given freely of his time to work with organizations helping terminally ill children. Every weekend during the race season, Tony spent time talking with fans, signing autographs, and doing public relations work for Home Depot.

But they could not ignore this major black eye Tony had given the company. I felt sure that Home Depot would stand by Tony, but at what cost?

For Tony's part, he wasn't so sure initially. "It crossed my mind that I might not be driving for Home Depot next year," he said later, "or for anyone else!"

Rumors to that effect swirled almost instantly following the incident. But in fact, Home Depot never wavered for a moment in its commitment to Tony. Nor did Joe Gibbs Racing.

Following some intensive meetings with Home Depot, the company put out a stern public statement:

Tony Stewart's actions following the Brickyard 400 do not at all represent the values and beliefs of the over 290,000 associates who comprise the backbone and spirit of The Home Depot. We value our relationship with the media, fans, and competitors of NASCAR, and the behavior displayed following the Brickyard 400 will not be tolerated from any member of our race team now or in the future.

In addition to the strong rebuke, Home Depot fined Tony fifty thousand dollars over and above the NASCAR fine of ten thousand dollars, the money to be paid to the United Way of Central Indiana to help fund children's after-school programs. Furthermore, Home Depot placed Tony on probation for the remainder of the 2002 season.

Tony looked at the incident as a personal wake-up call. He knew that our corporate sponsor would not respond lightly to further public relations nightmares. And he vowed to get a better handle on his anger.

TWISTS AND TURNS

The week after the incident at Indianapolis was extremely emotional for all of us as we tried to do what was right for Tony, our race team, our sponsor, and our sport. The next weekend we went to Watkins Glen, New York, for the second of the two road races on the Winston Cup schedule. Exploiting the twists and turns of Watkins Glen and Sonoma for a win and a top-five finish the previous year, Jeff Gordon had shown that the Winston Cup title could turn on a driver's ability to successfully navigate the road courses.

Tony qualified third, securing an important starting position near the front. He went on to lead thirty-four of the ninety laps, outdueling highly touted rookie Ryan Newman for the win! Sterling Marlin lost a cylinder during the race and limped to a thirtieth-place finish, enabling Tony to climb to within one hundred and four points of the Winston Cup leader.

I felt as though we were on a roller coaster ride, having reached the lowest point of our season at the Brickyard, then turning around and skyrocketing to a win the next week. In many ways, Watkins Glen was the turning point in the season for us. Yet two weeks later we were back at Bristol, always an intense race, and we finished a disappointing twenty-fourth when an oil hose broke on the #20 car.

In the wake of the Indianapolis incident, Tony became something of a lightning rod, attracting all sorts of accusations like bolts from out of the blue. The worst of these was when a female fan accused Tony of shoving her in the pit area at Bristol. Charges were brought against Tony, even though several people who accompanied him through the crowd that day said that the charges were preposterous, that nothing had happened. Nevertheless, the fact that assault charges were filed sent us reeling again. Fortunately, numerous eyewitnesses questioned the allegations, and a grand jury refused to return an indictment. The charges were dropped, and Tony was completely exonerated.

We experienced another disappointment on the track at Richmond, where Tony always seemed to have a great race. But with about forty laps to go in the Chevy Monte Carlo 400, the #20 car broke a ring gear and Tony finished thirtieth, dropping him to fifth place in the points standings.

Then a few weeks later, the Winston Cup points race took another surprising turn when Sterling Marlin fractured a cervical vertebra in a vicious wreck at Kansas, forcing him to sit out the remainder of the schedule. The following week at Talladega, Tony overtook Mark Martin to lead in points for the first time in his career—but we didn't dare get too excited yet. We remembered well our high hopes at Daytona, the dashed dreams at Indy, and the race in Richmond where we were running so well before a mechanical failure. All it would take was for one tire to blow, one bolt to break loose, or for Tony to get collected in a wreck, and our title hopes could be crushed in a moment.

RISING TO THE CHALLENGE

Going into the last race of the season at Homestead, Florida, Tony had an eighty-nine-point lead over Mark Martin. He could clinch the Winston Cup title with a twenty-first-place finish in the four-hundred-mile event. This had been the most hotly contested points race of all time, and our pit area was crammed with people standing around, anticipating a celebration. The place was a security nightmare, a real zoo! As Tony made his way in for his first pit stop, I stepped around the corner of our pit box and could hardly believe my eyes! There, to my complete surprise, were three stunningly attractive young women standing at the front of our pit box close to the wall—and our car was heading down pit road!

I freaked. I strode across the pit, motioned with my index finger, and with a facial expression I might have worn to lecture a linebacker in the NFL, yelled, "OUT!"

The young women made a hasty retreat from our pit area.

I later learned that one of them was pop singer Britney Spears, but it wouldn't have mattered to me if she had been the queen of England. They had no business being in the pit, especially near the wall as we were about to make a pit stop. Later, the guys on our team teased me about chasing away Britney Spears.

But it wasn't personal. The race was intense enough without such distractions. Tony's car didn't handle well all day, and Mark Martin was inching forward through the field. Tony fell a lap down, jeopardizing his chances for the championship. But he got the lap back and worked his way up to eighteenth, keeping us in contention. Then with just thirty-three laps to go, John Andretti's #43 car blew an engine right in front of Tony, spraying oil all over the track just as they headed into turn three. Tony slid down to the apron of the track and slid safely past the ailing car. Robby Gordon wasn't so lucky. Trying to negotiate his way through the smoke on the high side of Andretti, he hit the oil and spun out.

This had been the most hotly contested points race of all time.

On the restart, Tony again narrowly averted disaster. He got caught between the #28 of Ricky Rudd and the #7 of Jason Leffler as the cars raced three-wide through turns three and four. Rudd dove under Leffler to pass, forcing Tony dangerously close to the wall on the high side, but Tony kept the car under control. He held on from there to finish eighteenth. Mark Martin finished fourth, picking up fifty-one points—still thirty-eight shy of catching Tony. This was the only time Tony had finished out of the top fifteen during the last ten races of the season, but it didn't matter.

Tony Stewart and the Home Depot team were the 2002 Winston Cup Champions!

In the pit, we were all cheering madly, patting everyone on the back and yelling like kids. The emotion of the moment overwhelmed Greg Zipadelli, who broke into tears when he saw the checkered flag wave. "It's been a long year," Greg said. "It's been a tough year—up and down—but this makes it all worth it!"

Tony, too, was ecstatic in Victory Lane. "I think the coolest part about this whole thing," he said, "is that I finally did something that A J Foyt didn't do. Most people don't realize, but the first Indy car I ever drove was in a test for A J at Phoenix, and it was one of the most frustrating experiences of my life. But it was one of the best experiences of my life, too. The relationship that I built with A J that week will last a lifetime. I never got beat up as bad verbally as I did with A J for five days. His favorite comment, when I was proud of something I did, was, 'Just check the record books, big boy!' Well, A J, check the record books now!"

I was so proud of our team because of all the problems we had overcome in 2002 to reach this point. I credit Greg Zipadelli with holding the team together during the tough times and for inspiring us all to never give up. Tony Stewart respects Zippy immensely, and Zippy is one guy in the racing world Tony will listen to. They share a tremendous respect for each other. Zippy said, "What I tried to teach Tony this year is that no matter what happens, it's a personal challenge. Whether it's a rule change, a bad day, or something else, take it as a personal challenge and do better than everybody else."

I couldn't have said it better myself!

CHANGES

Bobby Labonte was another key player in Tony Stewart's success that season. Bobby and our Interstate Batteries team were struggling through one of the worst seasons we had had in eleven years of running the #18 car. We worked hard all year long, experimenting with adjustments to Bobby's car; but nothing seemed to work, which sometimes happens in professional sports. Bobby finished a disappointing sixteenth in the 2002 Winston Cup points standings.

Yet through all the frustrating times, Bobby never ceased to be an encouragement to Tony. After each of the last several races of the season, I hurried to the #20 hauler to check on Tony and to lend my support. But before I could get there each week, Bobby Labonte was already there, coaching Tony and advising him on his run for the championship. When Tony finally won the title, Bobby was one of the first guys in Victory Lane to congratulate him.

Bobby's crew chief, Jimmy Makar, had won two championships as a crew chief, and he, too, was helping and advising Zippy and Tony down the stretch. Jimmy was always there for Zippy to lean on, and Zippy appreciated Jimmy's help. But near the end of the 2002 season, Jimmy made the decision to step away from the track to spend more time with his family. He would not be returning as Bobby's crew chief for 2003, but would instead head up operations for both the #18 and #20 teams as team manager for JGR.

Bobby and Jimmy had worked together for eight years and had won nineteen races and a championship together. Like Jimmy, Bobby had two small children, so he understood Jimmy's desire to be home more. "It will allow him to spend time with his family," Bobby said, "and that will mean more to us than winning any race."

In late October, we hired Michael "Fatback" McSwain to take over as crew chief for the #18 team in 2003. Michael had been with Robert Yates Racing, working as crew chief for Ricky Rudd. We knew he was an intense competitor with fresh ideas—the kind of guy we wanted, especially since we had already made the difficult decision to move from Pontiacs to Chevys in 2003.

Once again, we took our entire team—more than one hundred and fifty employees and their spouses—to the Winston Cup presentation in New York. And did we ever have a ball!

Tony Stewart won $4.3 million for overcoming the challenges and adversity of the 2002 season. Tony, Bob Nardelli, Pat, and I were later invited to visit with President George W. Bush at the White House. When the president was introduced to Tony, President Bush joked for the press, "So you beat up photographers?"

Throughout the emotional highs and lows of that championship season, I relied constantly on certain cornerstone principles for living—principles which I will discuss throughout this book. These guidelines helped us to hurdle obstacles, confront problems head-on, overcome unexpected setbacks, and, against incredible odds, come out on top.

These principles have worked for me. I know they can work for you, too.

Seven Cornerstone Principles for Success

CAREER

Now that you know the track on which my career has run, you will better understand when I tell you that my strongest foundation for success has not been physical or material. Rather, it has been spiritual. And that's not a cute cliché or a thinly disguised attempt to trick you into converting to my style of religion, either.

Fact is, all the "religion" in the world will never lead you to success in this life or the next. I'm telling you straight out: The greatest factor in my success has been my personal relationship with God.

You can take it or leave it. I'm no theologian; I'm just a coach. But I know a good game plan when I see one, and I've found the best plan of all in the Bible. And I'm speaking from experience when I say this stuff works.

You may be an accountant, a writer, a homemaker, a schoolteacher, a football coach, or an expert in some other field; but whatever you do for a living, God wants you to do it well. He wants us to be great at our occupations, not just average, and He has given us the gifts and the help to make it happen.

He can also answer all kinds of questions about your life's calling. What are you supposed to be doing with your life, anyway? How can you achieve occupational success? If you will trust the Lord, He will guide you in your own career.

My advice is to check out God's game plan in the Bible. Find out what God says about achieving success in your vocational calling. Meanwhile, I can offer the following cornerstone principles that have proven to be true in my life. Consider these as starters.

CORNERSTONE 1

God created you for a special purpose, and He wants you to be successful at it. We are all made in His image, so think of your work as an honorable reflection of Him and an expression of God's creativity. As for success, "luck" and "chance" are foreign to God's plans. Personally, I don't believe in luck. As Thomas Jefferson said, "I'm a great believer in luck, and I find the harder I work, the more I have of it." I always felt that God wanted me to do something great, and He has something great for you to do, too!

CORNERSTONE 2

Your priorities should line up with God's plan. Occupational success, as God defines it, will follow. And remember, God knows what you need before you even ask! When you surrender your career to the Lord, He will honor you and teach you to use the platform He gives you to honor Him.

CORNERSTONE 3

All work done for the Lord is sacred. In God's economy, how you do whatever job you have is what matters most. Do your work as unto the Lord, regardless of what field you serve in. And don't imitate the attitude I used to have. I wanted God in the car with me, but I still wanted to drive! Let God be completely in charge.

CORNERSTONE 4

Personal integrity and honesty really matter. This is huge! Your reputation will precede you, just as God Himself went before the Israelites when He brought them out of slavery in Egypt. Employers will hire you and bosses will promote you because your integrity will make a way.

CORNERSTONE 5

Team players make the best players. The most successful individual is a team-oriented person who knows his own blind or weak spots. Only an honest, realistic, and cooperative individual can dare to seek out the counsel of others before making a difficult decision. A team player relies on others to help make up for his or her own personal shortcomings. And that will make both you and your team strong.

CORNERSTONE 6

Success comes to those who trust God. All jobs have their ups and downs. But the more you trust God, the more He will fortify you through the tough times. Show up early and finish your projects under budget and ahead of deadline. Know your boundaries and abide by them. Reject any conduct, speech, or attitudes that are out of bounds biblically, and God will honor you.

CORNERSTONE 7

Be gracious and a servant to all. Jesus told the people who worked for Him that He "did not come to be served, but to serve." Whether you are an employee or an employer, the head of the household or the youngest sibling, give your allegiance to those with whom you live and work. Serve one another. Remember, to be a good leader, you must first be a good follower. More often than not, the best head coaches were first good assistants.

Your Financial Success

Most of us, whether we admit it or not, believe that there is a God. I only know for sure about my relationship with God. I am continuously made aware of other people's relationships with Him as made known in their presence, in their manner of living, and in their character. Joe Gibbs's relationship with God must be among the best—his presence is inspiring, his manner of living evokes admiration, and his character is so obviously strong and good. In this book, you will find God reflected through Joe Gibbs. That reflection comes through in Joe's day-to-day business dealings just as clearly as a ringing bell. Whether it's God, God showing Himself through Joe, or just Joe Gibbs, he is a shining example for all of us. He is a shining example of how to do things the right way.

Charlie Cawley is the CEO of MBNA America, one of the world's largest financial institutions and a proud sponsor of Joe Gibbs Racing.

Who wants to be a millionaire? Who *doesn't* want to be rich? We all want to be successful and make a lot of money, but sometimes the two don't go hand in hand. It's possible to be very successful without making a great deal of money, and it's equally possible to make lots of money and be a colossal failure in life!

Besides, money is never about how much you have; it's always about how much money has you. In other words, money, or the lack of it, is never the real problem. It's how we use money that makes a world of difference in our lives.

How do I know that? I learned the hard way.

In this section, you'll find:

- How I went from winning the Super Bowl to being nearly bankrupt.
- How I learned to handle my finances according to God's game plan.
- What happens when we ignore God's game plan.
- Why a husband and wife should be in agreement about money matters.
- God's game plan for your finances.

NINE

FROM THE SUPER BOWL TO THE PORCELAIN BOWL

You might think that a Super Bowl–winning NFL coach would be rolling in money, but appearances can sometimes fool you. At the top of my game, while the sports media heralded my savvy as a field general, I was a few weeks away from losing everything my family owned. I was nearly bankrupt because of my own foolish financial mistakes.

It wasn't as though God hadn't given me several warnings. I just hadn't learned my lessons, and it was almost too late before I did.

The first warning came when I was in my mid-thirties, working as an assistant coach with the St. Louis Cardinals. I began playing racquetball for exercise, and I soon became addicted to the game, playing every chance I got. I practiced before work, blew off meals to play during my lunch hour, and competed in tournaments on evenings and weekends. I was getting pretty good at it, too. I competed in thirty-five-and-older tournaments all across the country and was fortunate enough to win quite a few. Racquetball served to satisfy my craving for competition, which I still have to this day.

About that time, the racquetball craze seemed to be taking the country by storm. I was certain that there was big money to be made in owning a racquetball court, so when a friend of mine in the construction business suggested that we build and manage our own court, I thought, *Hey, that's perfect!* My annual income was in the $35,000 range at the time, and with a wife and two growing boys to provide for, I was anxious to increase the balance in our checking account as quickly as possible.

It's important for a husband and wife to be in agreement on major financial decisions.

Pat was opposed to our investing what little savings we had in racquetball, but I pestered, badgered, and harped on her until she finally saw things my way. "If you have to do it, go ahead and do it," Pat sighed. To me, that was an endorsement. It was the beginning of an unwise pattern in our marriage when it came to the use of money.

While I always sought Pat's opinion on financial matters, I didn't always listen well when her views contradicted mine. Instead, if I wanted to buy a big-ticket item or invest in something about which Pat waved a caution flag, I immediately set about finding a way to sway her opinion. Eventually, I would wear her down. Even though Pat was extremely frugal, she loved me and wanted me to be happy, and the money wasn't nearly as important to her as our relationship. I had not yet learned that it's important for a husband and wife to be in agreement concerning major financial decisions.

Ironically, although I was never really arrogant about my success in sports, for some reason I had adopted an arrogance in my business dealings. When it came to money, I was overconfident for no apparent reason. It wasn't as though I had made a lot of money or developed a track record of wise investments. Nevertheless, I truly thought that I knew what I was doing when it came to financial matters!

MISGUIDED MOTIVES

Racquetball was huge in St. Louis, so I was sure that in no time we'd all get rich. I thought, *What have I got to lose?* Pat and I owned hardly anything to speak of. And because my share of ownership was a mere 10 percent, if the new business failed, my partners might lose a bundle, but I certainly wouldn't. So I rolled the dice.

From the day we opened our doors, the business took off. In 1976, I won the National Seniors Championship, further enhancing our prestige in racquetball circles. We soon built and opened a second court.

But then, almost as suddenly as the racquetball fad had begun, enthusiasm for the sport faded. We began losing money like a broken ATM spewing hundred-dollar bills. Several partners fell by the wayside, leaving only two of us, and we were still hemorrhaging money at the same alarming rate. I had entered the partnership with only a 10 percent investment, but I was now taking 50 percent of the losses. Finally, my partner and I swallowed hard and threw in the towel. Before we got out of the business, however, we had each lost more than $200,000!

In retrospect, it's easy to see that I got involved in the business with wrong motives, selfishly thinking that I had nothing to lose—that if anyone was going to lose money, it would be my friends, not me. I was simply trying to make some easy money. I refused to see it at the time, but when we closed the business in the early 1980s, the Lord was cautioning me concerning my attitudes toward money and get-rich-quick schemes.

Pat was great in the aftermath of the financial disaster. She never berated me or said, "I told you so!" Her attitude was, "Let's clean up this mess and move on."

SECOND WARNING

I should have learned my lesson from the racquetball fiasco, but I didn't. Although God had provided a good job and an adequate income for doing something that I enjoyed, I was still scouting the horizons, searching for a golden opportunity. I felt sure I could parlay my position as the head coach of the World Champion Washington Redskins into some sort of outside business that would provide for my family long-term. Nothing wrong with that, right? Sports figures do something like it every day.

The truth is, for all my reputation as a man of faith, I wasn't trusting God at that point. I was trusting in my own effort and financial acumen.

God was trying to get through to me: *Just coach! Just do the job I've given you to do, and I will take care of you and your family.* But I wasn't content with His provision. I didn't want to "just coach." I wanted to get rich! As it turned out, if I had simply obeyed God, handling my money according to His principles and investing wisely, I would have saved my family a lot of heartache—and our net worth would be much larger than it is today!

Instead, when another business opportunity came along—this time, a home nursing care business—I plunged in recklessly. I knew very little about the medical care business; it was completely outside the realm of my expertise. So not surprisingly, we again nearly lost our shirts. The price tag on my get-rich-quick schemes was getting higher, but I still ignored the red flags.

Amazingly, God loves us so much that He is willing to turn up the heat more and more if we fail to listen and obey His Word. And I was about to find out just how hot that flame could get!

THIRD AND LONG!

After winning the Super Bowl in 1983, I became acutely aware of how hard it is for a championship team to repeat. Although I had a three-year contract, coaching on almost any level is a "What have you done for me lately?" proposition; and under the intense scrutiny of the sports media in our nation's capital, I knew better than to relax and rest on my laurels.

I had no long-term guarantees. Anything could happen next season. I wanted to place my family's financial future on something more secure than an oblong ball that could bounce in any direction on any given Sunday. With the Super Bowl bonus money bolstering our bank account, I started searching for investment opportunities once again.

An acquaintance from college offered to let me become a partner in a tremendous real estate opportunity in Norman, Oklahoma, for a minimal amount of money. He was building homes and apartment complexes and developing other properties in the area, and the extent of my out-of-pocket expenses would be only a few thousand dollars for closing costs on each property. He planned to rent the properties until they sold, with the rental income more than covering our expenses. This was a no-brainer! I was going to be rich!

We can't lose money in real estate, I said to myself. Plus, it's the perfect place. Oklahoma is booming, thanks to the oil and gas companies, two commodities for which the demand is never going to die. I visited the properties with my friend and liked what I saw. I signed on in a simple partnership—my buddy built and I paid. Soon we were building and renting faster than I could keep up with it.

Pat was against the idea from the beginning. But I knew she just *had* to be wrong about this investment. After all, where else could we make so much money, so easily, with so little investment? This deal was too good to be true!

An old saying warns that when something seems too good to be true, it probably is.

One of my partners reassured me, "Joe, don't worry. Before you lose a dime, we'll lose everything we own!"

And they did.

After two years of enormous growth, during which we couldn't build properties fast enough, the oil-and-gas balloon suddenly burst and the local economy went bust. Then came the savings-and-loan debacle, and all at once people seemed to be staying away from Oklahoma in droves. A lot of people moved out of the area, and of those who remained, living in our properties, many couldn't make their payments.

Meanwhile, I was gearing up for the new football season in Washington, oblivious to the gathering storm clouds in Oklahoma. Then one day, I came home to find some odd mail. A late-payment notice had arrived from a bank that held a mortgage on our properties in Oklahoma. A few days later, another bank sent a late notice. Several of our mortgages on the development were past due.

At first, I didn't think much about the late notices. I simply sent them on to my partner in Oklahoma, and he promised to take care of them. But more and more late notices filled my mailbox. The Oklahoma economy had taken a nosedive. People were moving out, and businesses and industries were shutting their doors. Nevertheless, my partners were convinced that the downturn was temporary, so we continued to build more housing, anticipating the turnaround that many of the financial gurus said was certain to happen.

It didn't. Instead, things got worse. The partnership was in trouble, and I knew we had to take some drastic action. But what? How? The developments were in Oklahoma, and I was in Washington, sleeping at the office three nights a week as it was. I was working till two or three each morning and back in the office at eight, trying to field another Super Bowl team. I didn't have time to mess with the nuisance in Norman. I needed someone I could trust to handle the situation, and I knew just the right person.

A FRIEND INDEED

Just prior to the trouble in Oklahoma, I had begun working with a group of people in D.C. to develop a home for troubled and at-risk boys. Pat and I hadn't lived in the area long before we realized that while our nation's capital was one of the greatest cities in the world, it was also one of the most dangerous—especially for underprivileged teenage boys.

Everywhere I've coached, I have been involved in programs helping troubled youth, and I wanted to do something similar in Washington, D.C. For years I had dreamed of building a foster home where at-risk kids could live in a stable, family environment while learning Christian principles and job skills that could give them hope and save them from a life in the streets.

Several members of our Sunday school class met with a group of like-minded individuals, and they caught the vision. One member of that group was Don Meredith, a coolheaded, softhearted guy who loved God and loved people. Don was good at getting things done, especially beginning new organizations from scratch. He and his wife, Sally, became great friends to Pat and me.

Don is no relation to Dandy Don Meredith, the former Dallas Cowboys quarterback who later shared the Monday Night Football broadcast booth with Frank Gifford and Howard Cosell. But Don did find some common ground in Dallas at a home for children started by Olympic weightlifting champion Paul Anderson. The late Tom Landry, legendary Dallas Cowboys coach, and his former star quarterback Roger Staubach were on the board of directors of the children's home, along with Dallas Mavericks owner Don Carter and others. We decided to investigate what they were doing in Dallas to help kids, hoping to find some good ideas we could bring back to Washington.

Paul Anderson and his board were operating the Dallas-area homes under the careful direction of Jerry Campbell, a dedicated Christian with a heart as big as Texas. I was tremendously impressed with both the homes and the children whose lives they were impacting. Paul and his board agreed to help us open a similar home in Washington.

Naturally, I wanted to start big. We asked then–Vice President George Bush and Roger Staubach to speak at our initial fundraising banquet. We booked a well-known hotel in D.C. that could accommodate a crowd of 1,500 people for dinner, then worked like mad to publicize the event, filling every seat, and raising $150,000 for our new organization, Youth for Tomorrow.

We found a great spot to build the youth home, a 137-acre piece of property out in the country near Manassas, Virginia, and we purchased it for $320,000. Many people thought we were nuts to spend that kind of money, but today the same property is worth millions.

In the beginning, our group committed to raising our own funds, taking no government money and thus avoiding government strings that might prevent us from encouraging the kids to study the Bible and establish a firm relationship with God. Our fundraising group must raise more than $1 million every year simply to keep the doors open, but the home continues to this day, impacting the lives of teens in the Washington area. And in 2002 some substantial financial gifts made it possible for us to fulfill our dream of establishing an additional home for girls.

Because I had seen Don Meredith in action, working through the various challenges associated with starting Youth for Tomorrow, I felt comfortable in turning to him for advice on handling the Oklahoma real estate matter, while I focused on coaching. I asked Don if he would fly to the site and check it out for me.

What Don found was frightening. The partnership was millions of dollars in debt! The interest payments alone on the properties were more than $35,000 a month, in addition to the mortgages, and the partnership wasn't making its payments. "It's a huge mess," Don said somberly.

"But the partnership owns the properties!" I protested.

"Yeah, and you're a partner, so you're liable."

"Don, I'm at the beginning of a new season here. I can't take the time away from coaching to deal with this right now."

"Joe, I think I can help you with this," Don volunteered. "I'll go back to Oklahoma and handle this mess the best I know how till after the season."

Don returned to Norman to try to unravel the mess, which was far more complicated than either of us dreamed. He assembled a team of accountants, attorneys, and bookkeepers and spent sixty-four days going over every detail of the deal. He discovered that the partnership had borrowed irresponsibly, creating a complex maze of obligations, using one financial source to pay off another, much like many Americans juggle credit-card balance transfers, never really reducing the debt. Instead, the debt continued to deepen until there were no more places to find funds. Our mortgages were due, the rents weren't paying the bills, I had lost every cent I'd poured into the deal, and my financial obligations were mounting exponentially every day!

As a good friend, Don tried to shield me from the doom and despair he found in our development so that I could concentrate on coaching. All he said was, "We'll need to go down there to look at the situation after the season is over."

END OF THE LINE

The Redskins went 11-5 that year, but the Chicago Bears beat us 23-19 at RFK Stadium in the first game of the post-season playoffs. The football season was over for me, so I beat it down to Oklahoma, along with two accountants and two attorneys, only to discover that my other partners had already gone under and declared bankruptcy. As the only remaining partner, the entire financial responsibility was on my shoulders. Too late, I recognized the shocking truth: I was liable for everything the partners had done, whether I had been personally aware of the transactions or not.

As we waded through the past-due notices and other invoices, I felt a vice grip clamp on to my stomach, wrenching my insides tighter with each new bill the accountants turned up. We worked all day long trying to add up what the partnership actually owed. The bottom line: I was millions of dollars in debt with no means of repaying that amount of money! At the height of my career, at a time when I should be enjoying my success, I was wiped out. I was technically bankrupt.

TEN

WORKING OUT OF A FINANCIAL MESS

Amillion questions pummeled my mind. What was I going to do? How would this affect our family? Would the creditors take away our home, our cars, our furniture? How would this affect my job? Would Mr. Cooke, a man who prided himself on his financial successes, even want to keep me on as coach of the Redskins? If not, then what? How would this mess affect our children? What would Pat think?

Pat! I had to call her and tell her the devastating news. I excused myself from the others, went into a private room, and reached for the telephone. It was one of the toughest calls I've ever made.

"Pat, we're in debt," I said. "Deep, deep in debt." I tried my best to explain the vast scope of the financial mess we had on our hands, but I choked on the words.

The Lord extended His grace through Pat. She didn't lash out at me verbally, nor did she throw insults at my financial ineptitude. She didn't condemn me or heap further burdens of guilt on my already drooping shoulders.

After the initial shock wore off, Pat and I discussed further what the other partners had done. Finally, she said, "This is too much. You're going to kill yourself trying to deal with all of this. You were used, and you got taken. There's no use worrying about it. There's nothing you can do. File bankruptcy and come on home. We'll get through it somehow."

I was grateful for Pat's willingness to support me and help face the mess head-on. Nevertheless, my self-esteem plummeted through the floorboards. *How could I have been so foolish as to give my partners the power to sign my name without my approval? I should have...I could have done this...or that...Why? How? What now? I can't just walk away. People are depending on me.* Incomplete thoughts raced through my mind, each one opening a new Pandora's box of nightmares.

When we finished our first day of meetings, I returned to my hotel room and collapsed on my knees beside the bed. Not normally given to tears, I couldn't contain them any longer, as I cried to the Lord, "God, I am bankrupt! There is no question about it." I knew that I had trusted in my own financial scheming, rather than trusting God.

"I admit that I've been a fool," I prayed. "I've never felt more stupid in all my life. And I'm willing to go through it, if this is what You want me to do, but I don't feel like I should file bankruptcy. I feel that I have an obligation to these banks and to the people involved, and I would like to work this out. But You know I don't have the resources to do it. To me, this is the biggest mess in the world. Only You can straighten this out. Please show me what to do, and I'll do it."

I knew bankruptcy was a legal option for people in messes like mine, and some might say it was the wisest option. I had known of other people and businesses that had filed bankruptcy and rebuilt their lives admirably once they were out from under their financial burdens. I didn't feel that I was better than they were for not filing bankruptcy; nor did I feel that their problems were greater than mine. I simply felt that for me, bankruptcy was not the answer. I had gotten into this mess by trusting in my own abilities rather than God's. I wasn't going to attempt to manipulate, maneuver, or otherwise try to make something happen. I decided to trust God to pull me out of it.

As I acknowledged my own foolishness and inadequacy, God gave me a marvelous peace in my heart and mind and a fresh sense of His amazing grace. Theologians say that mercy is when God doesn't give us what we deserve and that grace is when He gives us *better* than we deserve. Seems to me He gave me double portions of both!

That didn't make it any less embarrassing for me to approach my creditors. Nevertheless, I made a commitment to personally contact everyone to whom the partnership owed money, to admit my mistakes and humble myself before them. Maybe we could work out some sort of payment arrangements.

MONEY MIRACLES

Nine banks were involved in the mess, eight in the Norman area alone. One bank held a $1.2 million note on some of my apartment complexes. There was also a $70,000 loan and seventeen unsold lots. Don Meredith and I met with the bank officer in charge of our accounts.

I leveled with the man. "I don't have the money to pay these debts, but I'm not going to file bankruptcy. I'd like to work out some sort of plan, so I can pay you what I owe."

The man studied the documents and said he'd get back to us. By the following day he had a proposal. I thought for sure the bank would want to salvage something, rather than risk losing all the money they had tied up in our partnerships, but I wasn't prepared for the bank officer's plan. "You turn over your properties to the bank, free and clear. We take your properties," he said, "and you give us $95,000. We'll put that money in a maturing note that pays us dividends for seven years. Does that sound manageable?"

"I guess," I replied. "That's it?"

"That's it. Do we have a deal?"

Don and I walked out of the bank with our heads spinning. The bank was literally offering to let me off the hook on more than a million dollars' worth of properties, for which they owned the mortgages, for the outrageously low sum of $95,000!

"What just happened in there?" I asked Don, as we made our way to the car.

"I don't know," Don replied out of the side of his mouth, "but just keep walking before they change their minds!"

There was only one problem with the deal: I didn't have $95,000.

Shortly after that, I was talking with Jerry Campbell, the director of the Paul Anderson Youth Home. I shared briefly with Jerry some of the trouble I was having. "Why don't you come to Dallas," Jerry suggested. "I'd like to introduce you to some people who might be able to help."

Don and I flew to Dallas to meet with Jerry and his friends. Jerry and a friend, Ralph Fellars, took us to a bank and arranged a loan for $125,000. I could hardly believe their kindness! Next, Jerry took us to see Don Carter, the former owner of the Dallas Mavericks, to see if he might loan me some money.

I was aware of Don's involvement in the business side of sports, but we had never met personally. "Joe, tell Don what's happened to you," Jerry prodded.

I was extremely uncomfortable talking about my personal financial fiasco in front of a man whom I had just met, but Don seemed so concerned that I soon found myself pouring out my story.

Suddenly, Don stopped me. "You don't need to tell me anything else, Joe," he said. "I don't need to know the details. Just tell me, what do you need?"

"Well, I'd like to borrow some money," I said quietly.

"Fine. Come with me," said Don. We went to the bank, and Don arranged a loan for $200,000 that same day.

Talk about a miracle! I left Dallas with $325,000 in loans from people I had just met a few hours earlier! Don Meredith and I returned to Norman, paid the money to the first bank, and then continued going from bank to bank, trying to work out a payment arrangement with each one.

One of the attorneys involved in our case was Robert Fraley, a bright, energetic lawyer whose Orlando-based company Leader Enterprises represented a number of high-profile athletes, including baseball greats Orel Hershiser and Frank Thomas, professional golfers Paul Azinger and Payne Stewart, and several NFL coaches. Robert and I hit it off immediately, and he eventually became one of my most trusted friends and advisors.

Robert and his wife, Dixie, were both dedicated Christians who brought their faith to bear on every decision they made, in their personal relationships as well as in business. Although younger than I, Robert seemed to have wisdom far beyond his years, and I soon learned to trust his judgment.

The weather was freezing the first time we went to Norman together. Standing outside in the bitter-cold wind, freezing his socks off in front of the motel, Robert pulled his overcoat tightly around his chest. "The next time you decide to go broke," Robert chided, "let's do it someplace warm!"

Robert negotiated a deal in which some of the banks could write off nearly a million dollars in exchange for $160,000 in interest. It made no sense the way these banks were dealing with us, but each step of the way when I expressed my desire to work out a payment plan rather than file bankruptcy, we found light where there was nothing but darkness.

Many people give up when they find themselves bogged down in debt. I've heard of families that filed bankruptcy because they were $10,000 in the hole. How sad! And how unnecessary! While any debt is serious, most creditors will work with people in trouble if you can show them you are sticking to a tight budget and will pay them what you can, as you can. Lenders would rather work with you than not get anything at all of what is owed to them. It's been my experience that if you will trust God and follow His plan, He will lead you through the darkness. You can make your way out without filing bankruptcy.

LIVING ON A BUDGET

Back in Washington, I still had enormous payments to make to nine separate institutions—and no ability to pay them, even with the payment plans we had worked out. One day, I received a card in the mail from a local banker in the D.C. area. The essence of the card's message was, "You've been recommended to us as a preferred customer, and we'd love to loan you some money." The card was hand signed by Tom Schaffer.

At first, I nearly laughed out loud when I read the card. Me? A preferred customer? They want to loan me money? What a joke!

But Pat and I had been praying throughout this ordeal, and our friends and legal representatives had been praying, too, so I thought, *Maybe this is an answer to prayer.* Don Meredith and I met with Tom Schaffer and poured out our hearts to him. I explained, "I've got this enormous debt in Oklahoma, with no real way of paying for it. I have a three-year contract with the Redskins, and I'm making a good salary, but it's not nearly enough."

We cut our expenses, eliminating luxuries that we had come to take for granted.

Tom listened carefully, made notes, and offered some suggestions. We found him to be an extremely competent banker and a wonderful Christian man. Tom worked with us to consolidate all the loans in Oklahoma, paying them off and establishing one large payment in Washington. Pat and I arranged to have my paychecks deposited directly to Tom's bank, and Tom doled out enough money for us to live on. Everything else went toward paying down the debt as fast as possible. We cut our expenses, eliminated many luxuries that we had come to take for granted as the family of a successful NFL coach, and learned to live on a budget.

When I informed Pat that we needed to cut back on nonessentials, I was thinking of those things that didn't matter much to me, such as Pat's extra trips to the beauty salon, shopping sprees, luxury vacations (although I had always enjoyed staying in nice places), expensive dinners at fancy restaurants—most of which I could live without rather easily. But Pat looked at our expenses and found that most of the big-ticket items were under my list of favorites, not hers. Still, I was surprised when I came home from work one night near the end of the football season to discover that Pat had canceled our country club membership.

The following spring, Pat heard our nine-year-old, Coy, out in the garage rummaging through some sporting equipment. "What are you doing?" she asked.

"I'm getting my golf clubs out," Coy replied matter-of-factly. "Me and Johnny and a couple buddies are going to the club to play golf." He'd already found his little white golf hat and was dressed to play. In previous years, Coy and his young friends often went to the club. I allowed him to use my account number, and he had grown accustomed to entertaining his friends, signing for malts after a round. The golf course was part of his life.

"You can't go," Pat told him.

"What?" Coy winced as he said the word. "Why not?"

"Because we had to cancel our membership at the club."

Coy threw his hat down on the floor, put his hands on his hips, and looked back at Pat in amazement. "Where am I supposed to play golf?" he nearly cried.

While our naive nine-year-old survived a few seasons without golf, the impact of our financial calamity affected the whole family in myriad ways. Certainly, because of my position as coach of the Redskins, our sacrifices were inconsequential compared to those of many families in a financial crunch. Nevertheless, the changes rocked our world, and each day we faced financial choices on matters that we had previously taken for granted.

For instance, just prior to learning of the fiasco in Norman, I had been shopping with J D for his first car. Cars were important to me as a kid, and I was thrilled to be able to now provide nice vehicles for my family. Yet I wanted my son to understand that things aren't just handed to you in life, so I made his first car an incentive to work hard in school. I had promised J D that if he kept his grades up and stayed out of trouble, I'd buy him a car at the end of his sophomore year in high school.

When J D turned sixteen, we went car shopping. He fell in love with a Chevy Camaro, and the salesman saw us coming. "For a few dollars more," he said, "you can move into a Z28."

When we looked at the Z28, we were sold. The car had to be special ordered, so J D selected the color and all the options, and we were like two kids in a candy store—an expensive candy store! We both could hardly wait the few weeks for the Z28 to arrive.

Then the dam burst in Norman. One night while I was working with Don at the development site, I called home late and talked to Pat. Much of our conversation, of course, centered on the dire circumstances we now faced. Pat and J D had been watching television together, and she thought that J D had fallen asleep. Actually, J D was listening to our conversation. When Pat hung up the phone, there were tears in her eyes. J D sat up and said, "Hey, Mom, I want to tell you something. I don't need that car."

His sacrificial attitude tore my heart out. I knew we couldn't afford that car anymore, but I was determined to find a way to keep my promise to my son, and I did.

That car became another lesson for all of us. When we give up something out of love, God often gives it back. J D was willing to give up the car he loved for the family that he loved even more. And when I saw that, I'd have moved mountains to make sure he got that car.

How much more, then, when we take our sticky fingers off those things we value so dearly, will our heavenly Father give back to us just what we need—and the little extras in life as well!

ELEVEN

BACK FROM THE BRINK

I t took more than four-and-a-half years of hard work, sacrifice, and commitment, but inch by inch our family walked out from under the dark financial cloud that had enveloped us. None of it could have happened without the counsel and help of a group of godly men who became my inner circle of advisors during and after the financial affair.

These friends included Don Meredith, Robert Fraley, Jerry Campbell, Don Carter, Tom Schaffer, and financial consultant Paul Kraus, who became personally involved and spent hundreds of hours helping to extricate me from my mess. Howard Dayton, president of Crown Ministries, also assisted us. (Crown Ministries has since merged with Christian Financial Concepts, headed by financial advisor Larry Burkett.) I still meet regularly with most of these men concerning my financial matters as well as the business aspects of our race teams.

Do you want to know one of the most amazing miracles I experienced in the midst of my financial quagmire? Despite the fact that I was a public figure and my name was on all the loan documents, not one word of my involvement in this mess leaked to the press. From the beginning of the debacle, one of my greatest concerns was how it might impact other people. Certain members of the media thrive on other people's calamities, and had my troubles become public knowledge, embarrassing features would no doubt have shown up on television, in newspapers, or in sports magazines. Overnight, I would have gone from Super Bowl champ to Super Bumbling Chump! I would have been an embarrassment to my family, my boss, my coworkers and team, and even my community.

But not one word surfaced in the media. For someone who has made his living on both sides of the media juggernaut, that's a miracle that ranks up there close to the crossing of the Red Sea!

TESTED BY FIRE

As we worked our way out of debt, Pat and I purchased very little that we didn't need. We applied every penny beyond basic living expenses and a few perks toward paying down the massive mountain of debt. Pat was especially good at keeping us on our budget and cutting expenses.

Nothing tests the fiber of your relationships more than a financial crisis.

As coach of the Redskins, I couldn't take on a second job, but Robert Fraley negotiated several side projects I could do to earn extra income to pay the debt more quickly. It was one of the toughest times of my life, and the financial stress spilled over into every aspect of our lives. But through it all, thank God, we didn't lose our home or our family.

Nothing tests the fiber of your relationships more than a financial crisis. Emotionally and physically, you're tired, stressed, and stretched much of the time. Many marriages explode under financial pressure. There's a tendency to be critical and short with the people who love you most. Some people lash out at each other; others beat up on themselves. The only way to avoid making matters worse is by turning the mess over to God on a daily basis and living the way His Word instructs.

Financial freedom doesn't happen overnight. We had to commit ourselves to a long-term program of financial responsibility, not just spending less than we earned, but also applying every bit of extra income beyond basic living expenses toward eliminating the debt. I emphasize this because it takes more than good intentions to get out of debt; it takes work. But you *can* do it!

THE AMOUNT DOESN'T MATTER

Another lesson I learned is that it doesn't matter if you are $16,000 in debt or $16,000,000; if you are unable to pay your bills, you experience that same awful feeling of horror and embarrassment. When there's too much month left at the end of your money, regardless of the amount, you know that wrenching in the pit of your stomach. Fall behind on a house payment or miss paying a medical bill and see how quickly the world seems to close in on you.

When the late notices flood your mailbox or the collection agencies call constantly, stark terror sears through your mind, and you feel as though you're being bowled over by a giant boulder. Life becomes a self-defeating process; the financial stress robs you of your creativity and your ability to think straight, which creates even more stress. You fear that you are going to lose everything you've ever worked for. *How am I going to handle this?* you fret. *It all seems so overwhelming.*

Shortly after I learned the severity of our financial crisis, I headed to Arkansas once again to see my friend and spiritual father, George Tharel. I wanted to get his take on how I might best handle the mess. And once again, I had trouble getting to Fayetteville. This time the car I rented overheated in the middle of nowhere.

It was late at night, freezing outside, and I was driving across a desolate section of Oklahoma that looked more like Siberia. No traffic approached or followed me; there wasn't a light to be seen anywhere! Steam curled from the edges of the car's hood. I knew the car was dying, but I decided to push it as far as it could go. I drove on with the temperature gauge bouncing in the red for more than a half hour. Finally, the car began to sputter and whine, and I knew the radiator could blow at any second. Whether out of frustration or sheer desperation, I floored that sucker and hoped I could get it up the next hill. The car barely inched over the crest of the hill when the radiator blew and the engine shut down completely. The car rolled down the other side of the hill, finally coasting to a stop—if you can believe it—right in front of a motel.

I checked in and called the car rental company. I recognized the name of the area where I was stranded and recalled that I had a friend from high school who lived nearby. He had contacted me once and invited me to visit. *Why not?* I thought. *I'm here. I may as well call him.*

My high school buddy was excited to hear from me. He picked me up at the motel and took me to his home, a small mobile home in which he and his wife were raising four kids. We swapped old football stories for a while and then got to the nitty-gritty of where I was coming from and why I was in the area. Strangely, I found it easy to admit my failures and tell my friend about the financial mess I was in.

He gazed at me in disbelief, and for a moment, I thought he was going to break down crying. He told me that he was in much the same condition. The numbers were different, but the facts were basically the same—he owed a debt he didn't have the ability to pay. His undoing had been an unwise loan of $16,000, and he had been paying it off slowly for a number of years. My first reaction was, *$16,000! I wish I owed that much!* But then I realized that the dollar amount was irrelevant. My income was greater than his, and my debt was deeper, but we were both in the same sinking boat. And we would both have to bail as hard and fast as we could to survive.

Dollars don't matter. For some people, it might take five million to bring them to their knees; for others, the amount may be five hundred. The good news is that when you're down on your knees, it's a good time to call out to God for help. God had warned me three times concerning my weakness of seeking security in money and get-rich-quick schemes—first through the racquetball club failure, then the nursing care business, and now through a real estate mess so enormous that I had nowhere else to turn but to Him.

He had some lessons He wanted me to learn—long, difficult, expensive lessons, but I finally learned them well. God didn't give me a financial gimmick to help get me out of the mess overnight. He did something much better. He pointed me to the Bible, where I found literally hundreds of verses of Scripture relating to money, how to handle it, and what my attitude should be toward it. I discovered that the Bible contained a virtual blueprint for success, and although I was a Christian and had attended church regularly for most of my life, I had missed it.

Life was simple for a boy growing up in Enka, North Carolina.

My father J C (front left), my mother Winnie, me, and my brother Jim (top right).

Pat and me, looking forward to a life together at her high school graduation.

My first hot rod, built in a Southern California garage.

Cutting up with quarterback Joe Theismann (far right) and the boys in the Redskins locker room.

I wasn't a pro prospect, but I played my heart out as a tight end, offensive guard, and linebacker at San Diego State University.

They call me Coach.

Going over the X's and O's in the Redskins locker room at halftime.

Talking things over with Jack Kent Cooke (left), owner of the Washington Redskins.

I fell to my knees and prayed as the Minnesota Vikings neared the Washington goal line in the final minute of the 1988 NFC Championship game.

On the sidelines at RFK Stadium with Don Breaux and quarterback Mark Rypien.

Five minutes into the final quarter of the 1983 Super Bowl against the Dolphins, with the Redskins facing fourth-and-one at the Miami forty-three, I decided to go for the first down instead of punting. John Riggins broke through the line and ran for a touchdown to put us ahead 20-17.

Returning on the Redskins team plane with the Super Bowl trophy and general manager Bobby Beathard (left).

Celebrating with Coy (left) and J D (right) following the Redskins' victory over the Buffalo Bills in Super Bowl XXVI.

George Tharel,
my spiritual father.

Putting on the ritz with Don
Meredith (left), my longtime friend
and founder of Christian Family Life,
at a function honoring Don and CFL.

Don Coryell (right) presented me for induction into the Pro Football Hall of
Fame in 1996. What an honor!

The Winston Cup cars of Joe Gibbs Racing—the #20 Home Depot Pontiac and the #18 Interstate Batteries Pontiac.

With Bobby Labonte (left), and Tony Stewart (right), two of the finest drivers in NASCAR.

In the winner's circle at Pocono Raceway in July 2001 with race winner Bobby Labonte (center), crew chief Jimmy Makar (right), and Bobby's son, Tyler.

The #18 Interstate Batteries pit crew in action during the Brickyard 400 at the Indianapolis Motor Speedway.

In his final race, the 2001 Daytona 500, #3 Dale Earnhardt leads the pack—#18 Bobby Labonte, #8 Dale Earnhardt Jr., #24 Jeff Gordon, #5 Terry Labonte and #20 Tony Stewart.

In the winner's circle at Bristol Motor Speedway in August 2001 with race winner Tony Stewart (center) and his crew chief Greg "Zippy" Zipadelli.

J D (left) and Coy hang out prior to a NASCAR Craftsman Truck Series race at Dover.

The #20 MBNA Chevrolet Silverado driven by my son Coy in the 2002 NASCAR Craftsman Truck Series.

Posing with the Winston Cup at the 2000 awards banquet in New York. From left to right are Coy, his wife Heather, J D, his wife Melissa, Bobby Labonte, his wife Donna, Pat, and me.

At the track with Interstate Batteries chairman Norm Miller (center) and Tom Landry (right), my former rival and legendary coach of the Dallas Cowboys.

The Gibbs family: J D, his son Miller, his wife Melissa, his son Jackson, me, Pat, Coy, and his wife Heather.

With Pat outside our home in Cornelius, North Carolina.

I committed myself to handling money God's way from then on. After we paid off the last debt, what a sense of freedom we felt! We celebrated and rejoiced. Pat and I had learned how to save money through our ordeal, so we didn't go out and do anything stupid. Instead, we remained in an offensive, "attack" mode; we took the same intensity that we had used in getting out of debt and applied it to rebuilding our financial house. Slowly but surely, following God's blueprint for success, we made headway, and before long, compound interest rates worked for us rather than against us. We were saving more, giving more, and enjoying what God had so graciously given to us.

> *God didn't give me a financial gimmick to help get me out of the mess overnight. He did something better.*

I soon had more money in my bank account than I'd ever had in my life. But my attitude toward getting money and acquiring material things had changed. Now I had money rather than money having me. More importantly, I found my security in the Lord rather than in my ability to provide a comfortable living for my family.

For quite a while, Pat and I didn't invest any major amounts of money in anything. But then one day, my sons and I began talking about starting a racing team.

HERE WE GO AGAIN?

Some people might think that when we started the racing team, we were plunging into another dangerous and risky get-rich-quick scheme. After all, those top-of-the-line stock cars are expensive to build, and you may have noticed that sometimes they hit a wall. Who was going to maintain the cars and fix them? Who was going to drive? How could we afford to hire and pay everyone we would need to make the team successful? What could possibly be more ludicrous than investing money in a car that costs $150,000 and gets less than five miles to the gallon?

All of these concerns were valid, and I considered each one carefully. But we built the race team on a completely different foundation—a biblical foundation, if you will. I received wise counsel, relying heavily on my inner circle of advisors. Most importantly, Pat and I were in agreement (after her sleepy introduction to racing in Charlotte, that is). Never again would I enter a major financial transaction without Pat's genuine approval. We prayed through every major decision, making sure that we weren't racing ahead of God or jumping into something unprepared. I realized in a fresh way that God had brought Pat and me together to be partners in life, and that included our business and financial life.

Don Meredith, J D, and I had done our homework before starting the race team; we knew as much as possible about what we wanted to do, even though we had no clue how it would actually work. From the beginning, we spent money in an extremely conservative fashion, carefully avoiding debt. After our experience with the partnership in Oklahoma, I was paranoid about spending money we didn't have. I met regularly with our accountants, attorneys, and advisors to make sure we were on solid financial ground, and I still do—as frequently as once a month.

I'm a case study that proves when you follow God's plan, it will work.

We didn't try to get rich quickly. Instead, we expanded slowly, paying our bills as we went, and we built the business from scratch following godly principles. Today, after ten years in the business, our race teams are consistent contenders, and Joe Gibbs Racing has become extremely successful. We went from the brink of bankruptcy to a business worth millions of dollars, employing more than two hundred people, and housed in a 135,000-square-foot, state-of-the-art race shop, with our own airplanes, transporters, and more than fifty race cars. I don't say these things to boast, but rather to encourage you that no matter how big your financial problems are, if you will trust God and do as He leads you to do, He can bring you out of that mess and give you a new start. I'm a case study that proves when you follow God's plan, it will work.

I needed to go through the financial fire in my life. Just as my experience in Tampa taught me how to handle losses and prepared me for the adversity and later success I experienced in Washington, my near-bankruptcy experience changed the way I handled money and prepared me for the prosperity God wanted to give to me all along. God had tried to warn me about the error of my ways, but I hadn't wanted to listen. I was such a bonehead that He had to flatten me, to break me, to bring me to the place where I'd trust Him and do things His way.

I'm grateful for the lessons learned, but I never want to make the same mistakes again. And with what I have discovered in God's Word, I never will.

A WORD ABOUT GENEROSITY

It's a funny thing about financial success. When the money starts flowing in, the only way to keep it coming is to give some away! Most truly successful people have proven the truth of the biblical principle, "Give and it shall be given unto you." If we hoard what we have, our supplies and resources soon dwindle. But if we give to others—whether out of our prosperity or our own need—multiplied blessings seem to come our way. Perhaps this is one of the reasons why prosperous people so often feel compelled to give something back.

Charlie Cawley, CEO of MBNA America Bank, as a boy attended St. Benedict's prep school in Newark. There Charlie learned the values that set him on the road to success. Charlie and his friend Al Lerner would later build from scratch one of America's largest financial institutions.

One day Charlie shared with me the story of his upbringing, and he took me to visit his old stomping grounds, including St. Benedict's. Charlie's fingerprints were all over that campus! Besides helping the school financially, he takes a personal interest in the students. When he attends NASCAR races as a principal sponsor of our race team, Charlie often brings along a planeload of kids from St. Benedict's as his guests. It's just one of the ways Charlie gives something back.

We all need to find some way to give back a portion of what we have received. As we do, the well of our resources will continue to be refilled.

Eleven Cornerstone Principles for Success

FINANCES

One Sunday morning, when I was in the depths of my financial despair, I glanced around my church and noticed several couples of various ages. Almost none were rich in dollars, but all were rich in love, peace of mind, and contentment. They all lived peaceful lives because they had learned the secret of contentment—how much is enough—and because they had applied God's principles of financial success to their lives.

The Bible has much to say about money. More than 2,300 verses relate to finances. About 500 verses talk about faith, while less than 500 pertain to prayer; but more than four times as many apply to money—our attitudes toward it, how we get it, what we do with it, and how we manage it. Jesus talked about money far more than He did about heaven or hell.

Frankly, I was surprised to learn that. But God is concerned about my finances because He knows that my money affects almost every other aspect of my life. It's an indicator of what I consider important. We may be slow to put our money where our mouths are, but we always put our money where our hearts are.

My attitudes toward money and my financial decisions are today based on the following principles. As you read through them, you might notice that I violated almost every single one before learning the hard way. But if you will take these principles to heart, you can avoid a lot of stress and save yourself a great deal of money.

CORNERSTONE 1

God is the owner of everything. We are merely the stewards of all that He provides. And since God owns it all, He can freely give good things to His children, which is exactly what He wants to do. We don't have to beg, manipulate, or trick God (as though we could!) into providing what we need. But we must be conscientious caretakers of the resources He gives us.

CORNERSTONE 2

There's no such thing as a self-made man or woman. We all need other people to help us—mentors, coaches, advisors, and nuts-and-bolts people, too. But most of all, we need God's help to prepare us, to put us in the right places at the right times, and to provide help and encouragement from sources He alone controls. Without Him, we don't have a prayer.

CORNERSTONE 3

Wealth and prosperity are fleeting and temporal. No matter how much you collect, only those things that are done for God with His help will last. The martyred missionary Jim Elliot once said, "He is no fool who gives what he cannot keep to gain that which he cannot lose." What legacy will you leave behind?

CORNERSTONE 4

Honesty really is the best policy. Yes, people can make money by shady means. But God's definition of success requires you to look yourself in the mirror and know that you have achieved your goals His way. Jesus said, "For what profit is it to a man if he gains the whole world, and loses his own soul?"

CORNERSTONE 5

Greed and envy are twin cancers. We tend to look at successful people and say, "I'll have what they're having." But God doesn't have a cookie-cutter plan for our lives. What spells success for one person may spell disaster for another. Do what God wants *you* to do, and He will supply what you need.

CORNERSTONE 6

Get-rich-quick schemes are to be avoided. Consistency and perseverance are the way to financial success. The overwhelming desire for a "quick score" will bring only trouble and possibly even self-induced destruction. Heed the advice of top financial counselors who caution, "The best way to get rich quickly is to get rich slowly."

CORNERSTONE 7

Don't co-sign on a loan unless you're willing to pay it off. It's never a good idea to put your own financial security at risk by agreeing to cover someone else's debts if they don't pay. And God makes a strong point in His Word that if you choose to co-sign for a loan, you must be prepared to pay it off yourself.

CORNERSTONE 8

Seek wise counsel before making any major financial decision. To be a truly successful individual, you must be a team player. Surround yourself with a group of people who will speak words of encouragement (as well as caution), people whom you trust to tell you the truth even when they think you are wrong.

CORNERSTONE 9

Avoid going into debt, if at all possible. Remember, getting into debt is easy; getting out is difficult and can be extremely painful. Personally, I like the way the apostle Paul put it: "Owe nothing to anyone except to love one another."

CORNERSTONE 10

Generosity yields great dividends. Most of us assume that generosity flows from financial success, but actually it's the other way around. A wonderful process is set into motion as we give to others: God gives back to us! When you're on God's team and trusting in His game plan, God can make a way in your finances. And His way is always better than our own.

CORNERSTONE 11

Only God is loyal; money favors no one. Money can be a vicious taskmaster, a false motivator, a hollow idol that sorely disappoints. Any way you look at it, you lose. But the person who trusts in God will never be disappointed, in this lifetime or the world to come.

Success in Building Your Team

Joe Gibbs embodies the qualities that make great leaders and inspire others to excel. His passion and resolve are infectious and ignite in others the desire to achieve what seems impossible. On the football field, at the race track, and in the boardroom, Joe has demonstrated an uncanny ability to build high performance into people the way it is designed into his race cars. Joe stretches horizons, challenges imaginations, and instills confidence in others. As a result, Joe's people are known for playing for the name on the front of the jersey rather than the one on the back. His success can be measured not only in championships, but also by each team member's reflections on being part of something that could not have been attained individually. And Joe lives what he teaches. Whether it's jumping in with his team to solve a problem or pitching in to build a playground in the inner city of Washington, D.C., as we did together, Joe Gibbs is right there setting the pace, making us want to do better, and showing us that working together will get us farther and get us there faster.

Bob Nardelli is chairman, president and CEO of The Home Depot,
the world's largest home improvement retailer with more than 1350 stores in
the U.S., Canada, Mexico, and Puerto Rico.

Few things in life are more exciting than gathering a group of people around you and watching them gel into a team that touches the world for good. Yet there seems to be a lack of information or teaching concerning how to best choose our teams. I am often asked to speak at seminars and conventions, and the number one topic people want to hear about is this: How do you build a winning team? How do you find good people and get them to buy into your program?

Through the years, I've been involved with football teams, racing teams, and business teams. I coached football for twenty-eight years, and I have owned a NASCAR team for ten. I've also been involved in a variety of business ventures—some of which have been enormously successful, and a few of which have been utterly disastrous. Through it all, I've come to recognize several components common to most successful enterprises.

The secrets that I am going to share with you in this section weren't learned at Harvard. The keys to my success didn't come from a philosophical approach to the subject. Nor did I glean my insights from focus groups or opinion polls. On the contrary, the lessons and team-building techniques I've learned were the result of on-the-job training—fumbling in the dark at times, operating by trial and error, and working my way through tough situations.

I have found that many of the key principles for success in professional sports are also necessary to be successful in business and other walks of life, including our personal relationships. I know these principles work, because I've used them again and again to motivate successful professional teams and to build successful businesses. If you will incorporate these ideas into your game plan for success, I'm confident that they will save you a lot of time and misery.

In this section, you will discover:

- Building a winning team starts with the man or woman in your mirror.
- How to learn from people who excel at what you want to do.
- How to lead by example.
- How to pick the right people for your team.

- Why it's important to demonstrate that every team member is important.
- How to deal with adversity.
- Why you need to confront problems head-on.
- How to keep your priorities in order.

TWELVE

BUILDING THE TEAM BUILDER

I looked over the crop of prospective players—a motley-looking group, to say the least. There was Chub, a badly-out-of-shape guy who could barely sprint ninety feet. Next to him was Goose, a tall, lanky fellow with good hands and big feet. Goose was a gangling sort of creature, but he sure could stretch to catch a ball. Then there was Jukie, a guy who could do it all—run, throw, hit, you name it. One by one, I considered my options. Who in this bunch could help me win?

Billie tossed the baseball bat to me, and I caught it in my right hand, grasping it just below the trademark. Billie put his right hand above mine. I put my left hand above his, and we choked up to the top of the bat. Billie's hand hugged the top of the bat handle, leaving less than an inch between his thumb and the knob.

"I win!" Billie shouted. "I get first pick."

"Oh no you don't," I yelled. "Scissors!" I made a V with my index finger and middle finger and shoved them around the bat handle. "I'll take Jukie."

I've always been competitive, but simply playing the game has never been good enough for me. My whole life, I've been trying to *win*. Growing up during the 1940s in a small town in the hills near Asheville, North Carolina, I spent most of my spare time playing baseball, basketball, or football with my friends. As soon as we finished our chores, we'd meet at the ball field—often not much more than a recently plowed tobacco field—and start a pickup game. There I quickly learned how to be a team player and how to pick good people. We had a limited number of guys to choose from, so making sound decisions concerning my team members was a key to winning.

And it still is today.

TEAM BUILDING IS TOUGH

It's tough to find people who will get as excited as you are about your goals and who will be as conscientious as you are about building your dream. You can start a company all by yourself, out in the garage, but as your business grows, you will need to bring in quality people and motivate them to move together in the same direction. You must be able to inspire them to share your dream.

Why is it so hard to find talented people who will willingly sacrifice their own goals for the good of the team? Because it goes against human nature. From the time a newborn child comes into the world, you will never need to teach that baby to be selfish, to look out for number one. But you'll spend years encouraging that child to share, to help others, and to do unto others as he would have them do unto him.

Even as adults, our natural tendency is to be extremely self-centered. We focus on *our* needs, *our* desires, what *we* want out of our relationships. Often, not until that first child comes along do we truly consider the needs of a human being other than ourselves.

In the NFL and in NASCAR, my role has been to bring people together to accomplish a common goal. My staff and I repeatedly remind our team members, "Look, you have to put aside your own agenda. You may have to stay late. You may have to work extra hard. You may even have to do menial tasks."

I would say to my football players, "We may need you to be a blocker instead of a ball carrier. You may have to play on special teams rather than be the star on offense or defense. But every position is important. And the kind of person you are and how you contribute—these things do make a difference, either positively or negatively. We are working together for the good of the entire team."

Because this concept goes against human nature, the first thing you must understand about team building is that it is *difficult* for people to lay aside their own interests for the benefit of the family, company, group, or team. But motivating people to work toward a common goal is crucial to building a strong team, and building a great team is absolutely essential for achieving success in any arena in life.

And it all starts with you. Can you be a good team member? Can you build a good team if given the opportunity? How will you do it? Where will you start?

LEARNING THE ROPES

If you are wise, you will learn from those who have already excelled at what you want to do. Fortunately, as I climbed the ladder of success in my chosen field, I had the advantage of learning from some strong role models and mentors.

During the years I worked as an assistant coach, I served under four separate head coaches, each of whom was extremely successful at motivating and leading people, yet each with his own distinctive style.

Don Coryell: Doing What You Love and Loving What You Do

Don Coryell was a brilliant coach, a master at developing strategies, incorporating new ideas, and working with people to bring out their best efforts. Ironically, Don was surprisingly uncomfortable speaking in public. He was especially cautious about speaking to the media. But he related well to team members and was excellent at selecting people to work with him.

Coryell was perhaps best known for his intense devotion to the game. As part of his preparation each week, Don spent hours immersed in the technical aspects of coaching, scouring game films, searching for any slight advantage against the upcoming opponent, and mapping out a sure-fire game plan. He lived and breathed football.

While coaching in San Diego, Don and his family lived atop a hillside, and when he went to work in the morning, his daughter usually rode in the car with him down to the foot of the hill. On his way, Don routinely took the trash to the dumpster each morning. But on more than one occasion, Don drove all the way to work with his daughter in the car and the trash in the trunk! His mind was already on the field. He was so focused on football, he had totally forgotten about everything else.

The man was consumed with what he was doing, and perhaps more important, he was able to transfer his intensity to the people around him. His enthusiasm was contagious. No doubt, Don Coryell would have coached football for free, because he loved the game and he loved his job. His attitude reminds me of the old saying, "Do what you love and the money will follow."

If you aren't passionate about what you are doing, if you are unwilling to do the work for low pay (or no pay), well, I hate to be the one to break this to you, but you probably will never succeed at that job. You ought to find another career—something that cranks your motor, something you can pour your life into and enjoy it. Life is far too short to labor for long at something that you don't enjoy.

Bill Peterson: Working Hard Leads to Success

At Florida State University, where I was an assistant coach to Bill Peterson, Coach Pete's approach to coaching was radically different from Don Coryell's.

He first sought out good, young assistants who had great potential. Once Coach Pete had rounded us up, he drove us like cattle. We stayed at the office from dawn to dusk, studying films and devising game plans. Coach Pete put a lot of pressure on everybody who worked or played for him.

Bill Peterson believed in hard work, not just for himself, but for everyone on his staff, as well. When Bill went out of town, he called back to the office early each morning. "Let me talk to Jim," he said to Ruby, his secretary.

"Okay," Ruby replied and started to press Jim's extension.

"Naw, wait a minute. Let me talk to Gary."

"Sure thing," Ruby replied and reached for Gary's number.

"Oh, that's all right. How about Joe? Is he there? Let me talk to Joe..." And he went right down the list of coaches, checking on the whereabouts of each of us. If Ruby said, "I'm sorry, Coach, but he isn't in yet," Coach Pete went berserk.

He maintained a high-pressure atmosphere in our football program, and he thrived on it. Although Coach Pete was one of the first proponents of a prolific passing game, he succeeded in big-time college football mainly by working extra hard. His secret to success was finding talented young guys who loved the game as much as he did and then putting the pressure on them to produce—which we did, racking up fifteen wins and only four losses during my two years with the program.

John McKay: Using Fear as a Motivator

At the University of Southern California, I worked under the legendary coach John McKay. McKay was a brilliant strategist—he knew every aspect of the game on both sides of the line. He wasn't physically intimidating, but he was extremely tough and very forceful.

A dictator on the football field, Coach McKay was a master at using fear as a motivator. Everybody who played or worked for John was scared to death of him. The coaches learned to keep an eye peeled in his direction on the practice field, shifting our positions so we could always see Coach McKay in front of us. Otherwise, you never knew when he might walk up behind you and shred you with a derisive comment.

Despite his reputation as a dictator, John was one of the funniest guys in the world—as long as he wasn't directing his biting humor at you. His wit and his whip were equally brilliant.

At one point during the time I was coaching the offensive line at USC, we barely eked out a win over a team that we should have beaten by four touchdowns. Coach McKay was furious! I was standing within earshot, when in the postgame interviews a reporter asked the coach about our star running back, Clarence Davis, on whom we had relied heavily that day. Everyone in the locker room expected McKay to talk about Clarence's possibilities of winning the Heisman Trophy. Instead, Coach McKay replied, "The way our offensive line is blocking right now, I predict that Davis will be dead in two weeks!"

Another reporter once asked Coach McKay, "What do you think of your team's execution?"

"I think it would be a pretty good idea," McKay deadpanned.

Of course, Coach McKay produced a great football program at USC and won national championships using this management style. During the two seasons I worked with him, the Trojans went 15-4-1, and I thrived in McKay's winning tradition.

Frank Broyles: Selling Your Vision

At the University of Arkansas, I worked for Frank Broyles, one of college football's most successful coaches. Coach Broyles could have been a top salesman in any company. He had a tremendous ability to persuade—he was well-organized, polished, and had the charm and charisma of a Southern gentleman. If Frank believed in something, he could sell it.

And Frank Broyles believed in the Arkansas football program. He sold the program to everyone he met—players, parents, assistant coaches, alumni. He sold us all on the idea that we could produce winning football teams. And we did!

LEARN FROM YOUR MENTORS, BUT BE YOURSELF

Now that you know a bit more about my mentors, you can understand why I believe that one of the first secrets to successful leadership is to learn all you can from your mentors, draw from them, but develop a leadership style that works for *you*. Be yourself.

I worked under four totally different kinds of guys who had managed to succeed in one of the most competitive jobs in the world. All were winners, but each man had his own style, his own way of doing things. All four coaches had learned a thing or two from their own mentors, to be sure; but each reached the pinnacle of success without trying to be somebody else.

This is a principle essential to success, regardless of the field you're working in. You are unique. You are special. Discover your God-given gifts, talents, and personality traits and use them. You can't be a phony. If you are not true to yourself, the team you're trying to build will see through your flimsy facade. For me to try to pattern myself as a coach after Coryell, Peterson, McKay, or Broyles would have been a sure-fire route to failure.

Did I learn from these men? Of course! I learned from Frank Broyles to be organized and how to be a good salesman. I learned from Don Coryell the value of intensity and the importance of being absolutely truthful, communicating to my team exactly what I think is important. I learned from John McKay that there is a certain part of being a good football coach, boss, or parent that involves using fear to motivate people. And then I saw in Bill Peterson a person who didn't have the raw talent on his teams or a flamboyant personality like the other three coaches had, but who succeeded nonetheless through sheer hard work. I learned from Bill that if you persist and work hard, if you are diligent and go after what you want, learning and improving your skills as you go, you can succeed at almost anything!

LEAD BY EXAMPLE

I recall seeing an old war movie in which a general was leading his troops on a difficult, desperate march. They stopped just long enough so the troops could eat. When a sergeant brought the general his meal, an elaborate lunch from the mobile galley, the general took one look and asked, "Is this what the men are eating?"

"No, sir. It is not," the sergeant replied.

"Bring me what the men are eating," ordered the general. "That way I'll know how far they can go."

This general was a leader, not simply a boss.

I have found that the most effective way to bring out the best in people on my team is to lead by example. The problem? You have to pay a price to be that kind of leader. You often have to be the first to work and the last to leave. You must be one of the hardest, most conscientious workers, producing the best quality product possible. Model the characteristics you want to see in your team members—hard work, self-discipline, diligence, honesty, and integrity.

Lots of managers don't care for this approach. They want to tell other people what to do. They want to delegate responsibility, to assign other people to do the dirty work while they get the glory, the awards, and the big paychecks. But if you're leaving early, passing the buck, and leaving the big decisions to someone else, believe me, that's the behavior your people will emulate.

No question, at times you must delegate responsibility—you can't do everything yourself. But there's a huge difference between *delegating* responsibility and *abdicating* responsibility. For example, a lot of head coaches, in both college and professional football, don't call the plays their teams run. Instead, they rely on their well-trained assistant coaches to study the competition and come up with just the right plays to be used at the most strategic moments.

Good leaders model hard work and self-discipline.

But delegating responsibility does not give you the right to be negligent, blame others, or look the other way when things go wrong. Dad, mom, pastor, manager, business owner, or head coach—the buck still stops with you and me!

PEOPLE WILL FOLLOW A TRUE LEADER

When I coached the Washington Redskins, one of our outstanding team leaders was wide receiver Art Monk. During practices or team meetings, Art rarely said a word, but he modeled the work ethic we highly valued. He didn't talk about it; he just did it. We held fifty-five voluntary workouts for our players during the off-season, and although Art was one of the most well-conditioned athletes I ever coached, Art attended every single voluntary workout!

And he worked hard on the practice field. Art was a premier player— a veteran with a couple of Super Bowl rings—but he was willing to lay down his body for the good of the team, to run a route across the middle of the defensive backfield to catch a pass, knowing full well he was going to get hit hard. Art did more than his share of the blocking, too. He was willing to pay the price. He was the kind of physical football player we sought for the Redskins and a guy other team members would follow.

At team meetings, when Art did speak up, it was an "E. F. Hutton moment"—everyone on the team shut their mouths and listened to what Art Monk had to say.

By contrast, the guy who shoots his mouth off and talks about all the stuff he's doing but is not paying a price—most players simply will not follow that guy. They'll say, "He's a joke, a flimflam artist. Big talk, no action." Leadership by example is the best and most effective way to bring about positive, successful results.

AHEAD, NOT ABOVE

Good leaders make conscious choices to stay in touch with the people they are trying to lead. Some corporate executives pride themselves on their inaccessibility, sequestering themselves in penthouses or off-limits corner offices. Team members may know their leader is in the building, but they rarely see or interact with him or her. Sadly, some kids get that same feeling from their dads—they know he's in the house, but he interacts with them for only a few minutes a day, at most.

At Joe Gibbs Racing, I try to interact with our team members as much as possible. When I walk through the race shop, I enjoy it when the guys working on the cars call out, "Hi, Joe!" Most of our employees call me by my first name, and I do my best to call them by name. When possible, I try to stop and talk for a few minutes with several of my employees every day.

In most organizations, divisions develop all too easily. In the NFL, when we lost a football game, everyone wanted to point the finger at someone else: "It's the offensive team's fault!" "You guys on special teams were terrible." "Hey, you and your buddies on defense didn't play well, so it's your problem." "It's your fault that we aren't winning."

Sound familiar? "I sat by that phone all night and you never called!" "It's your fault this relationship isn't working."

Sometimes that may be true. But more often, when things go well or things go wrong, the credit or blame can be spread around.

In our race shop, we house two highly competitive teams under one roof—the #20-car team and the #18-car team—but we make it clear that we are actually *one team*. We don't just say the words; we put our money where our mouths are. When one car wins, we all win, and all JGR team members get bonuses for the performances of both cars.

We also make a conscious effort to break down the barriers between management and employees. I encourage our team bosses to get out of their offices and spend time with the people they are leading. We try to cultivate a team atmosphere, in which everyone cares for his or her fellow team members. One of our shop guys said, "Hey, I know that if I have a problem, I can take it to my boss, because I know he cares about me. And he cares about my family."

That attitude can be encouraged in a lot of practical ways. If somebody has a problem, a good leader will be there to stand in the gap, to help in every way that he or she can. Mutual concern for other team members is contagious.

Recently, a family member of one of our employees was the victim of a serious accident and had to get around in a wheelchair. The employees in our race shop all chipped in and bought the family a van that would accommodate the wheelchair. You don't get that sort of concern if people feel that they don't matter, that they are merely a number or a name on a time card.

Certainly, it's more difficult to maintain a family atmosphere as an organization grows. You may employ tens of thousands of people, but in every way possible, you need to touch and talk with as many as you can. Bob Nardelli, CEO and president of Home Depot, told me that within the first two months of being the boss, he personally met with all 1,100 Home Depot store managers around the world. He listened to his employees' concerns and suggestions and shared his vision for the company. By visiting each store personally, he let the employees know that he cared about his people. That is leading by example.

Jimmy Makar, now team manager at Joe Gibbs Racing, also leads by example. He's a great coach, and he works hard at the track long after a race has ended. When Jimmy gets angry out there or barks out urgent instructions to someone on our team, they do what he tells them. Why? Because Jimmy's earned the right to be heard. Our guys know that Jimmy doesn't ask anything of them that he wouldn't do, or expect a level of performance that he doesn't expect of himself.

Other people are all talk. They *say* the right things, but they are not really *doing* the right things. They aren't following through with their actions. Those people are not going to be effective leaders over the long haul. They may see some temporary results. They may fool some people for a while, but eventually their character flaws will lead to their demise. It's hard to get people to follow you when you talk it but don't walk it.

THIRTEEN

A LEADER'S
TOUGHEST JOB

Put yourself in the position of a corporate CEO for a moment. As the leader of this international conglomerate, what do you consider to be your company's most important asset? If you answered money, materials, or machines, you need to think again. Your most valuable asset is your *people*. If you, as a leader, do nothing more than simply pick the right people, they will make you successful.

What was my most important asset with the Washington Redskins? I had great players. "Joe Gibbs is a genius," even the most cynical Washington sports reporters crowed when we won our third Super Bowl. No, I wasn't a genius. I just had the right guys out there on the field.

Of course, twenty-seven other teams came up short that year. Why? After all, we all had the same pool of talented college graduates to choose from. Why is picking the right people so hard? Because in football, as in business and in life, we tend to evaluate the wrong qualities.

The Redskins had seven scouts scouring the country, looking for great ballplayers, viewing college football games and films, visiting the parents of college players, and gathering information and statistics about players they thought had the potential to make it in the pros. Scouts love to evaluate candidates according to their physical attributes. *Let's see, the player stands 6' 4" tall. How much does he weigh? Wow, 224 pounds. How fast is he? He ran a 4.8-second forty-yard dash.*

What does all this information tell you about an athlete's potential to make it in the big show? Not a lot.

Physical stats and mental achievement tests could not provide us with the information we needed to evaluate a player's future potential. We needed to discover what was *inside* the person. *What is he made of? What kind of "heart" does he have?* A person with heart will outperform a person with mere talent in the long run. When you find a person with both talent and heart, you've discovered gold.

Effectively evaluating prospective team members is a problem for many businesses. When I spoke to the leaders of one of the biggest technology companies in Washington D.C., I learned that their personnel department had given up studying school records, using achievement tests, and reading résumés—the traditional methods for evaluating and selecting good people. Instead, they had resorted to analyzing handwriting!

So how do you pick good people? Here are a few simple keys.

KNOW YOUR PEOPLE

Given two people with similar skills, it's probably wise to pick the person you know best. Ideally, the best way to know somebody is to have worked with the person yourself or know someone who has. Having been in the trenches with the person, seeing how he or she acts under pressure in good times and bad, you will be able to make a much better assessment of that person's potential.

Obviously, such personal experience is not always available. If you need to bring someone in from the outside, someone you don't already know, at least make sure that he or she fits with your organization.

When our race team decided it was time to expand to two Winston Cup cars instead of one, we already had Bobby Labonte on board. As we considered Tony Stewart for the new position, we went through an elaborate evaluation process, looking into Tony's racing record, his intensity level, his character, and his personal life.

Besides being one of the finest racecar drivers in the world, we felt that he could represent a corporation in a positive way—a major issue for the sponsor of a Winston Cup team. Most importantly, Tony seemed to be extremely focused on racing. He was not out rabble-rousing, getting into trouble, or getting drunk before and after races. As we compiled Tony's history, we found that he'd been driving race cars of one kind or another since he was seven years old. And he was phenomenal at it!

We flew all over the country courting him and eventually had to buy out his contract in order to get him on our team, but it was worth it. Tony's success speaks for itself. He earned NASCAR Winston Cup Raybestos Rookie of the Year honors in 1999 and quickly established himself as a force to be reckoned with on the circuit. Tony would go on to win the 2002 Winston Cup championship and is poised to become one of the greatest NASCAR drivers ever.

PROMOTE FROM WITHIN

Many companies, churches, and civic groups prefer to promote from within. It's not xenophobia—a fear of foreigners—that worries them; nor is their practice based on nepotism, wanting to raise up "family" to run the show. On the contrary, many successful leaders have discovered that it is worth the time and effort to bring someone up through the ranks, someone who already has a heart for the organization, knows the system, and understands how and why the organization does things.

No doubt, that's why a number of families—such as the Pettys, Earnhardts, Waltrips, and Labontes—have been so successful in NASCAR. The kids grew up watching their elders race and learning the ropes, so when the time came, they were ready to take their place in racing, as well.

DON'T TRUST FIRST IMPRESSIONS

When I was hired to coach the Washington Redskins, one of my initial assignments was to "get John Riggins back here." Riggins had sat out the previous season due to a contract dispute. The inability of my predecessor to convince the Redskins' star running back to play was a major factor in his being fired.

I didn't want to get fired before I started, so I decided that getting Riggins back in uniform was a high priority. One day, without informing anyone on our staff and with no appointment to meet with Riggins, I booked myself on a flight to Kansas, where John lived, hoping that my showing up unannounced might demonstrate my sincerity in wanting him back. Besides, if I caught John by surprise, his guard might be down, and by talking man-to-man on his home turf, without the interference of agents and lawyers, I felt sure we could make some headway.

I got off the plane in Lawrence, Kansas, and rented a car. I stopped at a local gas station and asked the first guy I saw, "Can you tell me where John Riggins lives?" It was a small town, and the man was glad to give me directions. I drove out of town, down a dirt road, and pulled up in back of a farmhouse. I knocked on the door and John's wife, Mary Lou, answered.

Mary Lou's hair was up in rollers, she looked tired and frazzled, and the Riggins kids were running gleefully through the house. Mary Lou informed me that John wasn't at home but that *she* wanted John to return to the Redskins.

Aha! We might be able to do this, I thought. In my years of coaching, I had discovered that there were two ways to influence professional football players to do something. We could fine them, slapping them with a dollars-and-cents penalty for their actions: "You have to be on the plane at eight o'clock, and if you aren't there, you get fined." The pros understand that. Fine them $500 for being late, and they'll find a way to be on time.

The second way to influence a pro player is through his wife. If mama's happy, everyone is happy. I knew that if Mary Lou wanted John to play, I was halfway home. She and I talked briefly, and I gave her the number of the hotel where I was staying. That night, I received a message from Mary Lou: "You have an invitation for breakfast tomorrow morning with John."

The next morning, I was all fired up. I dressed in my best suit and prepared mentally for selling John on coming back to play for the Redskins.

As I pulled up behind the Riggins farmhouse, I noticed two men dressed in camouflage and carrying guns as they crossed the yard. Although I had never met him, I instantly recognized one of the men as John Riggins.

He and a buddy had been out hunting. It was only ten o'clock in the morning, and John carried a beer in his right hand.

After brief introductions, John and I went inside and sat down across from each other at the kitchen table. At first we talked genially over breakfast, and then I went into my sales pitch.

"John, things are going to be different in Washington. I'm the new head coach, and we're going to employ a new offense. We're gonna let you run the ball as many downs as you want. We're not going to ask you to block...." Employing every sales technique I'd learned from Frank Broyles, I was trying to sell the guy, pressing every hot button I knew.

> "You need to get me back there. I'll make you famous."

John didn't say a word. He just listened icily, not revealing his feelings.

For about fifteen minutes, I rattled off my list of power points, and all the while, John sat there staring at me, occasionally taking a bite of food but offering no encouraging signs that I was getting through to him.

Finally, John put down his fork, looked across at me, and said quietly but intensely, "You need to get me back there. I'll make you famous."

I was stunned. For a long moment, I didn't know how to respond. I stared blankly at Riggins, thinking, *This guy is an egomaniac! I'm going to get stuck coaching a kook!* In my negotiations with players over the years, nobody had ever said such an outrageous thing to me. Nobody had made such a bold claim.

Immediately, my mind began sorting through alternatives. What am I going to do? How can I get out of this? Suddenly it hit me. I know! I'll get him back on the team and then trade him. This is perfect. I get the guy back to Washington—that makes my boss happy. John will be back playing in the pros—Mary Lou will be happy. Riggins is worth a lot around the league, so I'll trade him for a first-round draft choice—that makes me happy.

I encouraged John to think it over and give me a call. Two days later, I received a phone call from John Riggins.

John got straight to the point. "I've made up my mind, and I'm going to play next year."

To myself, I said, Yes! This is perfect. I'll get him back and trade him. I don't have to coach a nut, and I'll get a great draft choice. I was really rather proud of myself.

John's somber voice broke into my silent celebration. "There's only one thing I want in my contract," he said.

"Sure, John. What's that?"

"A no-trade clause."

Whoooom! I felt the door of opportunity slamming in my face. A no-trade clause meant that I'd be stuck with Riggins. I gulped hard, swallowing my pride.

"Uh, sure, John. We'll work it out. Just plan to be ready to go the first day of camp."

As soon as John Riggins showed up at preseason camp, I knew that my first impressions of the man had been wrong. Riggins was not an egomaniac. The guy was a great producer and a great team player. He was super-smart about football, highly motivated, and one of the best football players I ever coached.

Clearly, the Lord above had been looking out for me, helping me to make the right decision, even when I had foolishly based my evaluation of a man on erroneous data. My first impression of John had been that he was not the kind of guy I wanted on my team, when in fact he was *precisely* the type of player I was looking for.

And you know what? John Riggins made me famous!

If you rely on your first impressions of people or their résumés, you can be easily misled. Simply knowing what school a job candidate attended or that he or she was a great producer during the past twelve months isn't enough. You need much more information if you hope to make the best choice for your team.

DO YOUR RESEARCH

Don't pick somebody based on their last year's performance, or even a year or two of good production. The Redskins' scouts tried to dig deeper into a player's background, to do some research and to assemble information on our potential players as far back as middle school and junior high if we could. We interviewed their teachers, coaches, and trainers, asking what kind of person he was when they knew him or worked with him. Was he somebody that cared about what he was doing? We'd do the same thing at a candidate's high school and college.

Why so thorough? The chances are pretty good that if somebody has been a stellar performer for ten years or more, in various areas of life, he or she will probably be successful in the future as well. On the other hand, if a potential player was a "one-year wonder," or you pick somebody on the basis of their having had a great senior year, you will probably be disappointed.

Although it flies in the face of modern fantasies and may seem terribly unromantic, the same principle is valid for evaluating a potential marriage partner. Has this person been faithful and loyal in other relationships? If he or she has a history of infidelity, recognize that this is a defect in the person's character and is likely to show up in your relationship, as well.

Don't ignore the obvious signs. Does this person complete the tasks he starts, or is he good at beginning new things but not so good at following through? Has she stood up for what is right in her life? Can you depend on this person? These are just a few of the practical questions you should ask when selecting your closest team member.

Certainly people can change. I'm a Christian, and I believe in the life-changing power of God. I've seen numerous people transformed by their faith. Sometimes a tragedy or an eye-opening shock to the system will cause someone to turn around. But apart from such a radical change, chances are high that a person's spots will remain the same. Don't be deceived. The real man or woman can be seen in the character that person has demonstrated over the long haul.

TEST FOR WHAT YOU NEED

Another important principle for picking good people is to test your candidates for their ability to do what you want them to do. When I first joined the Washington Redskins, we were using Scholastic Aptitude Test (SAT) scores to determine a potential player's mental capacity to play professional football. We were trying to evaluate the player's intelligence and ability to assimilate large amounts of information each week of the season, and using SATs seemed to make sense because the tests were designed to indicate academic potential.

We found, however, that some people didn't perform well on a written SAT test but were nevertheless "football brilliant." We actually turned away stellar athletes because they had done poorly on the test, only to have them picked up by other teams and become superstars in the NFL. Those guys may not have understood advanced math and may never have read Shakespeare, but they knew how to find a hole in a line or how to read a defense.

We also found the opposite to be true. Some people scored very well on the tests but couldn't seem to find their way around a football field in a game situation.

After all, what does a football player have to do? Besides having a natural ability to play the game, a player must be able to internalize and execute his team's game plan. Each week his coach describes and explains the game plan for the coming week. The player then must study the game plan (our playbook for each game was usually about an inch thick). When game time arrives, the player must physically perform his individual assignment against an offense or defense that is constantly moving, changing positions, adapting to our efforts, and trying to get ahead of us. Based on the information he has studied during the week, the player must make instantaneous decisions and adjustments that could have enormous ramifications for himself and the team.

Is that hard to do? You bet your life it is! Professional football players must be able to learn new systems almost overnight and be able to adapt quickly to the competition in order to achieve successful results. Not every player can handle that sort of pressure.

So Bobby Beathard, then the general manager of the Redskins, and I went to Harry Wachs, a learning specialist at George Washington University. We told Harry, "We're going to pick five of our smartest football players, guys who are football brilliant—proven performers on the field. Guys like Mark Rypien, Joe Jacoby, and Art Monk. We want you to test them and then develop a test that accurately reflects their skills and mental capabilities. We want a test that we can take on the road to compare and help evaluate the skills of potential players."

Harry did just that. He came up with a test that had little to do with reading, writing, or math, but instead placed a great emphasis on measuring directional ability, aptitude for circumventing obstacles, and ability to adjust to new situations. Our scouts used this exam to test nearly every player the Redskins drafted during the last seven years of my tenure as head coach.

After administering the test, if we still questioned a player's mental ability to handle our system, we brought the player to Washington, and Harry spent a couple of hours with him, administering verbal tests and asking the player to perform certain tasks following specific directions. The tests had nothing to do with academics, but they were the best indicators we ever used to determine whether or not someone was right for the Redskins.

Today, we test people before hiring for our race teams, too. We employ a wide spectrum of people—mechanics, engineers, salespeople, office workers, pit crew guys, and, oh yes, we have a couple of drivers, too. With over two hundred employees, I can't possibly evaluate each one personally, but our department heads do. The department heads know the specific job requirements, and they know the competition, the people who are doing the same type of job for other professional race teams. They know what we are looking for and the types of individuals who will fit with our team.

The key to effective testing is to make sure your test is relevant and actually provides the information you are seeking. It would be foolish to give a potential salesperson the same test you would give a prospective accountant. Good salespeople must be people-oriented. They must be persuasive. They must know when to be forceful and when to back off. And they must be able to handle rejection without taking it personally. Accountants, on the other hand, can tell you where every penny went after you made it; just don't ask them to talk anyone into buying anything!

CHOOSE PEOPLE WHO CARE

Winning team members care. They care about themselves; they care about the way they do their work and the influence they have on others. And they care about the team. They recognize that the team can achieve true success only when each person does his or her part.

In 1984, the Washington Redskins got off to a tough start. We had won one game and lost two as we prepared to play a nationally televised Monday night game against the St. Louis Cardinals in Washington.

As usual, just before we came out of the locker room before the opening kickoff, we paused for a team prayer. I generally talked to the team the night before a game, so my normal routine was not to say much of anything on game day, as everyone was already on edge, including me. But on that night, for some reason, before we got down on our knees to pray, I felt compelled to speak. "If anybody has anything to give to the Washington Redskins today," I said, "you need to give it, because we are in trouble." That's all I said.

Pick people who care!

When we stood up, I glanced around the locker room at forty-some players, twelve of whom would go to three Super Bowls with me, real leaders on the team. I noticed that a few of those great big football players had tears trickling from their eyes.

Were those men motivated by money? No. Most of the truly great players are not motivated by mere materialism. Money was important to them, and we were always glad when contract negotiations were over. But those guys *really cared.* They wanted to be the best—for themselves and for the team. They were the guys we turned to when the pressure was on. Their attitude was "Give me the ball, Coach, and I'll win this thing for you."

We also had a few guys who were content simply to be on the squad, glad to run in the middle of the pack. Their attitude was "Just give me the check." While merely making it may be good enough for some people, it will never bring true fulfillment, not if you know that you can do better. As a leader who is choosing your team, strive to find people who are not content to be mediocre. Recruit individuals who want to be the best they can be.

Currently, I deal with thirty-five companies that sponsor our race teams at some level. Most of the key individuals in those companies are passionate about seeing their organizations succeed, about achieving their companies' goals as well as their own. One of our sponsors is Ditch Witch, a small company in Perry, Oklahoma. The owner, Ed Malzahn, went to work for his dad in a machine shop at an early age. One day he looked around and said to himself, *I want to invent a machine to dig ditches, something better than what people are now using.* He worked and finally came up with a relatively small machine that could fit in the back of a station wagon. He carted that machine door-to-door to hardware and supply companies, trying to sell it, and that's how he started Ditch Witch. Today, when I visit the Ditch Witch factory and corporate offices, I am always amazed at the employees' intensity. They are sold on their product and committed to selling more than anybody else in their industry.

I'm also inspired by Norm Miller and his team at Interstate Batteries. I'm convinced that if some of Norm's employees were to cut a finger, they would probably bleed that distinctive Interstate green. They believe in what they are doing that much! Many of them came up through the ranks, and they care about the company. They refuse to be average employees.

In most organizations, those are the kinds of people that put you over the top. They are not always the most talented people in the world, but they are the ones who care deeply about what they are doing. They put their heart and soul into their work. Those are the people you want on your team!

MOVE PEOPLE TO WHERE THEY PERFORM BEST

You may have made a good choice when selecting a person, but perhaps you have put this person in the wrong position. Maybe you are asking the individual to perform tasks that don't fit his or her personality, talents, skills, or gifts. This person may be a hard worker, a person that cares for the company, but if your expectations are beyond his or her ability, both of you are going to be extremely frustrated.

I recall a great young football player for whom the Redskins traded two top draft picks. He was one of the most prized players in the draft that year, and we were excited to get him. We had done our homework; he performed well in all our evaluations. He was a tough athlete who played for a top-notch college program. He was accustomed to playing in cold weather, similar to ours in Washington. He had good size and speed, great hands, and appeared to have tremendous potential as a pass receiver.

The player was with us for only three or four weeks before we realized we had made a terrible mistake. He was not a good pass receiver. He wasn't good at making quick adjustments on the field, and he had a habit of not being where the quarterback wanted him to be on his pass patterns. Making matters worse, this player came to training camp a bit out of shape by our standards. We thought he was going to be the top young player in the NFL. Instead, he was not even going to make it onto the field.

Now the team was faced with a dilemma: What should we do with this player who had many good qualities and for whom we had spent enormous capital, a person on whom many of our hopes and dreams for the future were resting?

For the next year, our coaching staff tried their best to turn the player into a star receiver, but to no avail. Everyone was frustrated—the player, the coaches, and the team's owner. We were just about to cut our losses when someone came up with a brilliant idea: "Let's give him a try as a kick return specialist…"

To this day, the player remains one of the top punt returners in the history of the league. We were trying to make him into a receiver, but the player's basic skills, talents, and personality didn't lend themselves to that position. However, when given the opportunity (and a little daylight) to return kicks, the guy became a star. And to think we came mighty close to cutting him!

The key is to find out where our people's gifts, talents, and abilities lie and then help them use their gifts for the common good. In our office, we conduct periodic staff evaluations, in which everybody involved with our management team is assessed to determine their own strengths and weaknesses. Not surprisingly, we find not all of us are strong in the same areas. In some skills, some of us are "tens," whereas others are "twos" and "threes."

Richie Pettibone, one of our coaches with the Redskins, once put it this way: "You can't get in all the lines in heaven." In other words, none of us is a ten in every conceivable area of talent and ability. Yet everyone is gifted somewhere.

To get the best results at home or at work, you must have your people functioning in an area where they are strongest or most talented.

BE HONEST ENOUGH TO CUT YOUR LOSSES

Despite doing your best to evaluate your candidates and make wise, careful choices, it is still possible to make a mistake and select the wrong person. What then?

Recognize that you are probably not going to change that person in a few weeks. Adaptation or training may require a long process, and you will need to decide whether it is worth the effort. If not, then for everybody's sake, you must let the person go.

Occasionally, you will bring a person on board who just doesn't seem to fit with the organization. He doesn't share your goals, values, ethics, work habits, or other qualities that you regard as important. Or she may be self-centered and show little interest in the welfare of the company. If this person's presence is hurting the team, you, as the leader, must act. If you have made an honest effort to help this individual contribute and he or she still does not fit, then you must admit that you made a mistake. You picked the wrong person, and now you need to act decisively to get him out of there. Otherwise, you can lower the caliber of the entire organization. You will not be helping the person who doesn't fit in, and the negative impact this person has on others who are trying to do a good job can be enormous.

This is one of the major failures of modern managers and leaders. They are afraid to confront someone who is not performing properly. And they don't want to admit their mistake in hiring the person, so they perpetuate their mistake. This happens regularly in professional sports, particularly when a team pays a ton of money to an athlete or when they give up a high draft pick to get a player. The tendency is to say, "We'll make this work." Usually it doesn't.

DON'T EXTINGUISH A FADING STAR TOO SOON

What happens when talents begin to diminish, when you know that a team member was once a star, but now he or she just can't cut it anymore?

This is always a tough call, a situation we face in professional sports even more frequently than in most organizations. Usually, the people who can best make that decision are the people who are working most closely with the person in question. On our football teams, the decision to let someone go because of impaired or weakened abilities was made by the assistant coaches. They were the people spending eighteen to twenty hours per day studying the game films and observing the players on the job. If my assistant coaches suggested that a former starter could no longer contribute at an acceptable level, I usually agreed to let the player go.

Nevertheless, I've always found it better to keep a good producer too long than get rid of him too early. I've seen plenty of mistakes in this regard, where management said, "That guy is over the hill, and we need to get him out of here." The guy gets traded away and then plays successfully for five more years for another team! In at least one case, we let a player go from the Redskins, and he's still playing to this day. Another time, near the end of my coaching career, the assistant coaches felt that star defensive back Darrell Green needed to be traded. They were convinced that his career was winding down. I disagreed strongly, and we decided to keep him. And Darrell outlasted all of us, playing through the 2001 season!

If you are loyal to your people, they will give you 120 percent effort. Certainly, you can be loyal to a fault and allow your personal feelings to interfere with making good decisions, or you may allow an individual's needs to overshadow what is most beneficial for the team. But it's worth the risk. When your team members know that you will go to bat for them, that you are willing to stand up for them and keep them on the job as long as they can get it done, they will demonstrate incredible loyalty to the organization. Then you will have a strong team, today and tomorrow.

FOURTEEN

THRIVING IN TROUBLED TIMES

T ough times will come sooner or later to every individual, company, organization, team, and family. We all must deal with adversity, and what separates a great team from a merely good one is how well we overcome the obstacles in our path.

EVERY PERSON MATTERS

One way to prevent problems, or at least minimize their impact, is to make every member of the team realize that he is important, that each person is vital to the overall effectiveness of the team. Some leaders seem to have an innate talent for making people feel special—their very presence in the room somehow inspires hope and encouragement. Other leaders must make more of a conscious effort to validate their people, but whether or not it comes naturally to you, you must do it. A wise leader learns to express sincere appreciation for the contributions of each team member, regardless of his or her position or role.

Often it is the person deemed unimportant or insignificant that the wise team leader will recognize as having as much or more value than the super-stars on the team. When racing fans, clients, or vendors visit the Joe Gibbs Racing corporate headquarters and race shop in Huntersville, North

Carolina, the first person they see when they walk in the front door is the receptionist on duty, either Fran or Paige.

In many companies, the receptionist's job is considered to be an entry-level position. At our company, the receptionist is one of the most important people on our team. She is the person who makes the first impression on our clients and visitors. A person's opinion of Joe Gibbs Racing is often based almost entirely on their dealings with our receptionist. I frequently encourage Paige and Fran, complimenting them on the caring and efficient way they handle their responsibilities, and I remind them just how important they are to our organization.

Certainly, some people on the team get more public attention, but that doesn't mean they are more important. Bobby Labonte and Tony Stewart are the guys who climb up on the roof of their cars and spray everyone with champagne, but if the receptionist or the guys in the shop don't do their job well, there may not be any champagne for anyone on our team!

Early in our existence as a racing team, we told our employees, "When we win the Winston Cup, everyone on the team is going to celebrate—not just the guys at the race track. Everyone will get to enjoy it." It took us nine years to get there, but when we finally won the championship in 2000, we paid for all of our employees—every mechanic, every secretary, everybody and their spouses—to attend the gala NASCAR awards ceremony in New York. Every member of our team also received a championship ring similar to the large Super Bowl rings given to NFL champions.

Everyone participates when the company does well, and everyone participates when the company does poorly. This helps each employee to feel important and gives everyone a sense of ownership. When tough times come, everyone pulls together to overcome them.

LEARNING FROM ADVERSITY

The 1983 Washington Redskins were one of the greatest NFL football teams ever. We had Riggins at fullback, Theismann at quarterback, and a terrific bunch of guys like Dexter Manley and Charles Mann. Our regular season record was 14-2, and in both of the games we lost, we were beaten by a single point. We came within two points of an undefeated season, a feat that has been achieved only once in NFL history.

Accolades and affirmations came at me from every direction almost daily. "This Joe Gibbs guy is absolutely brilliant!" the newspapers and sports talk shows proclaimed. I was just a physical education major who had made good, but after three successful seasons, I was almost beginning to believe my own press reports!

We blew through the playoffs and went to the Super Bowl, where we faced the then–Los Angeles Raiders in Tampa. We had already beaten the Raiders once during the regular season, so I was extremely confident going into the game. Unfortunately, we got off to a lousy start in the first half. Everything seemed to go wrong! The Raiders blocked one of our punts, we failed to establish our running game, and we were hard-pressed to complete a pass. As we approached halftime, Los Angeles led by eight points. They punted to us, and we took possession at our own eighteen-yard line with eighteen seconds to go.

I had a tough decision to make. We had time to get off only one or two quick plays—and we were more than eighty yards from the end zone. What should I do? Just have Theismann fall on the football and run out the clock, hoping we could play better in the second half? That would be the safe move.

Had I been able to pause the action somehow and take a poll of the millions of fans watching on television around the world, not to mention the roaring crowd in Tampa, I doubt that even a small percentage would have suggested that we hunker down and run out the clock. I could hear a million voices in my mind: *Are you crazy, man? It's the Super Bowl! You're behind by eight. You've got to* do something. *Make something happen. Get this team moving so if nothing else, you can go into the locker room at halftime with some momentum!*

Besides the bedlam from the crowd, I had Theismann on the sideline yelling in my ear, telling me what he thought we ought to do, and two assistant coaches were yelling for me to do two different things.

I tried desperately to think, my mind searching through our options with only seconds to make a decision. Finally, in the midst of the chaos, I shouted to our players and coaches, "Everybody shut up! Now, here's what we're gonna do. We're going to throw a screen pass to Joe Washington and let him slide out of there and get us upfield a ways." If we could get anywhere near midfield, we would have enough time for Theismann to throw a "Hail Mary" pass into the end zone, in the hope that somebody with a red jersey would catch it. It seemed like a good plan at the time.

Theismann dropped back and set up as though he were going to throw a long pass, while our linemen slid out in front of Joe Washington, setting up the screen of blockers in front of him. That's when I saw something awful out of the corner of my eye. Raiders linebacker Jack Squirek had been playing man-to-man coverage on Joe Washington and had slipped behind the screen of blockers, positioning himself between our receiver and the ball. Theismann's pass was perfect—he dropped it right into the waiting hands of Squirek, who picked off the pass and danced virtually untouched into the end zone for a Raiders touchdown, sending us into the locker room fifteen points down at halftime instead of eight. Los Angeles's momentum from that play carried over into the second half, and they beat us badly, 38-9.

We can learn more from our failures than we can from our successes.

The next morning I picked up the *Washington Post*, and these words leaped off the newspaper at me: JOE GIBBS, A BUFFOON. Ouch! I had gone from brilliant to buffoon in less than eighteen seconds.

Unquestionably, if you are going to be a leader, you will take some shots like that. In the business world as in the sports world, you can be a hero one moment and drummed out of town the next. What will you do when those times of adversity come?

When adversity comes, learn all you can from it. There's an old saying that goes, "There's a kernel of truth in every lie." When criticism or calamities come your way, if you look carefully, you will find some positive things to learn from them. When adversity knocks, don't simply dismiss it. Study it, learn all you can from it, analyze it, and ask yourself, "What led to this?" Adversity is nearly always a better teacher than prosperity.

CONFRONTING PROBLEMS HEAD-ON

As an assistant coach with the San Diego Chargers, one of my responsibilities was to call the offensive plays during games. One Thursday night we played the Miami Dolphins in a nationally televised game. This was a big game for both teams, and as the clock ran down near the end of the fourth quarter, the Chargers were desperately trying to move the ball downfield and get into position for a last-minute field goal to win the game.

With the ball on the Dolphins' forty-yard line, I called an option play primarily designed for a short pass to the halfback, hoping to pick up seven or eight yards. As a secondary option, we had a wide receiver running a corner route.

Now, contrary to some opinions, defensive coordinators in the NFL are not stupid. They know that in such a situation the offense is likely to throw a short pass, so the Miami defense double-teamed our primary receiver coming out of the backfield. Our quarterback, Dan Fouts, spotted the double-team and instead smartly threw the ball downfield, intending to hit our secondary receiver who was running his route against a single defensive back. Chargers fans cringed as the ball dropped harmlessly onto the turf, an incomplete pass.

The ABC TV announcers, including the always opinionated Howard Cosell, had a field day at my expense, while fans in the stadium and in living rooms around the world chided me for making such a stupid call. "Throw the ball down the field with only seconds to go in the game? They only need ten yards or so to be in field goal position! What's wrong with these guys? Are the San Diego coaches nuts?"

Fortunately, we ran another play, picked up a few yards, and kicked a field goal to win the game. But the foiled downfield pass attempt still rankled some San Diego fans the following week.

While in my office preparing for the next game, I received a letter from a well-known San Diego attorney. The letterhead boasted a dozen or more names in the lawyer's practice, and he was the top dog. In his letter, the attorney ripped my hide up one end and down the other, blasting me for making such a foolish call so late in the game and risking the opportunity to win. He ranted, "You've got maybe one or two plays at the end of the game, you're trying to get a field goal, and you call this play downfield! What do you think you're doing? Are you an idiot?"

It was bad enough receiving such a snide, critical letter after a game we had won, but to make matters worse, the attorney sent copies of his letter to everybody in the Chargers organization, including the team owner, general manager, and head coach Don Coryell.

After reading the letter, I sat fuming at my desk for several minutes. I said to myself, *If I let it, this letter is going to bother me all day long.* I sat there for a few more minutes and finally dialed the phone number on the attorney's stationery.

I had to talk my way past several secretaries. "I need to talk to your boss about this letter he was nice enough to write to me..."

Eventually, my critic came on the line and in a quiet voice said, "Hello?"

"Hello, this is Joe Gibbs, and you were nice enough to write me a letter and copy everybody in the organization, so I just want to take time this morning to talk to you about your complaint."

"Well, you know, Howard Cosell said..."

I cut him off sharply. "First of all, Howard Cosell is an entertaining announcer, but Howard knows very little about what I am doing. I've spent twenty years of my life working eighteen hours a day studying football. To be quite truthful, I think I'm a fairly intelligent guy when it comes to football, and Howard doesn't always know what I'm doing on the field or why. Second, my job takes place in front of people who are watching on TV. When I make a mistake, millions of football fans see it. I'd be willing to bet that most of your mistakes are locked somewhere in jail!" I was on a roll.

"Now, let me tell you about that play," I continued, barely taking a breath. "That play was designed as an option route to the halfback. If the halfback was covered, which he was, the quarterback could go downfield to a receiver who should be relatively open in man-to-man coverage. The play was geared for the halfback to get seven yards so we could kick a field goal. But in some cases, the defense outguesses us and doubles our back. So we tried to get the ball downfield..."

About that time, the lawyer whined, "My wife told me not to write the letter."

We talked for a while, and before the conversation concluded, the attorney said, "I appreciate your calling me, and I feel so bad that I wrote the letter. You're right on this thing." To his credit, the attorney wrote an enthusiastic follow-up letter to everybody in the Chargers organization, extolling my football wisdom and generally apologizing for being an opinionated jerk. That attorney became one of my staunchest supporters in San Diego. When I got the job with the Washington Redskins, he wrote me a kind letter thanking me for a job well done with the Chargers and wishing me well with my new team.

My point is this: Good leaders confront problem situations head-on. Anytime something is bothering you or something is said or you don't like the way someone is performing, you must deal with the problem as soon as possible. Don't go home that night still stewing over something that happened in the office earlier that day. Don't allow open sores to fester and get worse. Get things out on the table and deal with them. Chances are, if a problem is bothering you, it is most likely bothering someone else, too.

Of course, you can't respond to every little irritation or every critical voice. When I was in Washington, a Supreme Court justice wrote a letter castigating me for keeping a particular player on the field late in a game. I had to laugh as I read the justice's letter. *Here is a person who could determine the future of our nation or decide the fate of somebody on death row, and he is writing me a letter about a football game!* But that's part of coaching in professional sports—you soon learn that everybody thinks they're experts on the game.

I once flagged a taxi in D.C. and immediately could tell that the driver had been in the country for only a few days. I asked him very slowly, "Can you get me to RFK Stadium?" He had no idea, but he started driving anyhow. After about five minutes, he looked in the rearview mirror and said, "Are you the coach of the Redskins?"

"Why, yes, I am."

"You need to throw deep more."

Everybody is an expert on football.

KEEP YOUR PRIORITIES IN ORDER

Whenever I speak at a conference or motivational seminar, I meet people who are looking for the one key that will help them revolutionize their lives or the lives of the people they are leading. One of the most important secrets to building and motivating a strong team is to *keep your own priorities in order*.

People tend to follow the leader, and if your priorities are out of whack, the people who are looking to you as a role model will be more likely to confuse matters, as well.

One sharply dressed young man approached me after a seminar and said, "Mr. Gibbs, I want to be a millionaire by the time I'm thirty-five. Shouldn't my career take first place in my life?"

"No," I told him. "If you want to be successful, the number one priority in your life should be God and your relationship with Him."

"Should my occupation be the number two priority?" the young man asked.

"No, I don't believe so. Your second priority in life ought to be your family and the influence you are having on others. Your career should rank third in your life."

Most of the people I know who have been unsuccessful with career, money, or personal relationships failed because they assigned an improper significance to their occupations. Many people allow their jobs to become their gods—they are obsessed with making it in their careers. They willingly sacrifice family, friends, or health on the altar of their false god.

Your career should rank third in your life.

Other people have the opposite problem. They allow their occupations to remain too *low* on their list of priorities. Their careers come in ninth or tenth on the list. I had a player with the Redskins who constantly made excuses for being late or missing workouts. One of his frequent excuses was "a death in the family." One day he came in and was about to launch into another lame excuse for being late, when I waved him off. "Don't tell me someone else in your family died, because I counted 'em and there's no one left!"

You've probably seen people with similar attitudes in your workplace. They always seem to have some reason to be late to work. They never have enough time to complete their assignments by the deadline. They cut corners on almost everything they do. Then they have the audacity to complain that they are not advancing in the company fast enough! That sort of person is simply not going to help the team succeed.

Remember, your relationship with God comes first. Your family comes second. Work comes in third. You may miss an occasional ball game or a special event because of work responsibilities, but never make your children or your spouse wonder if your career is more important than they are. Believe me, it isn't.

The most important legacies Pat and I will leave on this earth are our children, our grandchildren, and our influence on other people. Someday, I may be sitting in my rocking chair at an old folks' home, rasping to anyone who will listen, "I once coached the Washington Redskins!" The applause and the accolades of this world are fleeting, but the impact we have on our families will last.

After God and your family, you must guard your priorities tenaciously. Don't allow other people or circumstances to creep in above your third highest priority—using your skills, gifts, and talents to make a difference.

I believe that God wants each of us to be great—not merely good at what we do, but great! He has given each of us unique talents and abilities to help make us great, and one day we will give an account for what we have done with what he has entrusted to us. What a shame it would be to have wasted your God-given abilities.

Eleven Cornerstone Principles for Success

Team Building

I'm often asked, "Where did you learn how to motivate people the way you do?" "What book can I read, what formula can I use to encourage my associates?" "Who is your role model when it comes to building a team?"

My interviewers are often baffled when I tell them that my greatest mentor was not a football coach or car owner; He was a carpenter's kid. You see, I learned my most effective team-building skills from the greatest team builder of all time, Jesus Christ.

Hold on! Before you brand me a religious nut, think about what Jesus did. To spread the most important message the world has ever known, He selected twelve of the most unlikely candidates for leadership the world has ever seen! His hand-chosen *apostles* (or "sent ones") included a few uneducated fishermen (two of whom were known hotheads), a tax collector, a skeptic, a true fanatic, and a few other no-name guys you probably wouldn't have noticed if they'd passed you on the street.

Yet with the exception of one traitor, these men changed the world with a message of love, hope, faith, and forgiveness. Within a few years, even Jesus' enemies had to admit that His followers "had turned the world upside down."

If you want to turn the world upside down, I suggest you begin by checking out the following cornerstone principles of leadership and team building modeled by Jesus of Nazareth.

CORNERSTONE 1

Choose a leadership style that is right for you and your team. You must develop your own style. Jesus wasn't swayed by other people's opinions. He wasn't compelled to remind people that He was the boss. Instead, He led by example and instruction. Remember, to achieve true and lasting success you must learn to *serve* those you lead—help them achieve their own potential.

CORNERSTONE 2

Pick the right people and put them in the right jobs. Jesus selected His disciples based on what they could become—what He saw in them—not what they were at the moment. He then gave them the tools, authority, and power to do everything He called them for. Only after He had personally trained them did He send them out to represent Him and His Father. Successful team-builders develop a knack for recognizing the right people for the right jobs. They then train and equip those people to use their God-given gifts and talents for the good of the team.

CORNERSTONE 3

You must define your goals. Jesus' public ministry lasted only three years, but He had specific goals He wanted to accomplish—and He did! Furthermore, Jesus clearly defined those goals for His disciples. They did what He commanded them to do, even when they didn't always under-stand why. To be a successful team builder, you must clearly define your goals and always keep them before your team members. You must also regularly evaluate your goals and be willing to revise them when necessary.

CORNERSTONE 4

Success should be rewarded. Jesus recognized the accomplishments of His disciples and delighted in acknowledging them. And although His disciples made many mistakes, because they maintained a teachable attitude and a desire to follow Him, Jesus never gave them their walking papers. Great team builders will reward success that is consistent with biblical principles.

CORNERSTONE 5

The best communication is simple and direct. Jesus was the master communicator. His message was simple enough for a child to understand, yet confounded His most educated critics and enemies. Jesus chose His words carefully and intentionally, with each comment specifically directed to an individual or group at their point of need. In building your team, communicate simply, specifically, and as directly as possible.

CORNERSTONE 6

Problems must be confronted head-on. Jesus never ran from problems. Nor did He ignore or overlook them in the lives of His followers. Jesus confronted each conflict straight on, with truth and love and a keen sense of timing. He knew when to speak and when to remain silent. He drove the greedy money changers out of the temple with a fiery and holy rage, but He offered an equally passionate defense of the broken and abused of His day. Successful team builders don't ignore problems but address them in the appropriate manner and the right spirit.

CORNERSTONE 7

Play fairly and keep your team honest. Moral integrity was the essence of Jesus' life and the heart of His message. His followers proclaimed His impeccable reputation far and wide, and nobody could refute it. Furthermore, Jesus called His followers to a life of moral goodness that springs from the heart. The implication for us today? Team leaders and team members must all be accountable to each other and to God.

CORNERSTONE 8

We must learn to deal with adversity. Talk about adversity! Jesus met with opposition and rejection in nearly every town and village He visited, particularly from the local religious officials. But He didn't allow it to get Him down. In fact, Jesus made a point of preparing the disciples to persevere in the face of adversity. He knew that tough times lay ahead. Yet He assured His people that they could make it through the dark days and nights by maintaining their faith in God.

CORNERSTONE 9

Everyone is important. From the little children who gathered around Him to Judas, the man who betrayed Him, Jesus demonstrated that everyone matters to God. He made it clear that He didn't come to condemn people but to save them. He even prayed for His enemies as they crucified Him! Successful team builders know that each person matters to God, and each person should matter to us, too.

CORNERSTONE 10

Good team leaders model hard work and discipline. Jesus worked with one primary goal in mind—to complete the mission for which He was sent. One day the disciples were worried that Jesus had worked all day without eating. He responded to their concerns by explaining, "My food is to do the will of Him who sent Me and to accomplish His work." In other words, His energy was focused toward one end—to successfully accomplish His calling. If you want to build a successful team, you must model hard work and discipline before you can expect the same from your team.

CORNERSTONE 11

Keep your priorities in order. Jesus never swerved from His calling, and He made it clear that His disciples were to keep His Father's priorities in *their* lives. Simply put, if you want to be on God's team, you must do things His way. His two main priorities? Love God with all your heart, and love your neighbor as yourself. This principle of success is the keystone, the one on which everything else stands or falls. If you want to achieve true and lasting success, you must keep your priorities aligned with God's priorities on a daily basis.

I have found it tremendously exciting and fulfilling to build teams that honor God, serve others, and achieve true and lasting success. Now you know how Jesus did it, and you know what motivates me. It's your turn. Go get 'em!

Success in Your Personal Relationships

When I'm right in the middle of the action, as I have been from the beginning of Joe Gibbs Racing, I don't have to judge a man by his promises; I can judge by what I actually experience. Open and honest communication has always been at the heart of our relationship with Joe Gibbs. I'm a direct recipient of his prayers and encouragement, and in his presence I've witnessed how moments of anger and frustration give way to forgiveness and reconciliation. I have learned through the years that I can count on Joe without having to refer to a contract, and our partnership has developed into a friendship. We've raced and wrecked, won and lost together. Our relationship has grown through it all, perhaps because we have both tried to honor God by first considering the interests of the other at least equal to our own—and just as He promises, God has honored us both as a team and as individuals.

Norm Miller is the chairman of Interstate Batteries,
makers of America's bestselling automotive battery sold at
more than 200,000 retail outlets.

Let's say you've developed your craft, honed your skills, become famous in your chosen field, acquired a large amount of money which you invested wisely, and built a strong team around you. If, after doing all of this, you had nobody with whom to share the ride, would you consider yourself to be successful? In my book, I could never consider myself a success if, along the way, I somehow lost the people most precious to me.

When we think about relationships, we usually think in terms of male-female relationships or parent-child relationships. But the need for healthy relationships extends beyond the confines of our own families. While the principles I'm going to present in this section will help you become a better marriage partner and parent, they will also help you become a better coworker, a better friend, and a better citizen. In other words, it's not good enough to maintain a successful relationship with the person(s) closest to you. I want to succeed in all of my relationships, and, if I don't miss my guess, so do you!

In this section, you'll find:

- How we teach children to lie.
- That it's not enough to have it all.
- Keys to quality relationships.
- The value of great relationships.
- God's game plan for your relationships.

FIFTEEN

RELATIONSHIPS MATTER

I t was my last year of coaching, and I was working another late night at the Redskins office. I hadn't been feeling well for five or six weeks. My body was run-down, and the late hours certainly weren't helping. Sometime after two o'clock in the morning, I left the room where my assistant coaches and I were devising our game plan for that weekend's game, and I walked over to the kitchen area, looking for a Diet Coke.

Nothing.

As I returned to the office, I groused to myself, sat down, and dove back into the game plan.

About forty-five minutes later, I glanced up, and in the back of the room stood my good friend Don Breaux, one of our assistant coaches. Don and I had coached together off and on over the years, ever since we first teamed up at Florida State. We had been together so long, we almost didn't need words to communicate—Don knew instinctively what I was thinking.

In his hands were two six-packs of Diet Coke.

"Where'd you get those?" I asked in surprise.

"I just ran down to the corner store," he replied with a shrug.

"At this hour in the morning?"

"Yeah, no big deal. I thought you could use a Coke."

Don's incredible loyalty and kindness reminded me of a story in the

Bible, in which the future King David and his close-knit band of warriors were camped in a cave in the hills above Bethlehem, David's boyhood stomping ground. David relished the memory of the local well at Bethlehem from which he used to drink fresh water, and in the twilight, he allowed himself to say aloud, "Man, it would be great to have a drink from that well again."

One problem—the enemy was camped all around the well.

David didn't command his men to sneak into the enemy camp and risk their lives for a flask of water. Nor did he intend to do so himself. He was merely mumbling about a fond memory. But David's buddies overheard their leader's longings, and in the middle of the night they crept into the enemy's camp, filled a flask with cool water from the well, and tiptoed out undetected. They brought the precious water to their leader. David was so overwhelmed with their gesture that he refused to drink the water!

I guess that's where David and I differ—I drank Don's Cokes. But I think I understand some of what David felt at the willingness of his friends to take action to meet a need without being asked. That sort of loyalty cannot be commanded or coerced; it springs naturally from a strong relationship.

BLESSED WITH GREAT RELATIONSHIPS

God has truly blessed me with great relationships—with my wife Pat, our sons J D and Coy, our daughters-in-law Melissa and Heather, and our grandchildren Jackson and Miller. I also have wonderful relationships with a number of friends and business acquaintances. To this day, when I think that Don Meredith volunteered two months of his life to help me figure out my financial mess, I am amazed. How many of us have a friend who would do something like that?

Don wasn't on my payroll at that time. He wasn't making any money by helping me. In fact, it cost him money, time, and energy. A few years later, Don, his son Todd, and our friend Dave Alpern would be key players in starting our race team. But at the time, I could barely reimburse Don for his expenses. Yet because of our relationship, he felt compelled to do something far above the call of duty. Unconditional love will do that. Selfishness will drive some people for a season, but only love will last in the long run.

George Tharel was another friend that God placed in my life, a person who quietly passed key values on to me. George wasn't wealthy in terms of material possessions, but he was extremely rich in love and wisdom. He spent hundreds of hours talking to me by phone, writing me letters of encouragement, and speaking words of wisdom into my life. In the process, George subtly helped me to forge a value system based on biblical truth rather than on public opinion polls, the latest headlines, or popularity contests. By his own example, George taught me how to do things the right way.

We can teach the people around us to do things the right way or the wrong way. Through our actions we can promote values of honesty and integrity, or we can teach others how to shade the truth. When my grandson Jackson was just a toddler, I took him to Starbucks with me. While I enjoyed a strong cup of coffee, Jackson had a cinnamon bun. To be more accurate,

Only love will last in the long run.

he *devoured* a cinnamon bun! I couldn't keep from laughing as this two-year-old smeared icing and cinnamon all over himself. He had icing on his face, up his nose, in his ears—everywhere.

After I got him cleaned up, I told him, "Now, Jackson, let's not say anything about this to Mom or Dad. They'll get after Grandpa Coach for feeding you such a big bun." Jackson nodded affirmatively.

Wouldn't you know it? The moment we got home, Jackson went parading down the hall and through the house, calling out loudly, "Cinnamon bun! Cinnamon bun! I had a cinnamon bun!"

My son and daughter-in-law gave me one of those disgusted-parent looks. I shrugged my shoulders as if to say, "Hey, what did you expect? I'm a grandparent!"

It struck me, however, that children start out knowing only honesty and innocence, speaking the truth, even when it hurts—until we adults teach them to fib. Of course, we do have a choice. We can teach them values of truthfulness and integrity by modeling those traits instead.

Two of the great influences on my own childhood were my Aunt Louise and Uncle Walter. Aunt Louise instilled in me a love for the Bible, and it was Uncle Walter who first instilled in me a love for racing. He was like a big kid, working hours with me to build the best soap box derby racer. Then, in his early forties, Uncle Walter went blind as a result of diabetes.

Nevertheless, Uncle Walter attended all my games while I was playing football at San Diego State. He also taped the radio broadcasts of the games, and we had great fun together listening to his recordings and reliving the excitement of the games.

My uncle didn't have to tell me how much he cared about me, although he did that, too. He showed me how much he cared simply by taking an active interest in what was going on in my life. When Uncle Walter died in his early sixties, a victim of a diabetes-related heart attack, that too left a profound impression on me.

THE SORROW OF A MAN WHO HAD EVERYTHING

One of my most important relationships as an adult was with Jack Kent Cooke, the cagey, sometimes cantankerous owner of the Washington Redskins. I admired him immensely, and I learned so much—both positive and negative—from the man.

Mr. Cooke had a keen ability to read people, especially when it came to potential new employees. He could tell almost instantly whether someone would be a strong contributor to our organization. Occasionally, he nixed one of my prospective employees with a wave of his hand: "That person won't perform." "She won't work well under pressure." "He's not a team player." On the other hand, he sometimes saw character traits in someone that I may have missed: "Go ahead and hire that fellow. He's very loyal." Inevitably, Mr. Cooke's advice proved true, and when I ignored his insights, I was almost always sorry. He was rarely proven wrong when it came to people.

Although he was an enormously successful businessman, in one of our more candid moments Mr. Cooke acknowledged to me that his worst failures in life were in the area of his close personal relationships. With the exception of his son John, Mr. Cooke struggled to maintain lasting, meaningful relationships with anyone, and his inability to do so deeply saddened him.

He truly wanted to be close to those he cared for; he simply didn't have it within himself to do it. And his strong, controlling, sometimes abrasive personality didn't help when it came to expressing "love out loud." Consequently, he drove away the very people with whom he desired to be close.

Once near the end of my coaching career, I was driving through Middleburg, Virginia, when I suddenly felt strongly that I should stop to visit Mr. Cooke, whose home was in the area. I never dropped in uninvited to see the boss, but for some reason it seemed the right thing to do that day. When I knocked on the door, a maid answered. She was the only person in the house besides Mr. Cooke, and he was sick in bed.

Here was a man with all the material possessions anyone could ever hope to own, a man with financial resources most of us could never even imagine accumulating, yet when he needed love and care, he suffered all alone, with only a paid employee to look after him. It was a poignant picture—a graphic illustration of misplaced priorities that I have never forgotten. When Mr. Cooke died in 1997, I recalled that incident and couldn't help thinking, *How sad to come to the end of your life knowing that you missed the best part.*

THE RIGHT COUNTERPART

The most important relationship in my life over the past four decades has been my relationship with Pat. To have a good marriage relationship, the partners should be complementary—in areas where one is weak, the other is strong—and Pat has been a great complement to my life. She knows how to encourage me with just the right word, and she's been known to humble me, as well. If we let Him, God will give us just the right marriage partner—someone who will put us in our place once in a while.

In 1983, the Redskins beat the Atlanta Falcons 37-21 to run our record to 12-2 and send us into the playoffs with visions of the Super Bowl dancing in our heads. The Washington press corps hailed me as a brilliant field general, an intelligent coach with an incredible knack for engineering victories. I knew in my heart that I was merely a PE major who had gotten lucky, but it's funny—when everyone around you keeps telling you how great you are, after a while, you start believing them!

The following morning, before heading to work to begin mapping out a strategy against our first-round playoff opponents, the Dallas Cowboys, I was feeling my oats. I had enjoyed reading in the morning newspapers about what a great job I had done with the team and what a big game the Cowboys-Redskins battle was shaping up to be. I was strutting my stuff around the house, thinking how important I was, when Pat complained, "Would you mind picking up your bathrobe and socks?"

I stared back at her as though she had just belted me with a two-by-four. I thought, *The nerve of her! Speaking that way to such an important man! Doesn't she realize who I am?*

And then I picked up my socks and bathrobe.

Then she had the audacity to start talking to me about a problem with our boys.

Doesn't she understand? I railed internally. *Doesn't she read the newspapers? Isn't she aware of what a tough and important job I have to do this week? Why is she bothering me about the kids right now?* I'd had it! I stormed out of the house, slamming the door behind me.

Still steamed while driving to work, I tried to turn my attention to higher things. I had a habit of praying—with my eyes open!—as I drove to work each morning. It was always a good time to talk to the Lord, and He and I had enjoyed many good conversations during my commute. But this morning, it seemed He was about ready to get out and take the bus if I didn't straighten out this matter with Pat. I tried to pray about other matters, but God kept turning my attention back to the way I had reacted to Pat's everyday concerns. You see, Pat knew exactly who I was. Halfway to work, it dawned on me what I had to do.

When I arrived at work, the flurry of activity and anticipation that accompanies playoff preparation already permeated the air, but I knew that my top priority was to call Pat. I dialed our home number and said, "Pat, I'm sorry. Please forgive me for being such a dope this morning. I want you to know something. What you're taking care of at home with our two boys is far more important than what I'm doing here at work. I just want you to know that I know that."

The world sells us a bill of goods. Society says that a person cannot be successful without making money and gaining position, prestige, or power—or in my case, winning football games and, now, auto races. If you fall for the world's line, you will scratch and claw your way through life, trying to accomplish the goals and gather the trophies that the world values, only to discover too late that the most important matters of life lie elsewhere—in your relationships with God, your family, and the people around you.

SIXTEEN

THE KEYS TO QUALITY RELATIONSHIPS

I'm not a marriage counselor, a child psychologist, or a social scientist, but from personal experience with my family, coaching football, and owning racing teams, I have discovered several principles that are important to keep in mind if you want to establish and maintain strong relationships with your family, your coworkers, and any other people with whom you interact on a regular basis.

WE ARE ALL CREATED AS EQUALS

If you label or rank people according to their social status, financial power, or some other artificial standard, you are assigning value to what they have or lack rather than valuing people for who they are. You must understand that every person has intrinsic value, for in God's eyes each of us is a uniquely designed, one-of-a-kind miracle. That means I can draw my self-esteem from the fact that God thinks I'm pretty special. I matter to Him—and so do you!

There's no reason to think that you or I am better (or worse) than someone else. If you think you're better than another person simply because you are smarter, faster, better looking, or even more spiritual, you are setting yourself up to make a lot of mistakes in the area of relationships. Likewise, if you consider somebody to be better than you because they have money, talent, looks, or power that you don't, you are going to be intimidated and will not relate well to that person. And if you attempt to compensate for what you feel you're lacking, you'll make matters even worse. Consider, for example, the insecure teenage boy who turns into a bully because he doesn't have any real friends with whom he can relate on any other basis.

If you keep in mind that God created us all as equals, this will counteract many of the negative stereotypes that often cause trouble between male and female, black and white. That doesn't mean we won't have our differences, but it does mean that you can regard another person's differences without rejecting him or her as a person of value.

We rarely had problems with racial prejudice on the football teams I coached. We didn't think of players or coaches as black, white, yellow, red, or chartreuse—every person was simply an important part of the team. The same goes for our racing teams today.

God tells us to love others just as we love ourselves. That's a lot easier to do when you value others and when you value yourself equally with everyone else. That can be a struggle, as we all tend to be self-centered, but it is an important key that will open the door to success in this area of your life.

Remember, every person matters. We are all equal on God's roster.

GOOD RELATIONSHIPS REQUIRE QUALITY TIME

It's true that kids spell *love* T-I-M-E. In today's world, kids understand that Dad needs to work, and in many cases, Mom does, too. They recognize that you have obligations regarding your occupation that sometimes interfere with their lessons, games, or recitals. What they want to know is what's really important to you. In other words, where do you spend your free time? Are you glued to the television set? Do you spend your free time with friends? Do you spend your discretionary time at the mall, on the golf course, or on the tennis court? You can spout all the pious platitudes you want about how much you love your family, but your kids will decide for themselves what's really important to you by the way you spend your free time.

I messed up pretty good in this area when my sons were young. I competed in racquetball tournaments, playing four or five times a week around the country. There's nothing wrong with racquetball as a sport, but while I was out chasing trophies, my boys were growing up without a father. Oh sure, I spent time with them during their toddler years, and I played ball with them when they were old enough for elementary school. But my competitiveness got the best of me, and I became obsessed with racquetball. So on far too many weekends, I hopped in the car or boarded a plane just to compete for a trophy, while Pat's and my two greatest trophies were missing their dad.

> *Kids spell love T-I-M-E.*

Although winning the national seniors title was one of the greatest thrills of my life, it wasn't worth it. One night after a tournament in Detroit, it hit me. I thought, *I'm an idiot. I'm running around the country to all these tournaments, while my family is back home without me. No more. That's it. I'm taking the first flight out of here, and I'm not going to miss opportunities to be home with my wife and children.*

Fortunately, both boys were still under ten when I came to my senses, and I've tried ever since to keep my family as my top priority after God. But that doesn't mean I didn't miss some irreplaceable moments in their lives. Because I traveled so much in my work, Pat developed a habit of placing pictures of the boys where I could see them as I shaved. She changed the photos from time to time, and it always hurt whenever she put up an old picture of the boys from when they were little, when I wasn't there a lot.

Fortunately, a fringe benefit of coaching football and owning a racing team is that both sports have allowed for special periods of time with my family. During my football years, I encouraged our boys not to take summer jobs. The relatively few dollars they might have earned during the summer couldn't compare to the priceless memories we made together. We spent many wonderful hours at our lake house, skiing, racing bicycles, riding motorbikes, jet skiing, and doing all sorts of other activities the kids enjoyed. Early on, Pat and I made a decision to invest our discretionary

income and time in our family, and that decision has paid enormous
dividends.

Today, our boys work with me at Joe Gibbs Racing. J D is the president
of the organization and handles much of the day-to-day business. Coy, our
younger son, is helping to improve our family's prayer life by driving in the
NASCAR Busch Series. There's something about seeing one of your own
loved ones roaring around a track at a couple hundred miles per hour that
will keep you in close touch with God!

Pat attends many of our races and has been right there with us through
the good times and the tough times. Family has always been a big part of
NASCAR racing, among the teams as well as the fans, and to me, having the
family together is one of the best parts of our involvement in the sport.

Our sons and their wives, Heather and Melissa, live nearby, so Pat and
I now get to enjoy our grandchildren. Pat and I prayed for our sons' mates
from the time our boys were small. God honored those prayers, providing
the perfect wives for our sons. Heather is a creative entrepreneur, manag-
ing her own business in addition to Coy's racing career. And Melissa is the
world's greatest mother, in my humble opinion.

Recently, I received an outrageous offer to return to coaching in the
NFL. The salary and perks involved were far more than a kid from Enka,
North Carolina, could ever have imagined! Just for fun, and to remain true
to my commitment to run all major financial decisions past Pat, I told her
about the offer.

Without hesitation, Pat said, "You can go, if you want. I'm not. I'm staying here with our grandbabies."

I smiled. "Me, too," I said.

Relationships are far more valuable than money.

LOVING WITHOUT LOOKING FOR A RETURN

In evaluating my conduct and attitudes toward another person, I have to
ask myself some tough questions: Am I simply being kind to someone in
hopes that they will do something good for me? Or do I care unconditionally for that person, whether he can do anything for me or not?

We all know *users,* people who will trade on their relationships to get what they want, even if it means compromising their values or possibly squandering away the relationship. Like a used-car salesman in a loud sports jacket, they'll tell you anything they think you want to hear if it will help them get what they want. We probably can't avoid all the users we come across, but we can certainly keep from becoming one ourselves. The best way I know to avoid using another person is to love that person unconditionally, regardless of what he or she can do for you.

ACTIVE COMMUNICATION IS KEY TO A GOOD RELATIONSHIP

There are probably people in your life with whom you have a strong enough relationship that even if you haven't seen each other for a long time, all you need to do is hear that person's voice or see his or her face, and the two of you can pick up right where you left off. Most good relationships, however, require a more frequent flow of communication. Certainly this is true in marriage. Isn't it amazing that after being together for a few years, many couples cease to talk with each other, except for issues surrounding the children? Other couples fall into a habit of exchanging meaningless drivel.

"How was your day?"

"Fine."

"Great."

"Good night."

Try living with that for a few years, and it shouldn't surprise you when one day you hear the words "I want a divorce."

Good books abound on the subject of improving your communications skills. Entire television shows and radio programs are given over to the subject of communication in the family, so I won't bore you with the how-to's. All I'm saying is that you can't possibly have a good relationship without genuine opportunities to talk to, listen to, and understand one another.

I've also made it a practice of communicating with friends by means of brief handwritten notes. I keep a list of people for whom I pray regularly, so every so often, I'll sit down and jot a short note just to let the person know I'm thinking of them. Frequently my notes are only one sentence long: "Hey, I prayed for you this morning, and I hope things are going well." You never know how that simple note might impact someone's life. I know that similar notes I received from George Tharel often arrived at a crucial time when I really needed to know that someone cared.

Nowadays, you may prefer to use e-mail, video conferencing, or other means of staying in touch. But whatever you do, keep the lines open and the communication flowing if you want to build and maintain a lasting relationship.

BE WILLING TO FORGIVE

The truth is, we all mess up and make mistakes. Sometimes our misdeeds, inappropriate words, or unfortunate attitudes hurt the people we know and love. All too often we run roughshod over the people who are closest to us and care for us most. Consequently, we all need to be forgiven, and we all need to forgive others for the things they have done that hurt or offended us. No one is perfect, and as in a hotly contested NASCAR race, friction, bumps, and crashes can occur, even in the best of relationships. When bad things happen in a relationship, learn to forgive and forget as much as humanly possible. Holding on to bitterness, resentment, and grudges will not accomplish anything of value for you or anyone else.

The truth of this hit me when I was forced to deal with one of the most sensitive issues in my career as a NASCAR owner. At the end of the 1994 season our driver, Dale Jarrett, announced that he was leaving the team. Dale had been with us from the very beginning, before we owned so much as a tire or gas can. He had helped recruit his brother-in-law, Jimmy Makar, to become the first crew chief of our #18 car. Dale was behind the wheel when we experienced our first crash in our first race, and then in 1993, Dale was driving when we won our first race, the prestigious Daytona 500. I had a huge financial interest in having Dale behind the wheel.

Beyond that, however, I had a spiritual interest in Dale Jarrett. Dale had been with me during one of my early meetings with Norm Miller of Interstate Batteries. Amazed at Norm's willingness to invest millions of dollars in a start-up racing team, Dale asked Norm straightforwardly, "What do you hope to get out of this?"

Norm didn't even blink. Without a moment's hesitation, he replied, "I want to reach people for Christ."

Dale scratched his head. Norm's answer puzzled him. Money. Fame. Prestige. Publicity. All sorts of other motivating factors Dale could have understood, but "to reach people for Christ"? What was *that* all about?

Nevertheless, when I invited Dale and Jimmy and their wives to attend the 1992 Super Bowl chapel—which turned out to be my last as the Redskins' coach—they eagerly accepted. At the close of the chapel service, the speaker encouraged those who wanted to place their trust in Jesus Christ to stand up. Among the many who responded were Patti and Jimmy Makar and Kelley and Dale Jarrett.

After our season-opening win at Daytona in 1993, expectations were high. Unfortunately, our performance on the track fell far below our expectations, and by the end of 1994 it seemed everything was going wrong. With two years remaining on his contract with us, Dale came to see me one day and said, "I need to leave, for my future's sake." I had heard rumors that Dale was being courted by other race teams, but that sort of attention just comes along with winning...or losing.

Competitors frequently dangled perks and promises in front of most of my best football players at Washington. No contract or noncompete clause will hold a person if he or she really wants to leave your organization, but we were so confident about the relationships we had with our Redskins players and staff, we rarely worried about quality people flying the coop. The same was true of our racing team, so when the rumors started circulating concerning Dale's imminent departure, I ignored them.

Then Dale walked in my office and admitted that he had been offered a tremendous deal to drive for one of our competitors, and that he was seriously considering the offer if I would let him out of his contract.

I was stunned. I pondered the situation for several days, then finally told Dale, "Well, okay, but only if I can find the right person to replace you. I can't just let you out of your contract."

Although Dale's leaving was a shock to our team and a crushing disappointment to me personally, I didn't dare hold a grudge. I had learned long ago that grudges serve only to destroy the person who holds them. Furthermore, Dale was much more than my employee; he was a brother in the Lord. The fact that he was discontented and wanted to leave bothered me, yet I knew that I had to handle it as though Dale were my own flesh and blood—wish Dale well and trust God to bless us both.

Around that time, we heard that another team's sponsorship deal had blown up and that their driver's contract could possibly be purchased. I first approached the team's owner and worked out a financial deal with him. I then immediately sought to secure the services of his talented young driver, Bobby Labonte.

Today, Dale Jarrett and I continue to share a genuine friendship, and we have great respect for each other as competitors. Of course, Dale went on to win the Winston Cup in 1999, and Bobby followed him by winning the championship in 2000.

ADMIT YOUR MISTAKES

Three little words could save many a marriage: "I was wrong." Or better yet, "You are right." Admitting that you made a mistake can defuse a person's anger faster even than the words "I love you."

Pat is the frugal partner in our marriage, and I am the big spender. Early in our marriage, we discovered that she is much more capable than me when it comes to handling the finances. But one day, I complained about something I had seen in the checkbook.

"Well, if you think you can do any better, here!" She whipped the checkbook across the room at me and bounced it off my chest.

"No, that's okay," I replied. "You handle it."

Pat takes excellent care of our finances, so I don't usually worry about it. I just tell her when I need money, and she doles it out. Then one day I was out with some friends and we were talking about money. I confessed, "I don't even have a checkbook."

"You don't have a checkbook? How do you function?" one of the guys wanted to know.

"That's ridiculous!" another of my buddies blurted.

I got to thinking about it and decided they were right. I went home and told Pat. "I want a checkbook," I snapped.

"Okay, fine," Pat replied.

Can you guess what happened? Yep, within a few weeks, I had that checkbook so fouled up, it would take a team of accountants to straighten it out. Besides that, Pat gave me the third degree regarding nearly every check I wrote. "What's that for?" "You spent *how much* on golf shoes?" Finally, I got so frustrated, I nearly begged her to take back the checkbook, and I went back to operating on a cash basis. Once again, I had to come back and admit to Pat that I was wrong. She accepted my apology, reclaimed possession of the checkbook, and gave me a few bucks to spend, to boot!

Admitting to your spouse that you were wrong is not easy, but if you want a quality relationship, you'll save a lot of heartache if you learn to keep short accounts with your partner.

THE THREE MOST POWERFUL WORDS YOUR KIDS CAN HEAR

Sure, your kids need to hear those three affirming words, "I love you." But for many children, the most powerful words they will ever hear you say are "I was wrong." Admitting to your children that you were wrong will not undermine their respect for you; it will enhance it. When the kids know that Mom and Dad have the courage and integrity to admit their shortcomings, the children are freed from their own fear of failure. Then when the kids *do* mess up, they can come to you and seek your help. But if you insist on maintaining for them the illusion that you are perfect, that you *could never* stoop to such low, despicable conduct, don't be surprised if the bridge into your children's lives keeps getting longer and harder to cross.

SURROUND YOURSELF WITH PEOPLE WHO WILL HOLD YOU ACCOUNTABLE

You need friends who will hold you accountable for your actions. This is especially true in regard to marriage and parenting issues, but also in the way you conduct yourself on the job, with members of the opposite sex, and in your attitude toward your work.

Who can you talk to when things are going haywire in your marriage? Or when your teenage son or daughter is rebelling against everything you believe? Many people pay a professional to listen to their most intimate problems. With all due respect to their counselors, perhaps if these people had someone in their life who loved them unconditionally and would tell them the truth—based on God's Word—when they need to hear it, they wouldn't need a pill or a drink or another session with their shrink to make it through the day.

Most of us need frequent reminders to do the right things in life. Occasionally I meet someone who is offended at that. "I don't need anyone to tell me how to live!" he rails. Maybe you don't need anyone to help keep you on track, but I sure do. I want people close to me who will ask me what I'm doing with my spare time, who will check with me concerning the regularity of my Bible study and prayer life, and who will caution me concerning my eating habits.

Furthermore, I need daily disciplines in my life. For instance, I attempt to exercise nearly every day. I attempt to read a few pages from the Bible every day. I keep a list of people for whom I am praying. I put important meetings and things to do—even dates with Pat—on my schedule, rather than assuming I will get around to them one of these days. Writing things down helps me to plan for action, rather than leaving the disciplines of my life to chance or good intentions.

ACTIONS DON'T ALWAYS SPEAK LOUDER THAN WORDS

Clearly, words are important in our relationships. Positive affirmations can bless your marriage partner, children, friends, or coworkers, while needlessly negative comments can curse your relationships. But all the good words you spout will prove worthless if your actions don't back them up.

Of course, it takes both actions *and* words to make your team members feel valued. A member of our race team complained to me that I didn't praise him enough in front of the other team members. "Joe, you don't value my contribution around here."

My mouth dropped open. "Don't value you? I'm paying you a fortune! Doesn't that show that I value you?"

Granted, money alone is no substitute for a kind word of appreciation, but by paying this team member a generous salary, I thought I was affirming his worth to our company. But he needed more. He needed to *hear* that I valued him. So now I make it a point to verbally pat my people on the back whenever possible.

If we want to enjoy quality relationships, we must look for ways to both show and tell of our appreciation for the people around us.

CAN PEOPLE COUNT ON YOU?

Quality relationships require consistency. Sure, spontaneous activities are fun and can perk up a slumbering relationship, but over the long haul, most people want to know that you can be counted on to do what you say you will do, to be where you say you will be, to be the kind of person you claim to be.

That's the kind of person I strive to be—a man that Pat can count on as her husband and that my sons can count on as their father. Likewise, I want to be able to count on my close friends and business associates. Norm Miller, for example, has repeatedly proven his loyalty to our race team and to me. Norm has stood up for me through thick and thin, placing his money where his mouth is and counting on our program as a major part of Interstate Batteries' advertising thrust.

Lots of people tritely mouth the words "You can count on me," but when the pressures of life begin to close in, they are often the first to disappear. People who have done what it takes to form quality relationships can be counted on in the good times and the bad.

THE VALUE OF DEVELOPING STRONG RELATIONSHIPS

Is it really worth the time and effort that must be invested to develop great relationships? You might be asking, *What's in it for me? What am I going to get out of this?* I can think of several positive returns you'll reap when you take the time to nurture your relationships.

Quality Relationships Last

A good relationship stands the test of time. You probably know someone who struggles to maintain even one quality relationship. He or she may flit from marriage to marriage, bounce from one church congregation to another, or leave job after job, dissatisfied and hoping to find something better down the road. On the other hand, something tugs at our hearts when a couple celebrates their fiftieth wedding anniversary or the company presents a distinguished service award to a dedicated, longtime employee. Something in us wants to stand up, applaud, and shout, "Yes! That's the way it's supposed to be!"

Quality Relationships Lead to Wise Decision Making

After making a series of poor financial decisions—and manipulating Pat into going along with them—I finally learned to rely on my wife's wisdom and help in making decisions, especially concerning investments. I made up my mind not to invest in anything big unless Pat agrees.

Shortly after we had recovered from one of my early financial messes, a friend approached me with another opportunity that promised to make us *big* money.

"You need to get in on this, Joe," he said. "You'll make a fortune."

The plan sounded a bit dubious to me so, looking for a way out, I said, "Only if you can convince Pat." I chuckled to myself, thinking, *He has no chance! This is a pipe dream, and Pat turns away 90 percent of the investment opportunities that come to us anyhow—good, sound investments with solid track records, and she still says no! Surely she isn't going to buy into this guy's deal!*

But my friend felt sure he could convince Pat, so he came to our home to make his pitch, and pitch he did! He wrote out the details of the program, writing first with his right hand, then his left. I didn't say a word. I just sat back and waited for Pat to reduce him and his cool presentation to a puddle with her fiery refusal. Nearly snickering aloud, I watched as the man came to a dynamic finish. I could barely hide my amusement as Pat stood, looked the guy squarely in the eye, then looked over at me and said, "I think we need to do this."

I was dumbfounded! I could hardly believe what my super-frugal wife was saying. But I told my friend, "Well, hey! If Pat says let's do it, we're gonna do it!"

We got into the deal, and within two months we had made $75,000!

I gained much more than money through that incident; I gained respect for Pat's intuition, an understanding of the importance of unity in making financial decisions, and the blessing of better decision making as the result of a better relationship.

Develop strong relationships with your mate and with a few people who are walking closely with the Lord, and they will help you make better decisions, even when those decisions sometimes fly in the face of logic.

Quality, Lasting Relationships Make For a Better Team

The best team builders are not dictatorial tyrants, but men and women who have learned how to develop strong relationships with the people they are leading. This is true in any family, organization, or business. If you want to build a great team, you must understand people, know how to relate to them, and know how to bring out the best in them. In fact, without concern and consideration for others, it is almost impossible to put together a successful team or hold one together for very long. Even CEOs in charge of tens of thousands of employees understand that they can only succeed by developing quality relationships.

Norm Miller of Interstate Batteries genuinely cares about the people who work for him. Besides paying his people a fair wage and providing a pleasant, upbeat, fun work environment, Norm also provides his people with on-site chaplains, to whom employees can turn for spiritual guidance and inspiration. Loyal employees receive wonderfully generous retirement plans and other perks that Norm does not necessarily have to provide. He does these things because he is not interested in simply building an empire for himself. Norm has a relationship with his team members because he wants them to enjoy the company's success as much as he does.

Your Values Will Be Passed On

Intentionally or not, children tend to emulate their parents. Whether you foster good relationships or poor ones in your home, your children will sit up and take notice. They will see and remember the way you treat your wife or husband; the way you speak to and about your family members; and the way you express love, joy, excitement, pain, compassion, and sympathy. If you fail to cultivate good relationships in your home, not only will your children and grandchildren reap a meager harvest, any number of potential disasters await as they reap the ill whirlwind spun off by your actions and attitudes.

You may already have failed in relationships with your spouse, family members, or coworkers—but keep in mind, no problem is too big for God. If you ask, He will help you clean up the mess, even if it takes a miracle to do it. And He will help you restore and rebuild the relationships you have injured or ignored. It's never too late with God.

Don't misunderstand me. You may pay a high price for missing opportunities or failing to keep your relationships in their proper place on your priority list. A friend whose father passed away recently said to me, "I wish every day that I could call my dad on the telephone, just to tell him that I love him or to ask his advice about something in my life. I had so many opportunities to do that, and I missed them. Now they are gone forever."

Similarly, I know of a good, godly man who missed seeing his daughter grow up because the demands of his business took him away from home so much during her adolescent years. Now he wants to be a part of his daughter's life, but she is consumed with her own business activities and her friends, and she doesn't have time for him. It's a modern-day

"Cat's in the Cradle" story. She grew up to be just like her father.

Nevertheless, God can help that dad build new bridges into his daughter's life, if he is willing to take the time and make the effort to start over, this time according to God's game plan.

Strong Relationships Multiply Your Vision

Two are always better than one when it comes to solving life's problems. You can see, hear, and accomplish more in your life when you are in good relationships with others. God has given each of us a complement of gifts, talents, and abilities, but none of us can do everything. Where I am weak, I need someone else to be strong. That's where my relationships come in. Other people help make up for my deficits, and hopefully my assets help to balance out someone else's shortfalls.

For instance, in some areas in which I'm a ten, Pat may be a three, and I help to pull her up. In other areas, I am a three and Pat is the ten who pulls me up. Together we are stronger than the sum total of our individual gifts, talents, and energies.

Quality Relationships Change Your Outlook on Life

Just as Pat and I were beginning to peek out from beneath the enormous load of debt I had buried us under (see chapter 9), I was at the Redskins training camp in Carlisle, Pennsylvania, when I received a phone call from an attorney in Oklahoma. Some creditors had discovered two more apartment complexes for which I ostensibly owed another quarter of a million dollars. The creditors insisted that I had signed for the loan on the apartments.

I knew that I had never personally signed on the loans. Apparently, my name had been forged, but the creditors had documents with my signature on them, so as far as they were concerned, I owed them money.

I went berserk! Besides feeling unjustly charged, I was angry because I had thought that all of that awful, ugly stuff was behind me, that Pat and I could move on and rebuild our lives. Then suddenly, like the monster that wouldn't die in the B-grade horror movie, a sense of impending doom and despair was rising from the quagmire and threatening to smother us with slime once again.

In a fit of rage, I called my friend and spiritual advisor George Tharel for some advice. For the first few minutes of our conversation, I ranted like a wild man, going off in every direction about the newly discovered monster in Oklahoma. When I finally stopped long enough to take a breath, George quietly interrupted. "Listen to you," he said calmly. "Is God in charge of your life? Is God bigger than this? You sound like someone who is coming apart."

His words brought me up short, and I realized that he was right. Of course, there was no need for me to justify myself to George; he already accepted me and loved me unconditionally. Because of our relationship, George had earned the right to speak bluntly and directly into my life. And I was willing to accept counsel from him.

George's Christlike example and his mild rebuke checked me right there and sparked in me an entirely different attitude. No doubt, if someone whose spiritual authority I respected less had spoken into my life in such an overt manner, I may have rejected it and perhaps become a bit angrier. But because George and I had built such a close relationship, his comments helped change my entire outlook. It's amazing that a five-minute conversation with a godly person could have such a profound effect.

Good relationships can make such things possible, especially when a relationship is established and maintained according to God's game plan.

Seven Cornerstone Principles for Success

RELATIONSHIPS

Only a fool would not want to succeed in his or her personal relationships. The question is, how? How can you be a success in your career and at home, too? How can you juggle your job and your desire to be actively involved in your community and the lives of your family members and friends, without all the balls coming down to bop you on the head?

Nowadays, many people are resigning themselves to the bleak notion that it's impossible to have it both ways. You can't develop, nurture, and maintain quality marriage and parenting relationships and still be a success in the workplace, they say. One or the other will suffer.

Well, I'm convinced that most of us don't want to run away or drop out. Many of us hope to have great relationships, and we want to be successful in our jobs at the same time. We also want lasting friendships, and we want to be valued by others.

The key is not brains, brilliance, or the bottom line. The key is *balance*. The most successful people in the world work hard but still spend time with their family and friends. How? Because they have learned the cornerstone principles for developing good, solid relationships.

The following principles are essential for lasting relationships of every conceivable type. These are the wheels on which everything else rolls. Therefore, if you maintain them in your own life, you can run the race with confidence, whether you run in clean, open air or when the traffic is heavy, the track is slippery, and the heat and pressure are intense.

God will help you hang in there, even when the tough times come. His game plan will keep you from caroming aimlessly from one failure to the next. You can cross the finish line and hug the most precious trophies of all—the people you love.

CORNERSTONE 1

God wants a personal relationship with you. God is a God of infinite love, and He desires a relationship with you. He's the one who initiates love; He is pursuing you and me, even when we foolishly choose to ignore Him or stubbornly refuse to accept His love. He loved us and began courting us long before we even gave Him a second thought. That's truly amazing!

CORNERSTONE 2

Apart from God, all your relationships will end in failure. We are all basically selfish creatures. We were born that way, and we will continue to live that way until we allow God to change our nature. And sooner or later, without the pure love and the saving grace of God, that self-centeredness will be the kiss of death in any relationship, regardless of how well it begins.

CORNERSTONE 3

Each person in your life means *completion*, not competition. Each of us has specific strengths and weaknesses, but God knowingly places people in our lives with complementary strengths. We are meant to live in interdependent relationships, strengths complementing weaknesses and weaknesses complementing strengths. This principle is especially important in marriage and in the family of God.

CORNERSTONE 4

Having the heart of a servant changes everything. Just as successful businesses find ways to serve their customers, you must learn to help and serve others. That's how to make your marriage, your parent-child relationships, your friendships, and your workplace relationships thrive. Don't just look out for number one; seek the best interests of the people around you.

CORNERSTONE 5

A few close friendships are better than many casual ones. To have two or three solid friends who stay with you through thick and thin, start by developing a friendship with God and allowing Jesus to be your best Friend. Then ask God to bring some other close friends into your life. Finally, the old adage is right on target: To have a friend, you must be a friend.

CORNERSTONE 6

Forgiveness paves the way. Grant forgiveness to those who offend you, and seek forgiveness from those you've hurt. And remember, forgiveness doesn't mean that you must ignore or condone wrongs—we forgive because that's the way God deals with us. Arrogance, pride, bitterness, and resentment destroy good relationships. Love, humility, modesty, and forgiveness will nurture them and help you to reap huge harvests.

CORNERSTONE 7

Blessing your enemies pays incredible dividends. Instead of paying back evil for evil or trading insult for insult, try blessing your opponent. Returning blessings for evil brings blessings into your own life. God's blessings can turn around hurt-filled, painful situations.

Success and Your Moral Choices

Coach Gibbs, as I knew him, was the head coach of the Washington Redskins for eleven of my twenty years in the NFL. As an impressionable young kid still entering manhood, I had certain ideas about what it took to succeed in professional sports. I thought that to become a championship-level coach or player a man had to be tough, selfish, prideful, and arrogant. But Coach Gibbs shattered my assumptions. Coach managed to build a successful coaching career while still being a great husband, father, and friend. A famous man once said, "Preach the gospel every day; use words when necessary." This is exactly how Coach Gibbs has lived—as a model of integrity, honesty, and compassion. The NFL is not the most friendly and open work environment, but Coach Gibbs cared about the lives of his players on and off the field. He taught us that character allows a person to manage the ups and downs of life and that a person of character knows how to respond appropriately whether he's winning or losing. By living what he teaches, Joe Gibbs has left with me a moral legacy, and he continues to leave his mark on all who come into contact with him.

Darrell Green, founder of the Youth Life Foundation,
was named NFL Man of the Year in 1996 and was a seven-time Pro Bowl
cornerback for the Washington Redskins.

Biotechnology, blurred sexual orientations, personal integrity issues, political compromises, euthanasia, abortion, stem cell research, Internet pornography, the bombardment of traditional values in popular culture and in the classroom—these and many other issues require us to make moral choices on a daily basis. Regardless of a person's persuasions, to say "I don't want to impose my views on anyone else" is a joke. We all impose our values on the world around us in many ways every day!

The question is this: Whose values will you live by?

Perhaps you will find in these pages some ideas to help you sort through the moral morass. In matters of morality and personal convictions, you must consider:

- How your values will be passed on.
- The influence you have on others.
- Who will your decisions impact, positively or negatively?
- Your role as a citizen.
- Tough choices must be made, regardless of the consequences.

SEVENTEEN

REAPING WHAT YOU SOW

S hortly after I got my driver's license at the age of sixteen, I went out joyriding with my friends. We were gallivanting and goofing off, as teenage boys are prone to do, just having fun and getting into mischief. But suddenly our foolishness shifted gears dangerously, and before we knew what had happened, we were involved in a serious accident. Scared to death, I initially kept right on driving, leaving the scene of the accident; but as the driver, I knew that I had to take responsibility. I drove back to the scene and turned myself in.

Mom and Dad were out of town overnight and couldn't be reached. Consequently, the police locked me up in Juvenile Hall for the night. I was horrified to hear the cell door clank shut behind me. I tried to sleep in the stark accommodations—a thin cot, a small sink, and an open commode— but I was terrified about the trouble I was in, not to mention the taunts, yells, and screams from the other inmates. It was one of the longest nights of my life.

The next morning, I was taken to a room where the detention center superintendent was waiting with my mom and dad. When I saw the look on my dad's face, I thought for the first time that I might be safer in the cell! The officer nodded to a chair across the room from my folks, and I took a seat. I glanced at my mother, and the look in her eyes said it all.

She was horrendously disappointed in me, and I never wanted to see that look again.

The superintendent launched into a tirade about my being out so late at night and how my parents ought to take more responsibility for my behavior. Unaware that my dad was a former police officer himself, the superintendent read my dad the riot act, ripping him for not being a better parent.

After about five minutes of this, my dad suddenly bolted out of his chair, bounded across the room, grabbed me by the throat, and pulled me right up out of my chair! The chair caromed out from under me and flew across the room. Choking and gasping for air, my sixteen-year-old frame dangled precariously above the floor, while Dad reared back as though he was going to punch my lights out. "I'm gonna kill you!" he roared.

Mom and the superintendent jumped up, pulled Dad off me, and eventually got him calmed down.

"It's really not that bad," the superintendent said, flip-flopping from being my accuser to become my defender as he attempted to defuse Dad's fury.

I learned a number of lessons through that incident. Most important, perhaps, I realized that I had made a mistake by allowing myself to be improperly influenced by my peer group. I knew what we were doing was wrong, yet I let myself get swept along with the crowd and made my moral decisions according to what was popular at the moment. I was influenced by the voices I heard the loudest, and I didn't stop until someone got hurt.

An interesting thing about peer pressure: We usually talk to teenagers about its dangers, but peer pressure doesn't disappear with age—it merely changes forms. The temptation to go along with the crowd, to do what is expected, even when we know it is wrong, stays with us as adults. Ask any congressman or senator, or better yet, simply examine their voting records, and you will see where their true loyalties lie and on what basis they make their decisions.

Fortunately, my parents really loved me and were willing to discipline me for my inappropriate actions. My dad, of course, scared the wits out of me, but that look in my mother's eyes had an even more profound effect. After all my parents had done for me, working hard for every penny, scrimping and saving to help me get my car...I never wanted to cause them hurt and disappointment again. Those two factors—discipline and having someone who loved me—helped me to realign my priorities and kept me on the straight and narrow path (with a few relatively minor detours).

I lost my driver's license for a year. Mom and Dad didn't try to argue with the decision; they supported it as part of the price I must pay for what I had done. I learned that my actions, however frivolous they seem at the moment, can have serious consequences. One false move or irresponsible decision could cost me my license—or much more.

Today, a young man in pursuit of a moment's pleasure can take a needle into his arm and contract AIDS, decimating his life forever. Just one pre-marital sexual experience can leave a young woman pregnant and walking an entirely unexpected path. A man or woman may succumb to a moment of temptation and destroy a marriage. One incident of cheating or thievery can cost you your job. It doesn't take a lifetime of bad choices to reap destruction. Often, a single wrong decision leads to a mess for you, your family, and your friends.

That's why it is vital that we find an accurate basis from which we can make moral decisions daily.

TAKE A STAND AND EARN RESPECT

Once you establish and maintain a reputation for moral integrity, other people will notice. You may inadvertently have a positive influence on them, without having to toot your own horn to do it.

While coaching the Washington Redskins, I was once the butt of a scathing article written by a local reporter. We had lost a few games that year, and the reporter implied that team owner Jack Kent Cooke and I were at odds and that my boss was ready to give me the boot. I have always considered the source when it comes to negative media coverage, so I didn't let the article bother me too much. But when Mr. Cooke saw the article, he blew his top sky-high!

I was in my office when I received a phone call from Mr. Cooke. In his gravelly voice, he growled, "I'm going to bring this writer in here, and we're going to address this. You and I are going to confront him about the untruths in his article."

Mr. Cooke invited the writer to meet with us in his office, and the writer was foolish enough to accept. Our meeting had no sooner begun than Mr. Cooke was all over him. "You, my good man," Mr. Cooke railed, "have come between me and my coach. This man is like one of my sons!" Then Mr. Cooke delivered a series of searing four-letter words, calling the writer everything but *nice*. Every so often, Mr. Cooke paused just briefly, turned to me, and said, "Joe, excuse my language." Then he immediately turned back to the reporter and let loose with another diatribe with language salty enough to preserve a dead body!

I had taken a stand early in my career and chose not to use foul language to express myself. That's not to say I never got angry, and I was never reluctant to speak my mind. In fact, in my younger years, I wasn't bashful about cursing a blue streak. But after rededicating my life to God, I decided that such language was inconsistent with the lifestyle I wanted to lead. I didn't make a big deal about it, nor did I reprimand anyone on my staff for their language. After all, I was working in a rough-and-tumble world where blue locker-room language was considered normal. Yet for some reason, players, assistants, opposing coaches, and even Mr. Cooke were sensitive about using profanity when they were around me.

Live consistently according to your moral values. People will respect you for it.

Some people might say it's impossible to be a coach of an NFL football team without using profanity. But that simply is not true.

To curse or not to curse is a small issue to some people. But I mention it here because I am convinced that people will respect you more, not less, when you take a stand for what is good and right and live consistently according to your moral values. Other people may not agree with you; they may disapprove of the stands you take. But they will respect the fact that you are true to what you believe. Some of the least respected people in the world are hypocrites who claim to live on the moral high ground yet live another way entirely. In the Bible, Jesus reserved some of His most scathing rebukes not for the prostitutes, tax collectors, and thieves, but for religious hypocrites! (Check out Matthew 23:14–39.)

Moreover, a certain measure of professionalism should accompany the position of being a leader, and to me, profanity is simply an unprofessional way of speaking. When a leader publicly spews a litany of foul words, he or she breeds bad attitudes among the rank and file and lowers the caliber of the entire team.

I saw this principle in action at a meeting of executives for one of America's largest companies. One of the top executives was brutal about using foul language, even in the presence of women and younger executives who looked to him as a role model. I took part in a meeting he chaired, in which more than a hundred executives gathered in New York to glean from him. The man got up in front of the entire audience and told raunchy, profanity-laced stories, the likes of which I had never heard even in a locker room. The shock and disdain in that room was palpable.

Worse, this man's performance opened the floodgates. Following his lead, several junior executives took their turns at the podium and turned the air blue with off-color language, comments, and jokes. This guy had led his followers straight into the gutter and down the drainpipe.

Another reason for my decision to abstain from profanity was that I knew it was unnecessary. My uncle Gus Blalock ran a trucking firm during his younger years. Uncle Gus had a reputation for turning a phrase and knowing how to use words. His employees said, "He could take you down to the bottom and chew you out as good as anyone; he could wear you down to a nub without ever using a foul word."

Nowadays, the rationale for using profanity—even in its most offensive forms—is that "everybody is doing it." No, everybody is not doing it. Most of the people I'm around on a daily basis do not talk that way. Our pit crew guys work in hot, pressure-packed, sometimes dangerous situations, but they do not normally use foul language on the job. Oh, sure, if you hang around our race shop long enough, you'll probably hear a curse word or two, but that's the aberration rather than the norm.

Many contemporary movies and books are laced with profanity in an effort to emulate "reality." Whose reality? Certainly not mine; nor is it the reality for most Americans. Truth is, most Americans I meet don't speak as crudely as the characters in most modern movies and novels. Besides, diarrhea is part of real life, too, but that doesn't mean it's pleasant or something to be expressed in public.

Don't be afraid to buck the system when the system is wrong. Taking a stand for what is morally right will have a positive effect on your home, your business, maybe even your entire community. Seek to elevate the morale of those around you by speaking and acting positively.

LEAVING A MORAL LEGACY

When I was coaching in Tampa, a friend of mine owned a cigar store that sold rich, smooth cigars, and I got into the habit of smoking a good cigar while working at the office. I never smoked at home or around our children, but one day on the way home after work, I was enjoying a cigar and thinking about the game ahead. When I pulled into our driveway and got out of the car, our youngest son, Coy, was standing there. When I saw him, I realized that I was still holding the cigar, so I casually slipped my hand behind my back. Too late.

Always the inquisitive one, Coy ran straight to me, but he didn't stop. Without even saying hello, he slipped around me, looked behind my back, and stared at the still-lit cigar in amazement. His little eyes widened. He looked up at me, then back at the cigar in unbelief, as if to say, "Oh, my gosh! My dad is smoking a cigar!"

This caused me to stop and think, What kind of influence am I having on my sons by smoking?

And that was the day I gave up my cigars. I never lost the taste for them, and to this day, I sometimes long to smoke a good cigar, but I don't. I got involved in an "I Quit Smoking" campaign in Washington, and one of the greatest rewards I ever received was a letter from a woman thanking me that because of a commercial I had done, her husband quit smoking.

Coy grew up to be even more staunch in his belief system than I am! Coy graduated from Stanford University, an institution that prides itself on being one of the most liberal schools in America. His views and values were constantly attacked as being too conservative. Yet rather than undermining his beliefs, the challenges caused Coy to evaluate what he truly believed, which served to strengthen his faith and his values. I've always admired his courage when it comes to taking a stand. I nearly laughed out loud when I heard that one of his classmates said, "I didn't know there were still people who believed the way Coy does!"

Parents, you can influence your children either positively or negatively, but one way or another, you *will* pass on your values to your children. Some kids are raised in homes where Dad smokes a stogie every evening after dinner, and most of them turn out just fine; but too many of those children develop addictions of their own. Some people will tell you there's nothing wrong with drinking alcohol in moderation. "I only drink socially," they say. "A drink here and there won't hurt anything." And that may be true. But it's really difficult to discipline your children for using marijuana when you are holding on to your own drug of choice.

Moral choices fall into two categories: those that are guided by biblical principles and those that are left to our personal convictions. When the Bible says "You shall" or "You shall not," those points are not up for debate; I try to do what the biblical principle commands. Many daily choices, however, must be based on our own personal convictions—which car I drive, where we go for vacation, how I dress, and myriad other daily decisions that the Bible does not give specific instructions about.

For instance, the Bible doesn't prohibit drinking wine. Jesus turned water into wine at a wedding in Cana; the apostle Paul told his young preacher friend Timothy to have some wine to soothe his stomach. But the Bible *does* forbid getting drunk. For me, then, drinking wine is a matter of personal conviction. If a person wants to have a glass of wine with dinner, I'm not offended, although I personally choose not to drink.

When making moral choices, especially those that fall into the realm of personal convictions, I often ask myself, *Who am I influencing by this action? And who am I disappointing by doing this?* I surely don't want to disappoint God, nor do I want to set a bad example for my kids or grandkids. I don't want to disappoint Pat or have a negative influence on other people. If I determine that the consequences of my actions—and the influence they might have on others—may be more negative than positive, I'll often choose to abstain, even if it's something that I might really enjoy myself.

If I'm still undecided about an issue, I'll ask, *How does this make me feel about myself?* In my younger years, I made a raft of bad decisions about my priorities, and when I looked at the guy in the mirror, I didn't feel so great about myself. Something within me said, *You can do better than this. You were made for more than this.* Although I was frequently patted on the back by others for my "achievements," my self-esteem plummeted through the floorboards. I now believe that the Spirit of God was speaking to my heart way back then, encouraging me to become a better man and letting me know that God was willing to help me. I just didn't recognize His voice at the time.

HOW TO OVERCOME TEMPTATION

Temptations often come to us at the point where we are weakest. The strongest attacks may come on our "off days," because the enemy of our souls never takes a break. You and I may come out of the game for a rest, call for a time out, or take a vacation from our disciplines, and that is often when we are most vulnerable to the opposition.

I find the biblical account of David fascinating. Talk about courage! He went up against the giant Goliath with only a slingshot and a few stones to do battle—and he won! That takes a lot more courage than a guy covering a kickoff or driving a fast car. David did many mighty deeds that make for great reading.

On the other hand, David failed spectacularly during his reign as king because of moral compromise. He had a sexual affair with a married woman named Bathsheba, got her pregnant, and then arranged to have her husband killed in battle to cover up his sin. When the prophet Nathan confronted David about his heinous crime, David repented and God forgave and restored him. Nevertheless, David's moral failure had terrible consequences for his family, his nation, and even the world of his day. Unfortunately, David was not the first or the last strong leader to fall into compromise, immorality, and sin.

Two aspects of this story impress me. First, I am reminded of how easy it is for a person, even a godly king, to make wrong moral choices. That in itself should cause us to walk humbly with our God and to want to do justly before our friends and family. Second, when David truly repented, God was willing to give him another chance. That gives us hope. No matter what you or I have done, no matter how horribly we have failed, or how far reaching the influence of our deeds extends, if we are willing to turn away from doing wrong and ask God for forgiveness and the strength to live according to His value system, He will give us a fresh start. We are never too far gone—we can still become successful in life by accepting and following God's game plan. When God later spoke of David, He gave him an enormous compliment, calling David "a man after My own heart."

One of the best ways to avoid compromising your ethics and values is to maintain daily disciplines. I choose to begin each morning by reading the Bible and praying. Usually, I pray first. Then I read from a Bible that takes a through-the-Scriptures-in-a-year approach. For a goal-oriented person like me, the daily reading selections provide a tangible means of measuring my progress; I know that by following the program, I can read through the entire Bible in one year.

I've discovered that I live, work, and play better when I keep my appointments with God first thing in the morning rather than at day's end. I'm not going to get into too much trouble at night, but I face challenging issues every day that demand the wisdom, composure, and understanding that I can get only by spending time with God at the beginning of a day.

I've also found that it is extremely valuable to stay in close fellowship with a local group of godly men and women. Whether or not I get something out of Sunday's sermon is irrelevant. It's good for me to be in touch with a fellowship of other people who are walking with the Lord. They can help me, and hopefully, I can help them. That's why we have Bible studies at our race shop. It's not mandatory for our employees to attend, and no criticism is tolerated toward those who choose not to come. But most of our team members want to be there, because they've discovered a genuine source of strength far greater than their own.

I'm particular in picking the people with whom I hang out. I have many opportunities to brush shoulders with people in the world who do not share my values but to whom I can be a positive witness. But when it comes to the people I turn to for advice, encouragement, and spiritual fellowship, I prefer to be with men, women, and children who share my faith. Their fellowship lifts me up and challenges me to do better.

We cannot always select the people we work with. But successful people can decide whom they will spend the majority of their spare time with. In doing so, you will create your own track to run on and make choices that increase your confidence, your courage, and your self-worth.

Many aspects about this life are out of our control. We didn't choose the color of our skin, our natural abilities, or where we were born. But we do control our moral choices, and to make the right ones takes courage. We are not robots preprogrammed to do the right thing. God has made us so that we can shake our fist in His face and scream, "I want to do it my way!"—and amazingly, He will let us. But when we disregard His game plan, we are on our own, and we will suffer the consequences.

While God does not force us to do the right thing, neither are we moral weaklings who must give in to every temptation, instinct, natural desire, predisposition, thought, or whim. What separates humans from the animals is the fact that we can make intelligent moral choices. And when you start making your decisions based on God's game plan, He promises to help you find true success.

EIGHTEEN

MAKING THE TOUGH CALLS

Coaching professional football in Washington, D.C., can be a pretty heady experience. Besides the normal assortment of fans, we also had a contingent of high-profile government officials in the stadium on any given game day. I was frequently courted by senators and congressmen and even a few presidents. Some were bona fide football fans; others simply wanted to be associated with a winner. Most of the political figures I met in Washington were kind, compassionate, sincere individuals, but only a few got my vote.

Why? Because to me, character matters. I'm not too concerned about party affiliation, power trips, or the persuasive abilities of a candidate. I choose to support people who have personal integrity and the courage to stand for what is right, even when it may not be popular.

When determining how to cast my vote, I refuse to base my decision on the political winds, public opinion polls, or what some so-called authority has to say about a subject. The first place I look for answers is in the Bible. I don't apologize for that, nor am I intimidated by anyone who tries to demean the Scriptures as a valid foundation on which to make decisions regarding politics, ethics, and morality. What other people think doesn't sway me. The real issue is this: What does *God* think about the issue? He doesn't try to hide His standards from us. Just the opposite. God has laid out in His Word practical information that reveals *precisely* how He feels about important issues and how I *ought* to feel about them. Once I understand where God stands on a matter, I make my decision based on that information.

Having a biblical worldview helps me to decide which candidates I will support, what stands I will take in life, and what role I will play as a citizen in my local, national, and global communities. This worldview also comes to bear on where Pat and I choose to place our discretionary contributions. I feel that I have an obligation to support with my financial resources, my time, and my influences those people who best represent what I understand to be a biblical perspective on the issues of our day. For me, it's merely putting my money where my mouth is, and I'm glad to do it.

To make wise decisions concerning your responsibility to society, however, you must maintain a diligent study of the Bible. Otherwise, your good intentions can be easily manipulated by those in power or those seeking it. It's no secret that Adolf Hitler manipulated the German church to help him rise to power in pre-war Germany. Chuck Colson, who served as special counsel to President Richard M. Nixon from 1969 to 1973, speaks candidly today concerning the White House's overt manipulation of Christian ministers and other spiritual leaders. The effective strategy was to invite them to the White House, take some pictures in the Oval Office, and pick up the votes of their constituency. In recent years, Lincoln bedroom sleepovers and White House coffee klatches have been in the news as means of fund-raising and political pandering.

Many people nowadays are quick to describe themselves as "spiritual," even though they may be living in abject disobedience to biblical truths. Some unscrupulous leaders will use the Bible as bait rather than as a game plan to live by, and the only way you will know the difference is to study the Scriptures for yourself. Don't take my word on a matter; get God's Word on it.

WHEN WE DISAGREE WITH THE LAW

To be truly successful in this life, we must be the best citizens possible. The Bible is very clear on our obligations in this regard. We must pay our fair share of the taxes. We must abide by the laws of the land or work to change them if the laws are unjust. We must respect, support, and pray for our leaders, even when we cannot condone their actions or we disagree with their decisions.

Just because a law is passed does not necessarily mean that it is fair or just. History is replete with examples of laws that were wrong for society and wrong according to God's Word. At one time, for example, slavery was legal in England and the United States. Was it right for one person to own another human being? Absolutely not! Today, abortion is a legal medical procedure in America, but does that make it right to destroy a human life?

What should you do when you disagree with the law of the land? First, you must respect the law. Actions such as bombing abortion clinics and refusing to pay your taxes (or cheating on your taxes) cannot be justified and will rightfully bring the anger of God and the government upon you.

Second, you must work to change the law that conflicts with God's ways. Yes, politics can be a slippery, slimy slope; but that can change if the people involved change. As unappealing as it may be, we must get involved in the political processes in our communities and our nation. Admittedly, changing the minds of voters and elected officials is a daunting and often disappointing task. Getting a new law passed or a poor law changed is often easier said than done, but we dare not become discouraged or back down from what we know is right.

Third, if a law of the land conflicts with the rule of God, you must follow God's Word, but be aware that you will probably pay a price for doing so. Don't engage in civil or outright disobedience of a law and expect to get patted on the back for it. You won't be. Quite the contrary, you may be persecuted or imprisoned. But if the issue really matters, the cost will be worth it. Regardless, we must respect the rights and dignity of all people, even those with whom we radically disagree.

WHEN TOUGH CHOICES MUST BE MADE

It's one thing to oppose abortion or homosexual marriage or euthanasia on principle; it's quite another when the pregnant young woman is your daughter or girlfriend, the member of the homosexual couple is your son, or the person in the coma is your parent. Please don't misunderstand me: The biblical principles remain the same, but the decision to obey them doesn't always come so easily.

My brother, Jim, and I experienced such a dilemma as our mother struggled to stay alive after debilitating heart problems sent her in and out of a coma. For more than a month, she barely existed, rarely acknowledging family members. My mother had always said that she did not want to be kept alive artificially, hooked up to some machine, if there was no hope for recovery. Of course, when she was healthy and happy, we never dreamed that we would face such an issue.

Now, at two o'clock in the morning, the doctors informed us that she had a perforated intestinal wall. "If we don't operate, she's going to die," her doctor told us. "If we do operate, it is highly questionable whether she will make it through the surgery. What would you like us to do?"

My brother and I talked it over. We felt that our mother was a fighter, that it was worth the risk to attempt the surgery. The doctors immediately began emergency surgery procedures. An hour later I was sitting in the waiting room when a surgeon appeared in the doorway. "Your mother's heart has stopped," he informed me matter-of-factly. "We're going to try to bring her back if we can."

Time seemed to stand still, and in the moments that followed, I was suddenly overwhelmed with the responsibility of making decisions that affected the life or death of someone I loved. How do we make these life-and-death decisions? What does God say about life and its value?

My mother survived the surgery and lived for three more weeks. When she died, it was of natural causes, and I was thankful that she went home peacefully, without my brother and I having to make further decisions about prolonging her life. Nevertheless, the experience brought home the ethical issues of "playing God," and I had to evaluate what I truly believe about who is in charge of life. Sooner or later, you will, too.

We dare not say, "This person has little chance for a future quality of life, so therefore, we should put her out of her misery" or "This fetus has no chance at viability, so let's cancel the order and abort the baby."

A young couple in our company was told by their doctor that there was a chance that their baby was going to be born with mental and physical deformities and that they should consider aborting the child. The couple refused to accept the doctor's forecast and said, "We're going to have our baby, no matter what." Meanwhile, members of our racing team and others in the community prayed that God would take care of the problem. Today, the young couple has a beautiful, healthy child. Granted, not every situation turns out so happily, but if we choose to follow God's game plan when making moral and ethical choices, He will give us the grace to handle whatever we face.

WHEN THE TEST COMES (AND IT IS COMING)

At our race shop, we run hundreds of tests every week. We test everything from the strength of the metal used to build our race cars to how much heat and pressure the nuts and bolts in the engines can handle. We recently spent more than a million dollars on one piece of testing equipment. Why? Because we know that the *real* test is coming—when we put our cars out on the track under race conditions, we want to be ready. When Bobby and Tony climb into their cars, they need to know that they can trust their vehicles, that everything has been designed for them not simply to complete the race safely, but to win.

Every day, it seems, we are faced with more and more difficult ethical tests. How will you decide when presented with these delicate matters? What standard will you use to formulate your answers to the tough problems of life? Is your life ready to withstand the pressures of the race? How will you decide when it's time for you to hang it up?

For example, thanks to modern medicine and health standards, people are living longer nowadays. It's not uncommon to have relatives in their seventies, eighties, and even nineties, who are active and productive. And so more of us among the Baby Boomers are confronted with the issue of dealing with aging parents. *Should we put Mom in a nursing home or in a managed care facility? Or should we bring her home to live with us?* All too often, the overriding factors in many of our decisions are money and convenience rather than morality. *How much will it cost me? How is it going to inconvenience my life to care for my father?*

When my mother was sick, I was tempted to think about how much time her care was costing me. Time is more important to me than money. But then I thought back and recalled how much time my mother had invested in me—working long days, caring for me when I was sick, giving of her time in so many ways. How could I do less for her? The truth is that caring for our loved ones costs us time, money, and sometimes heartache. Although it flies in the face of society's *What's in it for me?* attitude, have the moral courage to do what is best for others.

> *You may disagree with God, but that won't change the truth.*

WHEN IT COMES TO DELICATE MATTERS

We are increasingly confronted with sexually related issues—rampant pornography, flagrant sexual immorality, homosexuality, and marital infidelity, to name a few. Here again, I don't take my sexual cues from society, nor do I impose my opinions on anyone else. After years of study and personal experience, I am convinced that the Bible is God's playbook for our lives, so I simply point people to God's Word. What does the Bible say about sex outside of marriage? What does the Bible say about homosexual relationships? How are men and women supposed to treat each other? God is very clear about sexual issues, and the information is easily understood by anyone genuinely seeking the truth. If you believe in God, it only makes sense that you'd want to check out what God says about these matters. You may disagree with Him, but that won't change the truth.

The same is true concerning racism. There is no place for racism in the life of a successful person—not because it is bigoted or unpopular, but because it is *wrong!* It's not wrong because I say so or because someone else says so; racism is wrong because it violates the biblical principle that men and women are created in the image of God.

Much of modern education purports that everything in life is relative—nothing is right or wrong because there are no absolute truths in life. And many educators insist on that *absolutely!* In God's Book, however, you will find many absolutes. He gave us ten basic commandments, for instance, and those who adhere to these principles will find that their lives stay on track, no matter how many bumps they encounter in the road or how many pit stops or repair jobs are required.

I spent years flopping around, looking for the secrets to true success and trying to find a way to win. I've found the answers in God's Book. And you can, too.

Seven Cornerstone Principles for Success

MORAL CHOICES

Our moral, political, and community choices evolve from our character. Personal integrity and our cultural value systems are intimately linked, whether we like it or not. Regardless of what we *say*, what we *believe* determines how we *behave*.

Unfortunately, in recent years many well-known people in our society have espoused traditional family values and made good, morally sound statements, but have behaved in ways that contradict any traditional measure of right and wrong. And while hypocrisy is certainly not new, it is alarming to see it seemingly so accepted in our financial dealings, politics, schools, and families.

In view of all this, I'm still not bashful about saying that character counts! The moral integrity of our leaders matters because they set the tone for the society and for the next generation. Consider, for example, the quandary of many parents and educators who were trying to teach moral values, including sexual purity and truthfulness, during the televised chronicle of the Bill Clinton/Monica Lewinsky affair. The actions of the president and the intern mattered, not simply for themselves but for the moral climate of the entire country.

I hear people discussing political leaders, and they are often quick to say, "Let's get off character and get back to the issues." But character *is* the issue!

Fortunately, God's truth is easy to discover, and it doesn't change with the whims of fools or the flagrant rejection of moral standards by tyrannical despots. The following biblical principles will give you a foundation on which you can build your own integrity—and a solid rock on which you can base your moral, ethical, political, and personal decisions.

CORNERSTONE 1

God alone is the judge of all truth. He is the one true lawgiver. Our lives play out on His field and should be lived according to His standards, which are the only rules that really matter. And though many people may disagree, that doesn't change the truth one bit. You can win only according to the absolute truth of God.

CORNERSTONE 2

God's perfect will is revealed in the Bible. Sadly, many people claim that the Bible doesn't address modern problems. Yet its truths are as valid now as the day they were written. The Bible may be a dead book to those who don't read it, but for those of us who do, it truly lives and breathes!

CORNERSTONE 3

God alone determines when life begins and when it ends. The sanctity of life always takes precedence over the quality of life. If you take this truth seriously, it will affect your perspective on every stage of life—beginning, middle, and end. And it will help you see God's perspective on issues such as abortion, suicide, euthanasia, surrogate-birthing, cloning, and the testing of fetal tissue.

CORNERSTONE 4

God's ideas about sexuality haven't changed. Those who disregard or violate His divine order insult God's wisdom and character.

CORNERSTONE 5

God expects us to care for the needy. In the Old Testament, He specifically instructed the Israelites to care for their widows and orphans. Paul says the same to the believers in the New Testament. Surely we can do no less, especially in the modern world with its manifest abundance.

CORNERSTONE 6

Good government requires good citizens. We are called to obey the laws and submit to governing authorities, so long as the laws and decisions of government align with God's laws. That means we have a spiritual obligation to pay our taxes and work to make our communities better places. Even when our leaders are wrong, we are to pray for them and encourage them as far as possible, without violating biblical principles.

CORNERSTONE 7

As you are in private, so you will be in public. What is in a person's private life will eventually surface in public, for good or evil. There is no such thing as a "private" sin; all sin is social, for eventually it all seeps out. There is simply no such thing as a wholly private person. Given enough time, public and private personas always merge.

Success and Your Health

Health is the great equalizer of mankind—illness does not discriminate against age, race, sex, or social and economic class. Our health impacts every aspect of our lives, including our mood, stamina, and relationships. We are obligated to spend time and energy to maintain good physical, mental, and spiritual health. And yet despite our best efforts, everyone will experience health setbacks, some serious and some minor. My friend Joe has been successful despite the chronic illness of diabetes mellitus. He understands the importance of health maintenance, and despite his hectic schedule, he adheres to a regular exercise program, a healthy diet, and a disciplined lifestyle to control his illness. I have seen many a round of golf interrupted momentarily while Joe checks his blood sugar. But most importantly, I have never heard Joe complain about his yoke of diabetes; instead, he chooses a positive attitude. He practices what the Bible teaches: "Be joyful in hope, patient in affliction, faithful in prayer."

Craig Greene, MD, is a pediatrician
with the Sanger Clinic in Charlotte, North Carolina.

Health and fitness experts tell us that most Americans eat far too much sugar, drink too much caffeine, and don't get nearly enough real exercise. Is it any wonder that so many of us are overweight and jittery? Unfortunately, for many years I made poor choices in the area of health and fitness. I didn't eat the right foods, I didn't get proper rest, I exercised sporadically, and as a result, my unhealthy habits nearly killed me. In this section, I will share with you a few stories to remind you:

- Good health is requisite for successful living.
- Bad choices bear consequences.
- There are some things over which we have no control.
- A disciplined diet and simple cardiovascular workouts can do wonders for you.

NINETEEN

UNHEALTHY CHOICES

S omething was wrong. A tingling sensation seared through both of my legs, all the way from my kneecaps to my toes. I grabbed on to the treadmill to keep from falling over.

During the last year that I coached football, I attempted to maintain a regular fitness regimen, working out and running on the treadmill for about forty minutes at least two or three times each week. I hadn't been feeling well for months, but I assumed that if I kept pushing myself, I could increase my stamina and stay well enough to finish the football season. I convinced myself that the sacrifices I was making were worth it.

I was still working ridiculous hours, drinking far too much caffeine and eating all sorts of high-sugar foods in an effort to stay awake and maintain my energy level. I had tried to get into fairly good physical shape during the off-season, but now, as I approached fifty years of age, the combination of constant stress, poor diet, three or four hours of sleep per night, and lots of sweets was taking a toll on my body.

Toward the end of the season, I found it harder and harder to keep up on the treadmill, and when I stepped off that night, the tingling sensation set in. The next day, I made an appointment with my doctor. After a checkup, the only unusual symptom the doctor found was that my blood sugar was elevated.

I went back to work, and as the season drew to a close, I frequently awoke in the middle of the night with tingling in various parts of my body. This was getting serious. I went to more doctors and most of them said the same kind of thing: Lose twenty-five pounds and it will go away.

When the season was over I went to the Mayo Clinic for a thorough examination. The doctors there said my blood sugar levels were elevated and that if I would lose twenty-five pounds, the tingling would go away.

So I began losing the twenty-five pounds.

But the tingling sensation in my knees refused to subside.

After another battery of tests, the doctors at Mayo found that I was diabetic. They said that even losing weight would not rectify the problem. I would have to give myself injections of insulin every day for the rest of my life.

BAD CHOICES BEAR CONSEQUENCES

Diabetes was a direct result of bad choices I had made over a prolonged period of time. While many people have a genetic predisposition toward diabetes and the problem runs in their family, I'm convinced that I brought the disease on myself. God had given me a strong, healthy body, and I had abused it.

One of the mistakes I made was the work/rest imbalance I had long imposed on myself. For close to fifty years, I lived by the adage "Work like a horse, eat like a horse, and look like a horse." My eating and sleeping habits were horrendous. I thought I could work like a maniac and catch up on my rest later. For most of my coaching career, I was convinced that the ideal NFL coach could get by with about three hours of sleep a night. Don Breaux was the only guy I had ever met who could actually do it, but I sure tried. I didn't notice the price I was paying while I was younger; but the ramifications for my body would later became apparent.

I was obsessed with the game of football, and I was certain that my method of getting ready for each week's game was the absolute best and most effective way of doing it. I kept my offensive coaches working together as a group until one or two o'clock in the morning on Monday, till two or three on Tuesday, and up each morning at dawn to get back to work. At first, the long hours were the exception; then they became the norm, and by the end of my football career, the long hours had become expected. I wasn't a tyrannical taskmaster; I was right in there with our coaches, working as hard as anyone. Looking back, I'm not certain we could have accomplished what we did without such committed workers and long hours, but the choices we made were costly.

To keep up my energy level, I would enjoy a piece of pie or a candy bar in the middle of the night, while we were working. I rationalized it like this: *Hey, I'm sacrificing in a lot of other ways—at least I can enjoy eating!*

Wayne Sevier, one of our special teams coaches, felt much like I did. Wayne made a "sweet run" to the store most nights, bringing back ice cream, cake, pies, and all sorts of candy. Instead of drinking coffee to keep me going, I downed many a half-pound chocolate bar, usually around midnight. (Mr. Goodbar was my favorite!) When Wayne passed away in 1999, I couldn't help but wonder how much our unwise habits had contributed to his early demise.

Part of the price for not taking care of our bodies is the impact our negligence has on those people who love us. If you become disabled at an early age due to an undisciplined approach to life, you are likely to become a liability to your spouse and children. Your ability to make a living or to play with your children and grandchildren, even your level of sexual intimacy may be adversely affected if you fail to adequately care for your body now. The apostle Paul wrote that love "always protects, always trusts, always hopes, always perseveres" (1 Corinthians 13:7), and your family and friends will love you no matter what. But the flip side of that is also true: If you love your family and friends, you owe it to them to take better care of yourself!

Sadly, you can do everything right in the other five key areas of life— have a great career, be financially free, build a tremendous team, enjoy strong relationships, and exercise wise moral judgment—but if you neglect your physical fitness, your success in all the other areas will be short-lived. To be a true success, we need to be disciplined in all six key areas of our lives.

A BLESSING IN DISGUISE

I exercised throughout most of my life. But I "binge-exercised," slacking off during football season, then pouring it on during the off-season. Like so many people, I lived in delusion, thinking I could eat anything I wanted and sleep as little as possible, as long as I maintained an occasional, rigorous physical fitness regimen. Not so. Even with a consistent workout schedule, you must pay careful attention to your diet. You may pride yourself on your sleek, toned, exterior appearance as a result of your exercise program, yet still be severely damaging your body by what you are ingesting. Other people turn to diet pills and steroids in their quest to stay looking young. What good will it be if you have a washboard stomach but shorten your life by twenty years? I'm not a dietitian, but I can say from experience that the old standbys—lots of fresh fruits, vegetables, and water—still work when it comes to caring for our bodies. (A plethora of diet and exercise materials are available today, and I recommend that you find a program that works for you. Beware the fad diets and bogus exercise gimmicks that make unrealistic claims, but don't allow that to be an excuse for ignorance of what your body needs.)

Perhaps a more fundamental mistake I made was to ignore the truth that my body is the temple of God's Spirit. Frankly, I wasn't taking very good care of His house!

Could I have been as successful in my occupation without compromising my health? I believe I could have been and *should* have been! Unfortunately, I harbored the nagging fear that I could only coach for so long, so I thought, *I'd better give it everything I've got while I can.* While hard work is noble, as we've said throughout this book, my extended work hours betrayed a subtle lack of faith that God could and would take care of me if I couldn't coach. *What in the world could I ever do to make a living if I goof up this career?* I sometimes thought. Obviously, God doesn't need football to provide for my family and me, but I didn't see that back then.

If I had it to do all over again, I would find a way to work hard yet maintain a better balance with the other areas of my life. I'd delegate authority more than I did, allowing other people to take on more responsibility so I'd have more time to rest. Certainly, I would change my eating habits, avoiding the high-sugar, fatty foods, and large doses of caffeine, and I'd commit to a more balanced diet. I would also commit to a more regular exercise program, much as I have today, working out three or four times each week.

I choose to regard the diabetes as a blessing in disguise in my life. I was on the fast track to destruction, and had I continued in the unhealthy patterns I was pursuing, I may well have been dead by now. Now if I want to live, I have no choice. I can't eat sweets. I can't go without rest for too long. I don't dare be undisciplined in my lifestyle and must monitor my body closely.

The way I look at it, God was telling me, "Joe, you've had enough doughnuts in your life! You had more than your share during the first fifty years, so you don't get any more." My coworkers used to tease that I walked into the office wearing a doughnut on each finger! *Excess* was my middle name. If one doughnut tasted good, I'd eat three or four!

Today, even with the hectic pace of my involvement in NASCAR racing, I lead a much more disciplined life, and I encourage our team members to do the same. One of the unique aspects about our race shop in North Carolina is the large, state-of-the-art fitness center overlooking the #18 cars and #20 cars in the shop below. Besides helping to keep our pit crews in tip-top physical condition, the gym is open to all our employees, and a personal fitness trainer is available three days a week. I also encourage our crews—especially crew chiefs Michael McSwain and Greg Zipadelli—to take at least one day per week to rest. God Himself rested on the seventh day, so we shouldn't feel that we're dogging it when we take a break.

As for me, I lift weights at least two or three times a week. I use a stationary bicycle, a stair climber, and a treadmill for three types of cardiovascular exercise. I play golf every chance I get. I also have a local doctor check my blood sugar and insulin levels every four months. And every eighteen months, I go to the Mayo Clinic for a complete physical. I still struggle against the temptation to overeat or to eat things I shouldn't, which isn't always easy when I pass the hot dog stand or the ice cream or cotton candy booth at the race track. But I've made the changes that the wise, disciplined life requires. Hopefully you will do the same, while there's still time.

TWENTY

SOME PROBLEMS CAN'T BE AVOIDED

While coaching with the San Diego Chargers, I came home from work one night late in the season and found Pat looking unusually somber. She looked as though she had been crying. "What's wrong?" I asked nonchalantly.

"I have something to tell you," she said. Normally upbeat, Pat's demeanor and tone told me this was serious. Pat had slowly been losing hearing in her left ear over a period of five years. She had gone to the doctor, and he had ordered a CAT scan. Pat had encountered similar problems back when we were in St. Louis, and a doctor there had informed us that the problem could be acoustic neuroma—a tumor that caused hearing loss. The doctors in St. Louis ran tests but ruled out a tumor. Pat had let the matter drop, so I did, too. During the next five years, Pat's diminishing ability to hear was a nuisance at times, but she didn't let it bother her. Not wanting to bother me while I was busy trying to win football games, Pat kept quiet about her condition. Finally, she had decided to go to the doctor on her own. In November, the reports came back that Pat did indeed have an acoustic neuroma. The tumor had been growing in her head for the past five years and was now the size of a golf ball!

"The doctor called today," Pat told me, "and said it's major. Really major." The doctor explained that the tumor was not cancerous, but it had to be removed as soon as possible. He recommended a specialist in Los Angeles.

I wanted to go along with Pat to her appointment, but she wouldn't hear of it. "I'll find out what he says and tell you everything," Pat promised. "You stay here and coach." Foolishly, I relented and agreed to let her go alone for the consultation and exam.

The specialist was a no-nonsense sort of guy. After the exam, he pushed some papers across the desk toward Pat. "You'll need to sign these," he said. "It states that you understand the risks of this type of surgery. It's possible that you could have paralysis on the left side of your face if there is nerve damage. Your eyelid could remain permanently open..." The doctor reviewed a litany of possible complications that might result from the delicate operation.

Shaken by what she heard, Pat was nonetheless blunt. "Just give me the bottom line," she said with more courage than she really felt. "How many patients with similar conditions have you lost?"

The doctor didn't even crack a smile. "We've only lost one patient in this type of surgery within the past twenty years," he replied.

"What happened?" Pat wanted to know.

"Hemorrhaging following the surgery."

The surgery was scheduled for the second day of the New Year. Pat and I talked and prayed together a lot during the interim. Sure, the odds were in our favor, but we knew there was always a possibility—a possibility we couldn't really fathom—that our sons might grow up without their mother.

The specialist and neurosurgeon who were to perform the operation explained in graphic detail what they were about to do. They planned to make an incision behind Pat's ear, then drill a hole through her skull into the acoustic canal, through which they would extract the tumor. Just hearing about the procedure made me nervous! But the specialist had done this procedure hundreds of times, with a near perfect success rate, and he made the operation sound like an oil change on one of our cars. The gurney swept my wife toward the operating room, and along with

Pat's mom I headed for the waiting room, silently praying for Pat.

The operation took nearly four hours—most of which I spent pacing and praying—but finally I saw the neurosurgeon and the specialist walking briskly toward me. Both were beaming, grinning broadly. "It went great!" said the surgeon.

"Just great!" added the specialist.

I breathed an enormous sigh of relief and gushed all over the doctors, thanking them profusely.

"She's in recovery right now," the specialist said. "We'll have someone call you when you can go in to see her."

I sat down and thanked God for protecting Pat and for guiding the doctors during the operation. And I waited...and waited. I glanced at my watch and saw that nearly an hour had gone by since the doctors had emerged. I knew that wasn't a particularly long recovery time for such a serious operation, but I was antsy nonetheless. After a while, I walked down the hall to the nurses' station and asked, "Do you happen to know the status of Mrs. Gibbs? She's supposed to be in the recovery room, and I'd like to..."

The nurse interrupted me. "Excuse me, sir, I believe they are paging you in the waiting room right now!"

I ran back to the deserted waiting room and grabbed the ringing telephone. The neurosurgeon's agitated voice pierced my heart. "Mr. Gibbs, we're taking your wife back into surgery."

"You're what?"

"Yes, we have some bleeding in there. I'll call you when we're through."

"Wait a minute!" I nearly yelled into the phone. "Let me talk to the specialist."

"I'm sorry, sir. He's gone. He's already left the hospital."

The specialist's recall of the only patient he'd ever lost in a similar operation echoed through my mind and lodged in my heart. The patient had died due to hemorrhaging after the operation. I felt as though I were going to throw up.

I slumped into a chair like a wet towel tossed in the corner. I had never felt so helpless—or alone—in all my life. I knew God had said that He'd never leave us or forsake us, so I cried out to Him, praying at first that He would spare Pat's life. My faith vacillated every few minutes; sometimes I felt that God was going to bring Pat through fine, while at other times I felt that I should prepare for the worst. Finally, I could only pray, "Lord, please take care of Pat."

The second operation seemed to take forever. Hundreds of unanswered questions pummeled my mind. Had they discovered the bleeding soon enough to avoid damage to her brain? Pat was a vibrant, active woman. What if she could never function normally again? Would she be able to see and hear? Would she even live? How would I tell J D and Coy?

I prayed and prayed, trying to wheel and deal with God. I'd have given anything for Him just to heal Pat on the spot. For a make-something-happen guy like me, simply being still and knowing that He was God and would do the right thing was one of the most difficult tests of faith I'd ever experienced.

Finally, word came that Pat was in the intensive care unit and I could go see her. I hurried to the ICU and was taken aback when I saw my wife. She was conscious, but a spaghetti-like mass of tubes stretched down her throat, choking and gagging her. Spunky even in this ordeal, Pat was trying to pull the tubes out, while several attendants fought to restrain her. Finally, they slapped leather wrist restraints on her so her arms wouldn't budge. For three hours she had to lie like that, until the doctors were certain it was safe to remove the tubes and that she was out of danger. Pat fell asleep, so I slouched toward the waiting room again.

For the next few days, Pat looked as though she had suffered a stroke. Her face was swollen and discolored, and she could hardly move the left side of her body. Her left eye was taped shut. Bruised and battered, she looked as though she had been on the losing end of a prizefight.

Another operation, and the doctors installed a spring-loaded clip in Pat's eyelid, supposedly to allow her eyelid to close. It didn't seem to be working quite right, but we thought it would get better with time. It didn't. Worse yet, Pat still couldn't move or feel the left side of her face.

She remained in the hospital for more than two weeks, and when she came home, the paralysis in her face had subsided a bit but not completely. Prior to the operations, Pat had been a gorgeous woman, with dancing brown eyes and a perfectly symmetrical face. Now her eyelid refused to close, and the left side of her face was permanently altered. She rarely complained to me or railed against God. Nevertheless, I knew that Pat was devastated by her appearance, as any woman might be.

"I hated myself," she said later. "I cried every day at first. I tried to avoid looking in the mirror. Then I cried once a week. Eventually, I only let it bother me every so often."

At first, she had a difficult time coping with our public appearances. Never one to seek the limelight anyhow, Pat was now even more reticent about being seen outside our close circle of friends. But as the wife of an NFL coach, it was inevitable that she would be seen in public, and I tried to reinforce Pat's self-image every chance I got. To me, Pat has always been strikingly beautiful, but her true beauty emanates from within. Quick to smile and laugh, she still lights up the room when she walks in. The surgery may have altered her facial features, but the surgeon's knife couldn't touch her spirit.

It's been more than twenty years since the operations, and Pat still lives with the effects. Most people who meet her today hardly notice her slightly distorted facial feature until she cracks a joke about it. She doesn't joke to put herself down but instead to let new acquaintances know that it's okay to notice her disfigurement and that she's okay with that. She is characteristically upbeat about all that she went through. "I belong to God," she says, "and I know that He allows things to touch our lives for a reason. He promises that things will always work out for good for those who love Him. He didn't say that everything would *be* good, but that He'd use it for good. Maybe my ordeal has helped me to be more sensitive to other people with problems."

Pat has more faith than I do. When I get to heaven, I'd like to ask the Lord why. "Why, God? Why did she have to suffer like that? Why did we have to go through it as a family? We always tried to honor you. Why did you allow this problem to come our way?"

You may have a few questions like that for God, too, and your suffering may be far deeper than ours, your grief more painful, your questions more poignant. Of course, when we get there, it won't really matter...but I'll still be curious.

Seven Cornerstone Principles for Success

HEALTH

We spend billions of dollars each year on food, vitamins, supplements, health clubs, exercise equipment, weight loss paraphernalia, and other health-related programs in order to maintain, prolong, or improve our quality of life.

We also support a massive industry of doctors, nurses, hospitals, and pharmaceutical companies to help us when something goes wrong.

Now, don't get me wrong! I'm *glad* we have the best health care system in the world. I appreciate the doctors, nurses, and other health care workers who have been blessings in my life, and I'm sure you do, too. Yet given the statistics concerning obesity, AIDS, and frequent cold and flu epidemics, it's obvious that something has gone haywire in the way Americans care for their bodies. And I'm convinced that it's because we have disregarded the connections between body, mind, and spirit.

When I buy a new car, I take some time to check over the manual, to see what the manufacturer says about how I should care for it. I need to know what sort of gas to use, what items need to be serviced periodically, and any warning signs to watch for in case something goes wrong.

Likewise, I consult the manufacturer's manual for my life, the Bible, to see how I should care for my body. As I've already mentioned, I didn't always take such things seriously, and today I'm paying a high price as a result. But by building your life on the following cornerstones, you can avoid many of my mistakes and make wise choices that will profoundly affect your own physical, social, and emotional well-being—both today and in the future.

CORNERSTONE 1

God created mankind in His own image. He is the primary cause of life; without Him, none of us would exist. I came to grips with this truth as a child—that God purposely made me and gave my life meaning. It's truly foundational. Without knowing this deep in your heart, you're likely to be blown off course by every wind that comes along.

CORNERSTONE 2

Our bodies are temples of God's Spirit. God does not confine Himself to houses of worship. When we invite Him to do so, He resides in each of us. Unfortunately, the fact that we belong to another flies in the face of human self-centeredness. But this truth has profound implications for our physical and moral health, for it speaks to sexual issues, alcohol and drug usage, overeating, lack of rest, and other means by which we treat—or mistreat—our bodies.

CORNERSTONE 3

We must live according to God's Word if we hope to function well. How can we expect our bodies to be healthy and physically fit if we choose to ignore the instructions provided in the manufacturer's manual? We can't. This doesn't mean that if you live according to biblical principles you will never sprain your ankle, catch a cold, or have to wear glasses. But making healthy lifestyle choices according to God's Word will help prevent many modern illnesses and emotional maladies.

CORNERSTONE 4

Sin can have detrimental effects on our health. Sin takes a severe toll. The good news is that we can be forgiven. In fact, the negative effects of sin are often indications of God's loving discipline in our lives, causing us to humbly return to Him. Not all sickness comes along because of sin in your life, but sin can certainly make you sick!

CORNERSTONE 5

Exercise and moderate habits are vital to our health and well-being. Anyone who says that exercise is a waste of time is either grossly ignorant or extremely foolish. A bit more moderation earlier in my life could have saved me a lot of medical problems and expenses later on, as it could for you. And your health can greatly affect your ability to develop and maintain good relationships with your family, friends, and coworkers.

CORNERSTONE 6

Doctors are not gods. Our faith must be in God, not the medical profession. When Tony Stewart was rushed to the hospital after a wreck at Daytona, my first response was to pray. Thank the Lord for our dedicated medical workers, but only God can heal a body. A doctor may set a broken arm, but God's power and the processes He has established cause the pieces of bone to knit together.

CORNERSTONE 7

No one gets out alive. Take all the vitamins you want, but you will still suffer an earthly death unless Christ comes back first. The question is, where will you be a million years from now? My hope lies not in my success in this life; my trust is in my relationship with God. And maybe you and I will eventually find ourselves on one of those heavenly golf courses, and you'll ask about my health. "Better than ever," I'll answer. "Better than ever!"

THE FINAL LAP

Sooner or later, we all have to make up our minds which game plan we will follow. Will we plot our course according to society's plan, our own ideas, or God's Word? To me, it just makes good sense to entrust my life to the One who created me, knows where I came from, understands where I am today, and knows what's going to happen in my future. It's the height of pride, arrogance, and foolishness to say, "I want to do it my way," when God says, "Trust Me, and I'll show you the way."

Displayed in our employee fitness center is a quote from Augustine that reads, "We must care for our bodies as though they were going to live forever, but we must care for our souls as if we are going to die tomorrow." Don't wait. Now is the time to decide whose team you're on.

When I speak to civic groups, I often compare sports to the game of life, and I share with them five important components to winning in sports and in the game of life:

- You need the right coach.
- You need good players who can count on each other.
- Understand that real success is achieved through a team effort.
- Realize the clock is running and make every second count.
- Follow the game plan—it's crucial to victory.

TWENTY-ONE

YOUR TURN TO WIN

The fact that you have read this far in this book tells me something about you: Like me, you want to win. You especially want to emerge victorious in the game of life. After all, people like you and me don't like to lose the race from one traffic light to the next—we certainly don't want to lose in the biggest game of all!

If you're going to win in any sport, you need at least five important components on your side. The same is true in life.

Let's see if you've been paying attention. In any team sport, what is the most important component for success? And please don't tell me it's the players!

GET YOURSELF A GREAT COACH

No, the most important person on a winning team is the coach. Whether the sport is football, swimming, golf, or NASCAR auto racing, to truly be successful, you must have a top-notch coach. Even Tiger Woods has a coach who helps him keep his swing in line!

Without a coach, the players all want to do their own thing and go their own way, so they end up bumping into each other, causing unnecessary wrecks, and wasting a lot of time, money, energy, and resources. Somebody must be in charge. Of course, the best coach is somebody who knows you and knows the best way to maximize your effort within the system. Ideally, this person put the system together and can direct you to run the most effective plays and maneuvers.

On our racing teams, crew chiefs Michael McSwain and Greg Zipadelli are the coaches. Although Bobby Labonte and Tony Stewart are two of the most talented drivers in NASCAR history, they would be foolish to try to negotiate the treacherous tracks they run on without a crew chief. The drivers depend on their crew chiefs to direct them to victory. Once, during our first year of racing, the radio communication system conked out between Jimmy and our driver, Dale Jarrett. It was a nightmare, as Dale tried his best to compete without the aid of someone who could see the whole track, what was in front of him, and the encroaching dangers behind and to either side of him. Also, Dale and Jimmy had no way to communicate regarding the changes that needed to be made to the car. To win in NASCAR, you must be in communication with the crew chief.

How about you? Do you have a Coach in the game of life? Are you in direct communication with the Crew Chief? God knows you better than anyone. He created you as a unique individual, with special abilities, and He knows how to maximize your potential. Not only that, but He devised the game! He laid out the race track. He knows how you can negotiate the twists and turns successfully. And He knows how to help you recover from defeats and losses. It makes all the sense in the world to seek Him out as your Coach. He loves you, wants to communicate with you, and is right there, waiting for you to call out, "Coach, I need your help!"

YOU GOTTA HAVE SOME PLAYERS

I've been privileged to coach some great players over the years, and I've had great relationships with most of them. My players didn't always agree with the plays I called. They didn't always fully understand why I did certain things, but most of them knew that I cared about them on the field and off. And they knew that I cared passionately about winning, so they trusted me.

You and I are the players in the ultimate game, and God is our Coach.

Does He care about us? Count on it. Even when we don't fully understand His ways or why He lets us go through some things in life, we can know that He always loves us. He proved His love by allowing His only Son, Jesus Christ, to die in our place.

I would step in front of a bullet for my sons, and you'd probably do the same for your kids and grandkids. Now, consider this: God had one Son, yet He was willing to send His Son to this earth to pay the penalty for our failures, our mistakes, and our sins by dying in our place. This is not a mythological fairy tale; it's a fact of history that Jesus was executed by Roman soldiers on a cross outside the city of Jerusalem around A.D. 29. Does God care about you? Absolutely.

Do you know why I'm so sure of that? Because I'm basically a "people person." I genuinely enjoy being with people. But as much as I care about other people, I wouldn't sacrifice one of my sons for you. And you wouldn't give up one of your children for me. But God did precisely that.

Don't let anyone fool you. God cares passionately about whether you win or lose in this life...and the next.

TEAMWORK: WE'RE IN THIS THING TOGETHER

One of the reasons I enjoy football and auto racing so much is that they're both team sports. People must count on each other in order to achieve victory. In football, the linebackers count on the defensive linemen to do their jobs, the safeties count on the linebackers, and they can only succeed by working together.

The same is true in racing. While most of the publicity in NASCAR centers on the drivers, it takes a total team effort just to make it to the finish line, let alone win the race. We count on each other in racing as much or more than do teammates in the NFL. Imagine if one of the guys in the shop didn't do his job correctly, and Bobby or Tony fired up their car only to have the engine blow up? All of the driver's courage, experience, and skill would be wasted. Or think what could happen if one of the guys on the pit crew didn't fully tighten the lug nuts on a wheel during a pit stop. The car might roar off pit road onto the track only to have a wheel fall off.

That happens frequently in life. Somebody is racing their way to the top of the charts, when suddenly the wheels come off. When that happens, it's good to be surrounded by people who care, people who love you enough to help you make whatever corrections are necessary to get back on the track again. That's where the church, the family of God, comes into play. Certainly, your local church is not perfect. After all, it's full of people who have sinned and fallen short of the glory of God. Thankfully, you don't have to be perfect to be part of the family of God. You just need to love God and commit yourself to following His game plan for your life.

There are people on your team who are depending on you, counting on you to lead the way. Your family, your friends, your coworkers or employees, your business associates, people with whom you brush shoulders every day, maybe even your mom or dad—somebody is counting on you to lead them out of the darkness and into the light. You can either lead them to heaven, or you can lead them to hell.

TIME MANAGEMENT: THE CLOCK IS RUNNING

Whether we were on the road or at home in RFK Stadium, we had sixty minutes to win a game. Every week we had six days to prepare, and then came the test. We went out there, played our best, and either won or lost. Sixty minutes—that's it. When the clock ran out, it was "game over." No more chances. No more excuses. It was judgment day.

In the game of life, is there a clock ticking for you and me? I believe there is. Time is a gift, not a promise, and we need to make every day count for God, for good, and for those we love. We need to take time out to hug a person we haven't hugged in a while. We need to be there for our children, our grandchildren, and our parents. None of us has any guarantee that we will ever have another opportunity to say "I love you" to the precious people in our lives. The clock is running...

Time ran out for my dad when he was seventy-two years old. My mom died recently at the age of eighty-four, after a good, long life, and I hated to see her go. I lost my spiritual father, George Tharel, at age seventy-four.

On October 25, 1999, my good friend Robert Fraley was at the top of his game. Forty-four years old and one of the brightest and sharpest attorneys I've ever known, Robert represented a number of stellar athletes and NFL coaches. He owned his own business, was financially secure, had earned the respect of his peers, and enjoyed the kind of relationships with his wife and friends that most of us only hope for. Robert had it all.

That Monday morning in October, Robert boarded a private plane in Orlando, along with professional golfer Payne Stewart, two other passengers, and two crew members. The plane and its passengers never made it to their destination in Dallas. Just minutes into the flight, the Learjet in which they were traveling experienced a mystifying decompression, and within seconds, everyone on board was dead. The jet continued traveling 1,400 miles across the United States, all the way from Florida to Mina, South Dakota, where it finally ran out of fuel and plummeted toward the earth. The jet hit the ground at more than 600 miles per hour. Robert, Payne, and the others on board never had a chance to say good-bye to their loved ones. They had no opportunity to make things right with their business associates, and it's doubtful that they had more than a few seconds to make their peace with God. In a few blinks of an eye, their lives were over.

Time is a gift, not a promise.

None of us who follow NASCAR racing will ever forget the late, great Dale Earnhardt. His legion of fans referred to him as "The Intimidator," but I always found Dale to be one of the nicest guys in the world. Shortly after I got involved in racing, I sat in the lobby of Dale's shop, waiting to discuss a business venture with him. I was expecting a hard-nosed, crusty, rough-around-the-edges type of guy, but when Dale came out to greet me, he was so kind and engaging that we struck up an instant friendship. Dale took me out to his farm, drove me around his property, and showed me his home. We had a great time. Friendly and easygoing, Dale was quick to extend a hand, quick to laugh, and quick to help when anyone was in need.

Don't get me wrong. Dale was indeed a tough guy. A few years ago, he was in a horrible wreck at the Charlotte Motor Speedway. His trademark #3 car flipped end over end, bouncing all the way down the straightaway before coming to a stop. Dale cracked his sternum in the accident and sustained several other serious injuries—but he didn't even let on that he was hurt. He crawled out of the car and *walked* to the ambulance!

When I next saw Dale in the garage area, I said, "I think you could have played linebacker for me!" Dale laughed heartily. He liked the fact that I recognized that he was a physically and mentally tough guy, and I always enjoyed kidding him about the career we could have had together, had he chosen to play football instead of racing cars.

At the 2001 Daytona 500, a horrific crash involving eighteen cars— including those of both Bobby Labonte and Tony Stewart—took place late in the race. Tony's #20 car catapulted over several cars, caromed off several others, bounced on top of Bobby's car, caught fire, and continued hurtling through the air. The enormous crowd of more than 200,000 people seemed to gasp collectively as the cars crunched to a stop amid smoke, dust, and debris.

As soon as I saw Tony's car airborne and careening out of control, I knew we were going to the hospital. My assistant, Mickey Berry, was instantly at my side, already talking on a cellular phone to the Daytona police, arranging an escort to get us through the throng of cars, trucks, and motor homes clogging the exits from the speedway.

"Let's go," I said. Mickey nodded toward the golf cart we used to get around at the race track. We tumbled onto the cart and Mickey wheeled us through the crowds to our van. We raced to the hospital as rapidly as possible, and there we found Tony Stewart in the emergency room. Amazingly, he was conscious and sitting up on a gurney.

"How're you doing?" I asked Tony.

"My shoulder's pretty sore. I'm a little groggy, and I have a headache, but other than that, I think I'm all in one piece," Tony said with a grin.

I breathed a sigh of relief. Mickey and I stayed with Tony for about a half hour, and the doctors decided to keep him overnight for observation. Both the doctor and Tony assured us that he was fine, so we headed back to the track to pick up Pat. Only then did I hear that Dale Earnhardt had crashed on the final lap of the race. Watching the replay on television, I didn't give Dale's accident much thought. It was obvious that he had taken a severe blow, but compared to the "big one" that had happened earlier in the race, Dale's accident seemed relatively tame. Besides, Dale had been in so many tough wrecks over the years, I never dreamed that he would ever get hurt. Time after time Dale had walked away from major crashes with only minor injuries.

But not this time. This time, the stopwatch had stopped ticking for Dale.

The speed, coupled with the angle at which Dale had hit the wall, had proven deadly.

Pat and I were back at our rented accommodations later that evening around 6:30 when we first heard the shocking news. We were getting ready to go out for dinner, when the phone rang. Greg Zipadelli was calling to report on Tony Stewart's condition. "I checked with Tony," Zippy said quietly, "and he's going to be okay..." Greg's voice quivered. "But I just got word that Dale didn't make it."

I was so shocked, I could hardly respond. I don't recall saying good-bye to Greg or even hanging up the phone. It was as though we had suddenly entered some surreal world where nothing made sense and everything was a blur.

We turned on the television, flipping the channels incessantly from station to station, trying to find out any information at all. Almost immediately, members of our race team and friends started showing up at our door, weeping in disbelief at the loss of Dale Earnhardt. It was already dark that February evening, but mourners began gathering at the Daytona Speedway decorating the fence with tributes to Dale—flowers, notes, and Earnhardt memorabilia. It was a long, traumatic night for everyone who loved Dale and loved auto racing.

Now they're all gone. Dad, Mom, George, Robert, Dale.

Sometimes I can't help wondering, *How many more ticks of the clock do I have in this life?* How many more do you have? Do we really need any more reminders of how quickly a vibrant life can be snuffed out?

Maybe you're young and thinking, *Those things only happen to older people.* Really? Let me mention a few other names you might recognize. Diana, Princess of Wales. John F. Kennedy, Jr. Pop singer Aaliyah, who died in a plane crash at the age of twenty-two. Korey Stringer, the twenty-seven-year-old tackle for the Minnesota Vikings, who collapsed on the practice field and never regained consciousness. And the thousands of successful young businessmen and women, heroic firefighters and police officers, and everyday people who lost their lives in the terrorist attacks on September 11, 2001.

The evidence is in. Life is a gift. It's fragile, and it can be taken away in a single tick of the clock—and the clock is running. When the final second ticks away for you, you want to be sure that you are on the winning team.

YOU MUST FOLLOW THE GAME PLAN

Life is not an exhibition game or a dress rehearsal. This is the real deal, and following the game plan is not optional. Here's the bottom line: There is a God, and He has drawn up the perfect game plan for your life. You may think, *Well, I'll just devise my own game and pursue my own game plan.* People play lots of games, every day, in cities and towns all over the world. Many of these games are pointless and have little lasting value. A person could waste his life away trying to win at these trivial pursuits, while losing the one game that really matters.

Tony Stewart loves to race anywhere and everywhere. His exploits of driving an open-wheel race car at the Indianapolis 500 and then flying to Charlotte to drive in NASCAR's Coca-Cola 600 on the same day are the stuff of which legends are made. Tony just loves to race! He drives me bonkers sometimes because he'll race anywhere, anytime, in any kind of car, against any competition. On Friday night, after his qualifying run for the Daytona 500, he'll drive in some obscure race for a paltry prize—on the same weekend of the big race!

While Tony is good enough (and young enough) to spread himself a bit thin, most people cannot do so without getting off track in life. Fortunately, you don't have to waste your time trying to win the world's acclaim or a bunch of fragile trophies. If you will follow God's game plan for your life, you will win where it really matters.

Consider this: If God is our Coach, you and I are the players, and He designed us to win not just a few puny prizes but the greatest prize of all— eternal life with Him in heaven—is there any way He would put us here

without a game plan? Of course not! God would no more ask you to operate without a game plan than Michael McSwain would expect Bobby
Labonte to run a race without a plan.

Every NASCAR race track is different and requires a slightly different
approach. A win at any track doesn't just happen by accident. We don't simply fill our cars with gas, crank them up, and hope that we can drive faster
or outlast our opponents. Every detail of the race is thought through,
including contingency plans and backup parts. We have a game plan for the
race, and we attempt to follow it as closely as possible.

The same is true in life. I mentioned earlier that I don't consider myself
to be real brainy. But you don't need to be Albert Einstein to recognize that
God has given us a game plan in the Bible—a game plan that works! If you
want to be a success in every area of life, the key is to study the game plan
and then follow it!

THE BIG QUESTION

Here's the most important question of all: Whose team are you on?

In the grand scheme of things, there are only two teams, really. You can
choose to play on God's team, or you can choose to play against Him. (I
wouldn't recommend that!) *You* must decide which team you will be on.
Nobody else can do it for you. If we refuse to acknowledge God as our
Coach, then by default, we will play against Him forever.

Think about that. In His Book, it says that God gave each of us a soul that
is going to live forever. Did you catch that? We're *all* going to live *forever,*
whether we want to or not. And forever is a long, long time! The only question is, where are you going to spend eternity? In heaven with God and His
family? Or apart from Him, separated and isolated for infinity? It's your choice.

YOU CAN'T LOSE!

How are you doing in the game of life? Maybe you've enjoyed a few victories; perhaps you've had some losses. You know from reading my story that
I've known some great victories. I've heard the cheers of the world, and I've

made a lot more money than I ever thought I would make. I have a great wife, two successful sons, two wonderful daughters-in-law, and the smartest grandkids in the history of the world! What more could I ask for?

But, as you know, I've also experienced some excruciating losses. My embarrassing financial messes, the physical struggles that both Pat and I have endured, and of course, the devastating loss of friends and family members who died long before I was ready to let them go.

But the good news is that by choosing to play on God's team, we can't lose. Not really. Jesus said that we would never give up anything in this life—houses, money, possessions, father, mother, spouse, or children—that our heavenly Father would not return to us a hundred times over in heaven. Isn't that great? God said, "If you join My team, if you play for Me, My promise to you is you will never lose in the end. Ultimately, you will not be disappointed."

Have there been disasters in your life? Career troubles, financial pressures, trouble finding your place on the team? Maybe you've made a mess of some precious relationships or made wrong moral and political choices or unhealthy and unwise physical choices. No matter how big your problem is, God is bigger. There's nothing too big for Him! He can solve it. He can see you through. His promise to those who will trust in Him is that you will not go down, but you will go through. Your race may be a long trek or it might be a short haul. God wants you to enjoy the ride to the utmost and to know where you're going when it's over.

Pat said after her surgery, "Joe, the bottom line is that I belong to God, and this is going to work out best for me in the end." That's faith. That's true success. That's racing to win.

You know by now that I'm a pretty straight shooter. I'm not one for beating around the bush. I never want to offend you, but I'd be remiss if I didn't ask you one more crucial question. Can you point to a specific time and place when you asked Christ to come into your life and be your Lord and personal Savior? Have you ever really said, "Okay, Lord, from now on, I'm trusting You; I'm willing to turn from my own way and live by Your game plan"?

Understand, I'm not asking if you believe in God. Almost everybody believes in God. The devil himself believes in God!

I'm not asking if you go to church. I'm asking if you know for sure which team you're on. Have you ever really signed up with God?

If you can't remember ever having done so, or if it's been so long ago that you really need to renew the relationship, I suggest you make that your top priority right now, before you do another thing. It will be the greatest decision you've ever made!

God made His game plan so plain and simple that even a child can figure it out. Hey, I figured it out when I was only nine! I'm sure you won't have any trouble understanding it, but just in case you get stuck, I've got some men and women on our team who will be glad to help you out. I'll give you contact information at the back of this book.

THE CELESTIAL TOUR

One night J D, Coy, and I were talking before bedtime. The subject of heaven came up, and I was telling the boys what a glorious place heaven is going to be. Honest to a fault, Coy looked back at me and said, "Dad, I don't think I'm gonna like heaven."

I was stunned. How could anyone *not* like *heaven?* No more sickness, no more pain. Streets of gold, walls of jasper, people rejoicing in the presence of God forever! What's not to like?

"Well, er...uh, Coy, why would you say that?" I finally managed to ask.

"Because in heaven, you can't lose," Coy replied.

Both J D and Coy are risk takers. They've both played football and driven race cars. To them, heaven sounded eternally boring.

"Coy, I think you may have a misconception of heaven," I said. "It sounds as though you've been led to believe that in heaven we're just going to lie around playing a bunch of harps. That wouldn't be heaven to me. Playing a harp and lying around throughout eternity would seem more like the other place to me!"

Coy and J D smiled in agreement.

"But if I understand heaven correctly," I said, "it seems that God is preparing for us a special place where we will have the best of everything that is good in this life and a lot more, as well. It will probably take us a thousand years to even appreciate heaven. So I think that in heaven, there are going to be some thousand-year football games and some thousand-year races!"

My sons' eyes lit up.

If you have a thriving relationship with God, the race is already on. You're just waiting for this race to end and the heavenly race to begin. Remember, life is tough, but it can also be tremendous! Race hard. Follow the game plan. Race to win!

If I don't see you before we go, I'll see you...you know where!

Why I Believe
the Bible

J oe, you can't be serious," my friend said. "Do you mean to tell me that
you are willing to let some old book be the guide for your life?"

"Yep, I am willing to stake my life on it," I replied. "It's the one game
plan that guarantees true success, if you will follow it."

How can I be so sure?

First of all, the Bible is no ordinary book. Every year, it is the bestselling piece of literature in the world. It has sold literally *billions* of copies
and has been translated into more than 2,200 languages. (Most published
works are not translated into foreign languages at all, and only bestsellers
are translated into more than a few languages.) People everywhere are
excited to discover the game plan that really works.

Scoffers say, "Aw, that's because it's one of those religious books. You can't
compare that to a Harry Potter novel or a book like *Who Moved My Cheese?*"

How right they are! Modern literature cannot begin to compare with
the Bible. For one thing, the Bible was written by forty separate authors
over a time span of nearly two thousand years and under the direction of
one Editor. Some of the guys who wrote the Bible were highly educated;
others had never been off the farm. A few were fishermen, one was a doctor, one was a tax collector, several were government officials, but only a
few were what we would consider professional theologians. Amazingly,
most of these authors never met or communicated with one another.

Despite this incredible diversity of human writers, the Bible has a
remarkable unity and coherence. If you picked forty of your friends and

asked them to write on subjects such as religion, ethics, science, creation, the meaning of life, and the end of the world, you would expect that their ideas would run a huge gamut and most likely would often contradict each other. But the Bible's writers and subject matter flow together in complementary fashion, weaving a grand story around one central theme: God's desire to have a relationship with you.

Yes, some skeptics and even sincere seekers have questioned the Bible's reliability. Most of these critics do not know the author personally, so it's no wonder they are skeptical.

Still, the Bible has a marvelous ability to withstand blow after human blow, without losing a bit of its staying power. The famous philosophical skeptic Voltaire once held a Bible in his hand and pronounced its doom. "In one hundred years," he said, "this book will be forgotten, eliminated!" Ironically, one hundred years later, Voltaire's house served as the headquarters for the Geneva Bible Society! Does God have a sense of humor, or what?

WISE GUYS

I've also been intrigued by what some bright people down through history have said about the Bible. For instance, George Washington could not imagine a political system devoid of biblical values. Washington said, "It is impossible to rightly govern the world without God and the Bible."

The great writer Charles Dickens was even more grandiose in his estimation of the Bible. "[The New Testament] is the best book that ever was or ever will be known in the world," he said.

Abraham Lincoln recognized that the Bible provides the moral basis for our decision making. Lincoln said, "This great book...is the best gift God has given to man. But for it, we could not know right from wrong."

My own perspective is similar to that of John Quincy Adams, who said, "The first and almost the only book deserving of universal attention is the Bible. I speak as a man of the world...and I say to you, search the Scriptures."

But can you believe the Bible? Here are five reasons why I do:

1. Jesus believed.

Jesus quoted from twenty-four books of the Old Testament, so He clearly believed its authority. Beyond that He specifically said that we could believe the Bible (see Matthew 5:18; John 10:35).

2. Science and history corroborate events in the Bible.

History, archaeology, and scientific evidence continue to authenticate the Bible's accuracy. Archaeological finds in the Middle East confirming the credibility of the Bible now number in the thousands. Current excavations continue to bear witness to locations and events in both the Old and New Testaments.

Christopher Columbus was so convinced that the Bible was a better guide for his life than the best nautical information of his time (which claimed the earth was flat), that he set sail for a New World. (You can find Columbus's inspiration in Isaiah 40:22.) Who knows what new vistas you will discover as you begin to explore the Bible?

3. Our source documents are accurate.

The quantity and the quality of the ancient manuscript evidence for the Bible far surpass that of readily accepted authors such as Plato, Aristotle, and many other writers of antiquity. In 1947, Bedouin shepherds discovered a number of scrolls preserved in jars in a cave near the Dead Sea. The Dead Sea Scrolls, some of which date from 200 B.C., virtually confirm the accuracy of previously known Old Testament manuscripts. And more than 5,000 Greek manuscripts of the New Testament have been discovered, some of which date back to within twenty years of the death of John the apostle, believed to be the last of Jesus' original disciples to die.

Why is that important?

Imagine if people today were to begin a new religious movement based on the idea that John F. Kennedy died in Dallas on November 22, 1963, but three days later rose from the dead and now reigns as the lord of life! Most people would say, "That's ridiculous!"

Why? Because there are still quite a few of us around who were alive the day President Kennedy died. We watched and grieved as the funeral procession made its way down Pennsylvania Avenue in Washington, D.C. We know where the president was buried and can visit the gravesite to this day. How ludicrous it would be for anyone to say that President Kennedy is still alive!

That's how foolish it would have been for people to circulate the story that Jesus died, was buried, and rose from the dead—unless He had done so. At the time the New Testament documents appeared in public, many people knew the details of Jesus' life, death, burial, and resurrection. On one occasion after his resurrection (see 1 Corinthians 15:6), Jesus appeared in front of more than 500 people! The people of the day could easily have contested the facts presented in the Scriptures, had they been distorted. The overwhelming evidence, however, was that Jesus was who He said He was. Critics have tried to disprove the resurrection of Christ, but they can't. Quite the contrary; enough evidence exists regarding the resurrection of Jesus to prove the case in any fair trial.

4. Bible prophecies have been—and continue to be—fulfilled.

The Bible contains hundreds of prophecies that have been fulfilled specifically, word for word, not in the vague way that psychics and other so-called prophets today speak, dealing in ambiguities and general time frames. Many of the biblical prophecies were given hundreds of years in advance, were fulfilled to the letter, and are historically verifiable.

Some of the most interesting prophecies in the Bible relate to the coming of the Messiah, who would bring salvation to God's people. For instance, the prophet Micah said that the Christ would be born in Bethlehem (see Micah 5:2). The prophet Isaiah graphically described His death (see Isaiah 53). Interestingly, more than 300 specific Old Testament prophecies were fulfilled in the life, death, and resurrection of Jesus Christ.

Like you, perhaps, I'm especially interested in what the Bible has to say concerning the future. In that regard, the Bible also has an incredible track record. For instance, the Bible predicted that there would be a nation of Israel again back when Israel didn't even exist! Nearly 1,900 years prior to the nation of Israel being reestablished in 1948, the biblical writers predicted that Israel would one day be formed once more as a nation and that the Jewish people would return to Israel from the far corners of the earth. My generation has lived to witness these amazing events.

More specifically, Jesus proclaimed that Jerusalem would be back in Jewish hands shortly before His return to earth (see Luke 21:24–28). That, too, took place in my lifetime, following the Six-Day War in 1967. For individuals born since 1948, who have grown up with the nation of Israel and simply take its existence for granted, the importance of that event is sometimes blurred. We are the first society to witness Jerusalem under the control of the Jewish people in almost 2,000 years!

Sure, the Bible contains many things that I don't understand. But I believe that the same God who fulfilled biblical prophecies in the past will also cause the prophecies concerning the future to come to pass.

5. The Bible changes lives.

Perhaps most importantly, the Bible continues to be confirmed as the Word of God through its power to transform lives today. I can attest to that myself. I start every morning by reading from the Bible. To me it's not just an inspirational book; it's life. God's Word is like air, water, and food—something I can't live without. I find guidance and direction for my life in His book. He speaks to my heart, mind, and conscience through the Bible, and I can communicate with Him through prayer. It's a winning combination.

Millions of people have come to the logical conclusion that the Bible is the best game plan for life that a person can ever discover. I hope you do, too.

If you want to know more about becoming a member of God's team, visit www.needhim.org or call 1-888-563-4422.

You can write to Coach Gibbs at:

Racing to Win
P.O. Box 3116
Huntersville, NC 28070-3116

Keep up on the activities of Joe Gibbs Racing at joegibbsracing.com.

What the Bible Says About Success

God's Word gives us strength, courage, and wisdom far beyond what we could ever have on our own. What's the catch? We have to read the Bible for ourselves and think about it. With that in mind, I've pulled together a few key Scripture references that will help you to further investigate God's winning game plan as it relates to the six areas of life covered in this book.

At first glance, some of these passages might not seem to fit your circumstances, but many will—and therein lies one of the mysteries of the Bible. Since God was speaking to all people down through the ages, He couldn't specifically say, "Look, Myron, I told you to get your degree *before* you got married!" Yet the words of His book are still clear, relevant, and often amazingly appropriate to what we're going through right now.

And remember, the foundational principles written down in the Bible are far more important to your long-term success than calling the right play on a given Sunday, throwing a touchdown pass in the big game, or making a daring maneuver to take the lead on the final lap at Talladega. So look up these passages and read God's Word for yourself. Your ultimate success depends on it.

SUCCESS IN YOUR CAREER

Unless the LORD builds the house, its builders labor in vain. Unless the LORD watches over the city, the watchmen stand guard in vain. In vain you rise early and stay up late, toiling for food to eat—for he grants sleep to those he loves. (Psalm 127:1–2)

Lazy hands make a man poor, but diligent hands bring wealth. (Proverbs 10:4)

All hard work brings a profit, but mere talk leads only to poverty. (Proverbs 14:23)

"For I know the plans I have for you," declares the LORD, "plans to prosper you and not to harm you, plans to give you hope and a future." (Jeremiah 29:11)

Also read:

Genesis 1:26–28; 2:2, 15; 3:17–19

Exodus 20:9

Joshua 24:13

Psalms 104:23; 128:1–2

Proverbs 3:5–6; 10:9; 10:16; 11:1, 3, 28; 13:4, 11, 22; 16:18–19, 26; 20:7, 18; 21:17, 25; 24:15–16; 28:19, 25

Ecclesiastes 1:3, 8; 2:10–14, 18–24; 3:13; 4:9–12

Matthew 11:28–30

Mark 12:28–31

Luke 10:7

John 6:27; 10:10

Romans 12:6–8

1 Corinthians 3:8; 10:31

2 Corinthians 7:5–6

Ephesians 6:5–9

2 Thessalonians 3:6–13

Hebrews 10:36

YOUR FINANCIAL SUCCESS

Give generously to him and do so without a grudging heart; then because of this the LORD your God will bless you in all your work and in everything you put your hand to. (Deuteronomy 15:10)

Whoever trusts in his riches will fall, but the righteous will thrive like a green leaf. (Proverbs 11:28)

Watch out! Be on your guard against all kinds of greed; a man's life does not consist in the abundance of his possessions. (Luke 12:15)

We brought nothing into the world, and we can take nothing out of it. But if we have food and clothing, we will be content with that. People who want to get rich fall into temptation and a trap and into many foolish and harmful desires that plunge men into ruin and destruction. For the love of money is a root of all kinds of evil. Some people, eager for money, have wandered from the faith and pierced themselves with many griefs. (1 Timothy 6:7–10)

Also read:

Deuteronomy 10:14; 16:17

Joshua 23:14

1 Chronicles 29:17

Job 1:21

Psalms 15:1–5; 24:1; 37:21; 41:1

Proverbs 3:5–6; 10:4, 9; 11:1, 3–4, 15, 24–26, 28; 12:22; 13:11; 15:22, 27; 16:3, 16–17; 17:18; 18:11, 16; 19:17; 20:7, 18, 21; 21:5, 17; 22:1, 7, 9, 16, 26–27, 29; 23:4–5; 25:21; 28:19–20, 25; 30:8–9

Ecclesiastes 11:1

Isaiah 58:10

Jeremiah 29:11

Matthew 6:19–33; 10:42

Luke 1:37; 6:38; 12:33; 16:14–15

Acts 11:29; 20:35

Romans 13:8

2 Corinthians 8:9–15; 9:6–7

Galatians 6:6

Ephesians 6:8

Philippians 4:6–7, 10–13, 19

Colossians 3:5, 23–24

1 Timothy 5:4, 7–8

Hebrews 11:6; 13:5

James 4:13–14

1 Peter 5:6–7

1 John 3:17–18

SUCCESS IN BUILDING A TEAM

The LORD said, "If as one people speaking the same language they have begun to do this, then nothing they plan to do will be impossible for them." (Genesis 11:6)

Plans fail for lack of counsel, but with many advisers they succeed. (Proverbs 15:22)

Blessed are the peacemakers, for they will be called sons of God. (Matthew 5:9)

Your attitude should be the same as that of Christ Jesus: Who, being in very nature God, did not consider equality with God something to be grasped, but made himself nothing, taking the very nature of a servant, being made in human likeness. (Philippians 2:5–7)

Also read:

Job 42:2

Proverbs 14:22; 21:30

Isaiah 53:3

Matthew 5:1–10, 29; 12:34–37; 18:1–14; 19:13–15; 21:12–13

Mark 1:35–38; 3:13–19; 6:7–13; 9:30–50; 10:17–21, 32–45; 12:28–31; 16:15

Luke 3:1–14; 6:12–16; 10:17–20; 15:1–32; 18:31–34; 19:17

John 3:1–21; 4:1–26, 34–38; 5:30; 6:38; 8:1–11, 29; 13:12–17; 15:18–21; 16:12–13, 33; 17:5–8, 14–18; 21:15–19

1 Corinthians 10:13

SUCCESS IN YOUR PERSONAL RELATIONSHIPS

He who walks with the wise grows wise, but a companion of fools suffers harm. (Proverbs 13:20)

When you stand praying, if you hold anything against anyone, forgive him, so that your Father in heaven may forgive you your sins. (Mark 11:25)

Get rid of all bitterness, rage and anger, brawling and slander, along with every form of malice. Be kind and compassionate to one another, forgiving each other, just as in Christ God forgave you. (Ephesians 4:31–32)

Do nothing out of selfish ambition or vain conceit, but in humility consider others better than yourselves. Each of you should look not only to your own interests, but also to the interests of others. (Philippians 2:3–4)

Also read:

Genesis 2:18, 23–24

Psalms 51:17; 138:6

Proverbs 3:3–4; 5:18–19; 6:16–19; 11:2; 15:33; 16:19; 17:1, 17; 18:16, 22, 24; 20:17; 22:4, 24–25; 25:6–7; 27:2; 29:23

Ecclesiastes 4:8–10; 8:14–16; 9:9

Isaiah 57:15; 58:10

Micah 6:8

Matthew 5:3, 31–32; 9:38; 18:2–4; 19:4–6; 20:25–28

Luke 10:21; 14:11

John 3:16, 30; 15:9, 13–17

Romans 3:10–18; 7:1–3; 12:3, 17–18

1 Corinthians 7:1–17, 25–40; 10:12; 11:3; 12:12–20

2 Corinthians 2:7–8; 9:6–7

Galatians 6:1, 14

Ephesians 5:22–33

Philippians 2:3–11

Colossians 3:12–14, 18–19

2 Timothy 3:2–4

Hebrews 13:4

James 4:6, 10

1 Peter 3:1–2, 7–12

1 Peter 5:5–6

1 John 4:9–10

SUCCESS AND YOUR MORAL CHOICES

But if serving the LORD seems undesirable to you, then choose for yourselves this day whom you will serve....But as for me and my household, we will serve the LORD. (Joshua 24:15)

In everything, do to others what you would have them do to you, for this sums up the Law and the Prophets. (Matthew 7:12)

Do not be misled: "Bad company corrupts good character." (1 Corinthians 15:33)

Let us not become weary in doing good, for at the proper time we will reap a harvest if we do not give up. (Galatians 6:9)

Also read:

Genesis 1:14–27; 2:7

Leviticus 25:35

Numbers 15:30–31

Deuteronomy 15:7–8, 11, 15; 16:8–20; 32:4

1 Samuel 2:7–8

Psalm 12:5; 41:1–3; 47:2, 8; 72:12–14; 103:19; 109:31; 119:1–8, 89, 105, 160; 139:13–16; 145:13

Proverbs 13:13; 14:21, 31; 16:10–12, 20; 17:7; 19:17; 20:11; 21:1, 13; 22:22; 24:21–22; 28:12, 15, 27; 29:2, 7, 12; 31:1–9

Ecclesiastes 6:7

Daniel 2:21; 4:17, 34–35

Matthew 5:1–2, 10–14, 42–48; 6:1, 33; 10:28, 39; 22:21; 23:14–39; 25:34–36, 40

Luke 3:11; 6:38; 14:12–14; 18:22

John 15:7–8; 17:17

Acts 4:18–20; 5:29; 20:35

Romans 1:21–32; 7:12; 13:1–8

1 Corinthians 6:18; 10:31; 15:58

2 Corinthians 9:6

Ephesians 4:28

1 Timothy 3:10

2 Timothy 3:16

Titus 3:1–2, 14

Hebrews 13:4

James 2:1–9, 14–16

1 Peter 2:8, 13–17; 3:13–17; 4:15–16

1 John 3:17; 4:21

SUCCESS AND YOUR HEALTH

Worship the LORD your God, and his blessing will be on your food and water. I will take away sickness from among you. (Exodus 23:25)

Do not be wise in your own eyes; fear the LORD and shun evil. This will bring health to your body and nourishment to your bones. (Proverbs 3:7–8)

Come to me, all you who are weary and burdened, and I will give you rest. Take my yoke upon you and learn from me, for I am gentle and humble in heart, and you will find rest for your souls. For my yoke is easy and my burden is light. (Matthew 11:28–30)

Do you not know that your body is a temple of the Holy Spirit, who is in you, whom you have received from God? You are not your own; you were bought at a price. Therefore honor God with your body. (1 Corinthians 6:19–20)

Also read:

Genesis 2:7

Deuteronomy 32:39

1 Samuel 2:6

1 Chronicles 16:28–29; 29:10–13, 15

Job 1:21; 10:9; 13:15; 14:1–2; 19:25–27

Psalm 8:5; 18:46; 19:1; 32:3–5; 38:1–8, 18; 46:10; 50:14–15, 23; 86:9; 90:10–12; 99:9; 103:2–3, 13–16; 115:1

Proverbs 4:20–22; 5:20–23; 12:4; 14:30; 15:30; 16:24; 17:22; 23:1–3, 20–21; 25:16; 30:7–9

Ecclesiastes 7:16–18

Isaiah 2:17; 25:1; 57:2; 64:6

Jeremiah 17:14

Matthew 4:23; 5:16; 8:16–17; 9:22; 10:1, 8, 28; 19:2

Mark 7:32–35; 16:17–18

Luke 5:17–25; 6:17–19; 13:10–13; 18:35–43

John 13:31; 17:4

Acts 3:16; 5:14–16; 8:6–7; 19:11–12; 28:8

Romans 1:24–27; 4:20; 8:18–19; 11:36; 14:9; 15:6, 22–23

1 Corinthians 3:16; 9:24–27; 10:31; 12:28; 13:7

2 Corinthians 4:16

Galatians 6:9–10

1 Thessalonians 5:23–24

1 Timothy 4:7–8

2 Timothy 2:5

James 4:13–14; 5:14–15

3 John 1:2

Revelation 5:13; 11:13; 14:6–7; 15:4

The authors gratefully acknowledge the contribution of Dr. Barry Leventhal, who researched and compiled the Scripture passages and references used in this book.

The publisher and author would love to hear your comments about this book. *Please contact us at:*
www.multnomah.net/racingtowin

Don't Miss *Racing to Win* on Audiocassette or CD!

4-pack audiocassette
ISBN 1-59052-056-4

6-pack audio CD
ISBN 1-59052-062-9

Victory Is Within Your Reach!

Joe Gibbs is the only coach in history who has won prestigious championships in two world-class sports: NFL's Super Bowl and NASCAR's Winston Cup. A proven winner in motivating himself and others to succeed, the former Washington Redskins coach and current NASCAR team owner reveals the keys to success in *Racing to Win*. Through fascinating inside stories about stock car racing and football, Gibbs candidly admits his own mistakes and shares the life lessons he's learned. Football and racing fans, as well as anyone interested in balancing work and family responsibilities, will find *Racing to Win* both a page-turner and a valuable resource filled with practical truths.

GET ON TRACK!

"Run in such a way as to win the prize."
— 1 Corinthians 9:24

In the fast paced race of life, don't get sidelined by an error in spiritual judgment. Learn the key principles of Scripture that Hall of Fame coach Joe Gibbs has depended on through a lifetime of personal and career challenges. Get a winning game plan for these six areas:

- Career
- Finances
- Team Building
- Personal Relationships
- Morality
- Health & Fitness

The *Racing to Win Study Guide* will show you how to integrate biblical values into your daily decision making. Coach Gibbs outlines a winning strategy that will help you to go the distance in pursuit of the high calling of God in Christ Jesus. Everyone who finishes, wins!

ISBN 1-59052-054-8